INVITATION TO FLYING

INVITATION TO FLYING

A MANUAL FOR STUDENT AND PRIVATE PILOTS

BY ROBERT S. HUNTER

ZIFF-DAVIS FLYING BOOKS
NEW YORK

Copyright © 1979 by Robert S. Hunter.
All rights reserved.
No part of this book may reproduced in any form
without permission in writing from the publisher.
Printed in the United States of America.
Library of Congress Catalog Number 79-63217
ISBN 0-87165-032-0
First Printing
All Cessna 152 photographs
courtesy of Cessna Aircraft Company

TABLE OF CONTENTS

SECTION		PAGE
	Table of Contents	v
	Introduction	ix
1	What You Need to Get Your Private Pilot Certificate	1
2	Preparing to Obtain Your Private Pilot Certificate	4
3	Your Student Pilot Certificate	6
4	Your Cessna 152 (or 150)	7
5	The Controls of Your Airplane	9
6	The Gyroscopic Flight Instruments	11
7	The Powerplant, Fuel and Electrical Systems	13
8	Weight and Balance	16
9	Before You Go to the Airplane	20
10	How to Preflight your Cessna 152 or 150	23
11	Starting Your Airplane	25
12	Taxiing Your Airplane	27
13	The Runup	29
14	The Takeoff	31
15	Normal Flight	37
16	Your Altitude in Flight	40
17	Your Speed of Flight	45
18	Your Direction of Flight	50
19	Areas in Which Your Flight May Be Restricted	53
20	Other Important Flight Rules	56
21	Special Hazards in Flight	58
22	Wake Turbulence	61
23	Slow Flight and Stalls	64
24	Using Your Flaps	70
25	Airports	71
26	Airport Lighting and Navigation Aids	78
27	Landing Your Airplane	81

#	Title	Page
28	Procedures after Landing	87
29	Radio Facilities	88
30	Technique in Using Your Radio	92
31	Tower Controlled Airports	97
32	Terminal Control Areas	102
33	Radar Services for VFR Pilots	104
34	Terminal Radar Programs for VFR Aircraft	108
35	Automatic Terminal Information Service (ATIS)	110
36	Using Your VOR	112
37	Using Your ADF	116
38	Using Your Transponder	118
39	The Weather	120
40	Procedures When Lost	128
41	The DF Steer and Approach	132
42	Emergency Operations	134
43	Forced Landings	137
44	Instrument Flying	141
45	Night Flying	144
46	Your First Solo Flight	147
47	Planning the Cross-country Flight	151
48	Filing Your VFR Flight Plan	158
49	Making Your Cross-country Flight	163
50	Required Maneuvers and How To Perform Them	165
51	Accidents and How to Avoid Them	170
52	Reporting Accidents and Near Collisions	173
53	Keeping Your Logbook	175
54	Getting Ready for Your Flight Test	177
55	Your Flight Test	180
56	Flying Your Check Ride	185
57	After You Get Your Private Pilot Certificate	195
58	The Wonderful World of Flight	198
	Glossary of Aeronautical Abbreviations	201
	Glossary of Aeronautical Terms	224
	Index	237

TABLE OF FIGURES

8.1	Loading Graph	27.1	Landing Distances for the Cessna 152
8.2	Computing Weight and Balance	29.1	Reception Distances for VHF Radio Signals
8.3	Center of Gravity Moment Envelope	29.2	Radio Aids to Navigation and Communications Boxes
14.1	Takeoff Distances of Cessna 152	30.1	The Phonetic Alphabet
14.2	Crosswind Component Chart	30.2	The Vocabulary of Radio Communication
16.1	Reading the Altimeter	31.1	Airport Traffic Areas on Aeronautical Charts
16.2	Obstruction Depiction on Aeronautical Charts	31.2	Traffic Control Light Signals
17.1	Pertinent Airspeeds for the Cessna 152	33.1	Aircraft Receiving Radar Traffic Information
17.2	Airspeed Indicator Markings for the Cessna 152	38.1	Transponder Terminology
17.3	Cruise Performance of Cessna 152	43.1	Approximate Glide Distance of Cessna 152 (or 150)
18.1	An Isogonic Chart of the U.S.	47.1	Index of Sectional Charts
19.1	Airspace Information on Aeronautical Charts	47.2	Flight Log
22.1	Diagram of Wingtip Vortices	48.1	United States Time Zones
22.2	Vortex Movement in Ground Effect - No Wind	48.2	Conversions to Greenwich Mean Time (GMT)
23.1	Stall Speeds of Cessna 152	48.3	Flight Plan
25.1	Airport Symbols and Data on Aeronautical Chart	48.4	Special Equipment Suffixes
25.2	Runway Markings	50.1	S-turns Along a Road
25.3	Traffic Pattern	50.2	Eights Along a Road
26.1	The Visual Approach Slope Indicator (VASI)	50.3	Eights Across a Road
		50.4	Rectangular Course
		50.5	Turns About a Point
		50.6	Eights Around Pylons

INTRODUCTION

For any one or more of dozens of reasons, you want to fly. You want to join the ranks of the 700,000 active pilots in the United States who fly in general aviation. General aviation includes all pilots other than those who fly the airlines and in the military. Whether you want to fly for pleasure, for business, or both, all you have to do is make the effort. Flying is within the reach of nearly everyone. Even if buying a plane is too expensive for you, nearly everyone can afford to rent one. Rental aircraft are available at surprisingly reasonable rates in nearly every community.

You will have to pass a medical exam. Most people have no difficulty in passing it. Even people with serious handicaps may be able to get a license. But be sure that you can pass before you spend much time or effort in learning to fly.

Your training will follow two separate paths. You will have to take a ground school or an organized home study course in order to pass the written private pilot examination. In addition, you will have to have flight instruction in order to pass the private pilot check ride. You will get the best results if you do both at the same time. Your ground school can help you to understand flying the airplane. Your flight instruction can help you to understand the material needed for the written examination.

When you have passed both tests, you will receive your Private Pilot Certificate, which gives you freedom to fly almost wherever and whenever you want. It does not, however, give you the right to fly in cloud or commercially or for hire. Those activities require further training and passing other written examinations and checkrides. A Commercial Pilot Certificate requires that you pass a somewhat more difficult medical exam.

You may receive either your ground school or flight training from a FAA certificated school or through independent licensed instructors who will conduct a ground school and give flight training.

The people who conduct much of the business at an airport are known as the Fixed Base Operators or, more commonly, FBOs. Most of them provide instructors. The quickest way to get started in flying is to visit the FBO at your local airport and see if he has an instructor who can prepare you for the written examination and the flight check.

If you are in a hurry and have the time and money, the best, quickest and often the cheapest way to get your Private Pilot Certificate is to contact one of the 2,500 FAA approved flight schools, sign up, take the course in a relatively brief period and get your license.

On the other hand, for most people who cannot leave their schools or jobs or come up with the total cost on short notice, learning to fly through an FBO is much more convenient. It permits you to learn as you have the time and the money. You can do it as quickly or as slowly as your supply of time and money will permit.

While there is an enormous amount of literature designed to help you to become a good pilot, it is scattered in many places, often inaccessible to the student. Such information is contained in the *Airman's Information Manual (AIM),* the *Federal Aviation Regulations* (FARs), *The Pilot's Handbook of Aeronautical Knowledge,* Advisory Circulars (AC), VFR *Exam-o-grams,* and many other places.

The object of this book is to combine all this scattered material in one handy place. This guide is *not* a substitute for a good ground school and a good certified flight instructor. Rather, it is designed to supplement them. Read the book through before beginning your flight instruction. Then read the pertinent chapters *before* your instructor covers the material; next, review it after your flight lesson. Make notes. If he has a different or additional ideas, note them in the margin. Continue to review the material from beginning to end until you have your Private Pilot Certificate. Then review it periodically and particularly before your Biennial Flight Review. If an abbreviation or contraction bothers you, look it up in the Glossary of Abbreviations and Contractions. If it is a term, check the Glossary of Aeronautical Terms. I hope to help your instructor to do an even more effective job and to save him or her from answering the more obvious questions. With this book as a constantly available refresher, I hope to permit your instructor to concentrate on those important techniques that make you a good pilot.

I have based this book on the Cessna 152 (and 150) for a number of reasons. It is a well-built, safe airplane, designed to "forgive" many of the mistakes that students make. It is the most popular of all training planes. More students learn to fly in the 152, or its predecessor, the 150, than any other airplane. It is readily available in nearly every community.

The Cessna 150 was manufactured from 1959 through 1977. Since that time, the Cessna 152 has been manufactured. There have been numerous changes during that time. Few of those changes make much, if any, difference in the way the airplane is flown. Most of the statistics and figures in this book relate to the 1978 or 1979 Cessna 152. It is very important that you study the Pilot's Operating Handbook for the plane *you* are flying so that you can determine *any* differences between the plane you are flying and that which is discussed herein.

I earnestly hope that this guide will aid more people to become pilots. More important, I hope that it will make it somewhat easier to learn to fly. Most important of all, though, is the objective of making flying *safer,* particularly for you, the student, and all the others in the sky around you.

Robert S. Hunter
Quincy, Illinois
February 20, 1979

Section 1
WHAT YOU NEED TO GET YOUR PRIVATE PILOT CERTIFICATE

1. The Federal Aviation Agency (FAA) controls the licensing of pilots and the flight of aircraft in the United States;
    a. the FAA has adopted rules controlling the issuance of certificates, known as the Federal Aviation Regulations (FARs);
    b. there are many other rules regulating flight can be found in the *Airman's Information Manual (AIM)* and Advisory Circulars (AC);
2. To obtain the Private Pilot Certificate, you must:
    a. meet the eligibility requirements (Sec. 1.4);
    b. pass a written test (Sec. 1.5);
    c. have certain aeronautical experience (Sec. 1.6);
    d. pass a flight test (Sec. 1.7).
3. To obtain your Private Pilot Certificate, you must have:
    a. at least a Restricted Radiotelephone Operator Permit, before you can transmit on the airplane's radio;
        (1) it is issued by the FCC, Gettysburg, Pennsylvania 17325;
        (2) complete and mail Form 753-A with a check or money order for $4.00;
        (3) this permit does not expire but may be revoked for improper usage of the radio;
    b. at least a third-class medical certificate;
        (1) this examination can be administered by any FAA approved medical examiner in your area;
        (2) you can obtain the names of certified physicians from your flight instructor, fixed base operator, your closest Flight Service Station (FSS) or General Aviation District Office (GADO);
        (3) this certificate expires at the end of the last day of the 24th month after it has been issued;
        (4) you must have it before your first solo flight.
4. To be eligible for a Private Pilot Certificate you must:
    a. be at least 17 years of age;

b. be able to read, speak and understand the English language, or have such operating limitations placed on your pilot certificate as are necessary for the safe operation of the aircraft, to be removed when you show that you can read, speak and understand the English language.

5. Before you obtain your Private Pilot Certificate, you must pass a written test on the following subject areas:
    a. the FARs applicable to private pilot privileges, limitations and flight operations, accident reporting requirements of the NTSB, and the use of the *AIM* and FAA Advisory Circulars;
    b. VFR navigation, using pilotage, dead reckoning and radio aids;
    c. the recognition of critical weather situations from the ground and in flight and the procurement and use of aeronautical weather reports and forecasts;
    d. the safe and efficient operation of airplanes, including high density airport operations, collision avoidance precautions and radio communication procedures.

6. Before you can get your Private Pilot Certificate, you must:
    a. hold a Student Pilot Certificate (Sec. 3);
    b. have proper endorsements to show that you are entitled to solo and fly cross-country;
    c. have a total of 40 hours of flight instruction and solo flight time which must include:
        (1) 20 hours of flight instruction from an authorized flight instructor, including at least:
            (a) three hours of cross-country;
            (b) three hours at night, including 10 takeoffs and landings for applicants seeking night flying privileges,
            (c) three hours in airplanes in preparation for the private pilot flight test within 60 days prior to that test;
        (2) 20 hours of solo flight time, including at least:
            (a) ten hours in airplanes;
            (b) ten hours of cross-country flights, each flight with a landing more than 50 nautical miles from the point of departure, and one with landings at three points, each of which is more than 100 nautical miles from each of the other two points;
            (c) three solo takeoffs and landings to a full stop at an airport with an operating control tower;
    d. FAA certificated pilot schools may obtain approval of a private pilot (airplane) training course which provides for a total of 35 hours of flight and special instruction time.

7. You must pass a practical test administered by check ride examiner after you have logged instruction from an authorized flight instructor in at least the following pilot operations:
    a. preflight operations, including weight and balance determination, line inspection, and airplane servicing;
    b. airport and traffic pattern operations, including operations at controlled airports, radio communications, and collision avoidance precautions;
    c. flight maneuvering by reference to ground objects;

d. flight at critically slow airspeeds and the recognition of and recovery from imminent and full stalls entered from straight flight and from turns;
e. normal and crosswind takeoffs and landings;
f. controlling and maneuvering an airplane solely by reference to instruments, including descents and climbs using radio aids or radar directives;
g. cross-country flying, using pilotage, dead reckoning, and radio aids, including one 2 hour flight;
h. maximum performance takeoffs and landings;
i. night flying, including takeoffs, landings, and VFR navigation;
j. emergency operations, including simulated aircraft and equipment malfunctions;
k. your instructor must endorse your logbook finding you competent to perform each of these operations safely as a private pilot.

Section 2
PREPARING TO OBTAIN YOUR PRIVATE PILOT CERTIFICATE

1. Your course of instruction falls into two separate but closely related categories, the first of which is *ground school.* This is some form of home study or classroom instruction in the various fields of knowledge that you will need in order to understand the principles of flight, the weather, flight rules, etc.
    a. a primary purpose of your ground school is to prepare you for the Private Pilot written examination;
    b. while you may be able to do this in your own home study course, this demands an enormous amount of self-discipline;
    c. a home study course must include a program of study of the government publications which cover all areas included in the written examination;
    d. if you organize and follow a home study course, you should take one of the weekend ground courses mentioned below since they suffice, in themselves, to meet this requirement;
    e. if your ground school consists solely of a home study course, you must take the aviation home study course with you to the examination; the inspector will review it and may question you to determine that you have completed the course;
    f. several of the major aircraft manufacturers, including Cessna, have developed fine ground school programs, which are conducted at many of their dealers;
    g. ground schools are offered by flying schools, which may be either FAA-approved schools or non-approved schools which may be very satisfactory;
    h. many candidates for the Private Pilot written examination get great help from the intensive courses offered by the AOPA, 7315 Wisconsin Ave., Washington, D.C. 20014, 800-638-0853, Accelerated Ground Schools, Inc., P.O. Box 43548, Atlanta, Georgia 30336, 800-241-4992, and Aviation Seminars, Box 294, Princeton Junction, New Jersey 08550, 609-799-2120. A certificate that you have completed one of these courses will normally suffice to meet the training requirements.
2. The other required course is your flight instruction. This is personal instruction by a certified flight instructor (CFI) that will enable you to:

a. solo your airplane;
b. pass the Private Pilot check ride and thereby complete the requirements for the Private Pilot Certificate;
c. be a good, safe pilot;
d. be prepared to move on to your instrument rating and your Commercial Pilot Certificate.

3. There are various ways to arrange for your flight training:
   a. there are numerous FAA approved flight schools which you can find by:
      (1) checking the "List of Certificated Pilot Flight and Ground Schools," which you can obtain without charge from the U.S. Department of Transportation, Publications Section, TAD-443.1, Washington, D.C. 20590;
      (2) checking the advertisements in the numerous aviation magazines, such as *Flying;*
      (3) obtaining this information from the FAA General Aviation or Flight Standards District Office;
      (4) checking with FSS personnel and fixed base operators who are acquainted with the certificated flight instructors in your area.

4. You can also obtain flight instruction from a Certified Flight Instructor in your own community:
   a. most FBOs have CFIs available;
   b. whether or not he is affiliated with an FAA approved school, the CFI must have demonstrated an understanding of the learning processes, a knowledge of the fundamentals of teaching, and the ability to communicate effectively with his students.

Section 3
YOUR STUDENT PILOT CERTIFICATE

1. Before you can solo any airplane, you must have a Student Pilot Certificate;
    a. the eligibility requirements are the same as for a Private Pilot Certificate (Sec. 1.4) except that you need to be only 16 years old.
2. The Student Pilot Certificate may be issued by an FAA inspector or designated pilot examiner;
    a. obtain FAA Form 355, "Application for Student Pilot Certificate," from your flight instructor, complete it and send it to the District Office along with a valid medical certificate, which will be returned to you with your Student Pilot Certificate;
    b. you can obtain a combined Medical Certificate and Student Pilot Certificate from a designated medical examiner;
        (1) however, he is not permitted to issue the certificate if it is subject to operating limitations due to inability to read, write or speak English.
3. Your Student Pilot Certificate expires on the last day of the 24th month after it was issued;
    a. it cannot be renewed but a new one can be issued upon application and by presenting the old certificate and valid medical certificate;
    b. if a new certificate is issued, it will bear the same endorsements as the certificate it replaces.
    c. a medical examiner cannot transfer endorsements to a new Medical and Student Pilot Certificate. You should keep your old certificate as a record of those endorsements.
4. As a student pilot, you may *not* act as pilot in command of an aircraft;
    a. that is, carrying a passenger (your instructor is not a passenger; he *is* the pilot in command as long as you are the student);
    b. that is, carrying property for compensation or hire;
    c. for compensation or hire;
    d. in furtherance of a business;
    e. on an international flight, except that you may make solo training flights from Haines, Gustavas, or Juneau, Alaska, to White Horse, Yukon, Canada and return, over the province of British Columbia.
5. As a student pilot, you may not act as a required pilot flight crewmember on any aircraft for which more than one pilot is required, except when receiving flight instruction from an authorized flight instructor on board an airship and no person other than a required flight crewmember is carried on the aircraft.

Section 4
THE CESSNA 152 (or 150)

1. The Cessna 152 or 150 is extremely well built and a very safe piece of equipment if kept in good condition and flown carefully;
    a. the 150 was manufactured from 1959 to 1978 and is the most popular training plane in the world;
    b. the 152 came out in 1978 and is very similar, in most respects, to the 150;
        (1) the most important change is the conversion to the Lycoming engine, rated at 110 horsepower and using 100 octane gasoline;
        (2) the Continental engine in the 150 uses 80/87 octane, which at times has been in short supply;
    c. each year, there have been changes in the 150 and 152 but these do not make any substantial change in the way they are flown;
        (1) nevertheless, it is important that you consult the Pilot's Operating Handbook for the plane you are flying;
        (2) for convenience, note any important differences between your plane and the 1978 Cessna 152 right in this book.
2. The maximum weight of the Cessna 152, which includes the weight of the plane and everything aboard, is 1,670 pounds, or 70 pounds more than the Cessna 150. (Sec. 8).
3. The normal capacity of your airplane is two people, but you can have a child's seat installed in Baggage Area No. 1.
4. The engine and fuel system, as well as the electrical system, are discussed in Section 7.
5. Engine ignition is provided by two engine-driven magnetos and two spark plugs to each cylinder;
    a. the right magneto fires both left and right upper sparks and the left magneto fires both left and right lower sparks;
    b. ignition and starter operation are controlled by a switch on the left subpanel;
    c. the engine should be operated on BOTH magnetos except when you are checking, or during emergency use (See Sec. 42.1).
6. The pitot-static system supplies ram air pressure to the airspeed indicator and static pressure to the airspeed indicator, rate-of-climb indicator and altimeter;
    a. the system includes a heatable pitot tube mounted on the lower surface of the left wing and an external static port on the lower left side of the forward fuselage;

      b. pitot heat is applied by turning on the pitot heat switch during possible icing conditions (particularly if you blunder into cloud in cold air) but should *never* be left on otherwise;
      c. the rate-of-climb indicator is discussed in Sec. 17.8;
      d. the airspeed indicator is discussed in Sec. 17.5 and following;
      e. the altimeter is discussed in Sec. 16.4.
7. At 65% power and at 6000 feet, with the tanks full, the Cessna 152 has a range of about 375 nautical miles;
      a. any time you plan a cross-country flight, check the performance charts for *your airplane,* to estimate the ground speed, fuel consumption and endurance.
8. The normal rate of oil consumption is 1 quart every 5 hours.
9. The service ceiling of your airplane is 14,700 feet; see Sec. 16 for a discussion of problems relating to altitude.

Section 5
THE CONTROLS OF YOUR AIRPLANE

1. The flight of the airplane is governed by the use of controls which cause it to turn about on one or more of its three axes.
2. The ailerons cause an airplane to turn on its longitudinal axis, sometimes called the roll axis;
    a. the longitudinal axis extends from the nose of the airplane to its tail;
    b. the two ailerons are located on the outer trailing edge of each wing;
    c. the ailerons are controlled through the control wheel (which also controls the elevator);
    d. a turn of the control wheel to the left causes the left aileron to go up and the right aileron to go down;
        (1) with the left aileron up, the left wing has less lift and goes down; the right wing, with the right aileron down, has more lift and goes up;
        (2) the result is a roll or bank of the airplane on its longitudinal axis;
        (3) the opposite action takes place in a turn of the control wheel to the right.
3. The elevator causes the airplane to turn on its lateral axis, sometimes called the pitch axis;
    a. the lateral axis is a line that extends from wing tip to wing tip;
    b. the elevator forms the rear part of the horizontal tail assembly and moves up and down;
    c. the elevator is also controlled by the control wheel (along with the ailerons) and is moved upward by pulling back on the control wheel and downward by pushing forward on the control wheel;
        (1) when the elevator is *down,* the lift of the horizontal tail surface is increased, causing the tail to move upward and the nose to move downward;
        (2) when the elevator is *up,* the lift of the horizontal tail surface is decreased, causing the tail to move downward, which results in raising the nose.
4. The rudder causes the airplane to turn on its vertical axis, sometimes called the yaw axis;
    a. the vertical axis is a line that passes vertically through the center of gravity of the airplane;
    b. the rudder is fixed to the vertical stabilizer, or fin;
    c. the rudder is controlled by the feet as they push the rudder pedals;

(1) pushing the *left* pedal causes the rudder to swing to the left, which causes the tail to go to the right, with the result that the nose goes to the left;

(2) pushing on the *right* pedal has the opposite effect.

5. The elevator trim tab is used to adjust the flight of the airplane so that it will neither climb nor descend at any particular throttle setting, unless the elevator is raised or lowered;

    a. it is also used to maintain a fixed airspeed during a climb or descent without exerting forward or back pressure on the elevator;

    b. the trim tab is adjusted by rotating the trim tab control wheel;

        (1) rolling the wheel forward increases the tendency for the nose to go down;

        (2) rolling the wheel backward increases the tendency for the nose to go up;

    c. using the trim tab should not be thought of as the primary method for changing altitude; this is primarily the function of the throttle;

    d. you use the trim tab to relieve the pressure you are required to apply to maintain straight-and-level flight, and to reduce back pressure while ascending;

    e. some airplanes have a rudder trim tab, which is used primarily during takeoff and climbout to reduce the need for right rudder.

Section 6
THE GYROSCOPIC FLIGHT INSTRUMENTS

1. Your airplane has an engine-driven *vacuum system* that provides the suction necessary to operate the attitude indicator, the directional indicator and in some planes the turn and bank indicator;
    a. the turn and bank indicator of the 152 is operated by electricity, as a safety precaution, so that if the vacuum system fails, you will still have one instrument that helps you to know your airplane's attitude;
    b. the directional indicator is discussed in Sec. 18;
    c. the system consists of a vacuum pump mounted on the engine, a vacuum relief valve and vacuum system air filter on the aft side of the firewall below the instrument panel, a suction gage and instruments on the left side of your instrument panel;
    d. the normal range is 4.6 to 5.4 inches of mercury and a reading below this indicates the indicators are not reliable.
2. The *turn and bank indicator* is sometimes known as the turn coordinator, or the turn and slip indicator and consists of two instruments, a ball and a turn needle;
    a. the ball is a check on your coordination and tells you the "quality" of a turn, that is, whether your airplane has the correct angle of bank for its rate of turn;
        (1) in a coordinated turn, the ball is centered between the two markers;
        (2) skids and slips are discussed in Sec. 15.6;
    b. the *turn needle* indicates the rate at which the airplane is turning about its vertical axis; this rate is expressed in the number of degrees per second the airplane is turning;
    c. unlike the attitude indicator, this instrument does not tell you the banking attitude of your airplane but, for any given airspeed, there is a definite angle of bank necessary to maintain a coordinated turn at a given rate;
    d. the faster the airspeed, the greater the angle of bank you must maintain to obtain a given rate of turn;
    e. while turn and bank indicators may be calibrated for either a two minute or a four minute turn, yours has a two minute turn needle;
        (1) if the miniature airplane points squarely at the mark either to the left or right of center, that means that you will complete a 360 degree turn in 2 minutes;

(2) this means that you are turning at 3 degrees per second;
(3) before you fly an airplane, be sure that you understand exactly how your turn and bank indicator indicates a standard rate turn.
3. The attitude indicator is also known as the artificial horizon or gyro-horizon;
    a. your bank attitude is known by a pointer at the top of the indicator;
        (1) it has index marks at 10, 20, 30, 60, and 90 degrees on each side of the center mark;
        (2) the banking scale indicator moves in the direction in which the airplane is banked;
    b. your pitch and roll attitudes are shown by the miniature airplane in relation to the horizon bar, giving you an accurate picture of the attitude of your airplane;
    c. there is a knob at the bottom of the instrument so that you can adjust the miniature airplane to the horizon bar for accurate readings;
        (1) sit in your normal flying position when you make this adjustment;
    d. this instrument gives an instantaneous indication of the slightest changes in attitude;
        (1) it has virtually no lead or lag and is very reliable.

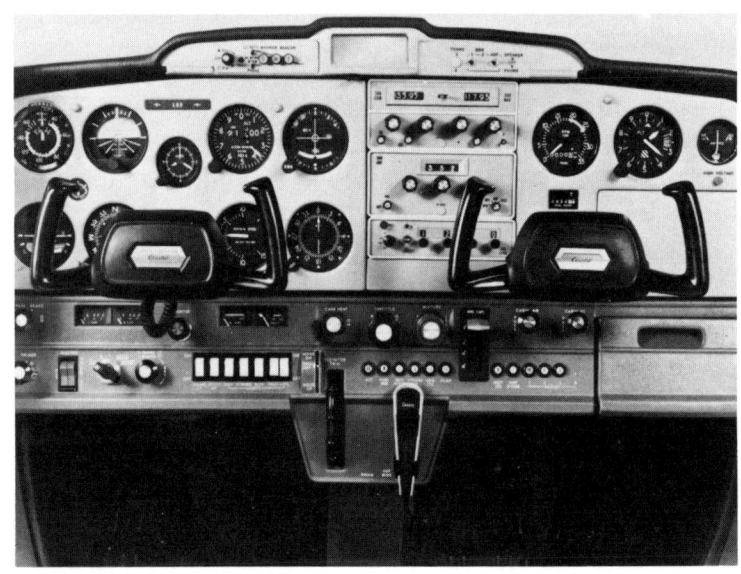

Section 7
THE POWERPLANT, FUEL AND ELECTRICAL SYSTEM

1. The Cessna 152 engine is a Lycoming 0-235-L2C rated at 110 horsepower at 2,550 rpm;
    a. it is a four-cylinder, overhead valve, air-cooled, carbureted engine;
    b. the 150 is equipped with a Continental 0-200-A rated at 100 horsepower at 2,750 rpm.
2. Your Cessna 152 may be equipped with either a standard fuel system or a long-range system (the latter is not considered here);
    a. the system consists of two vented fuel tanks (one in each wing), a fuel shutoff valve, fuel strainer, manual primer and carburetor;
    b. fuel flows by gravity from the two wing tanks to a fuel shutoff valve.
3. The standard tanks on a Cessna 152 will hold a total of 26 gallons, or 13 in each tank;
    a. of that amount, 1.5 gallons cannot be used; this leaves 24.5 usable;
    b. it uses 100 LL grade aviation fuel (blue) or 100 (green);
    c. because of the cross-feeding between fuel tanks, the tanks should be retopped after each fueling to assure maximum capacity;
    d. fuel contamination, caused by water or dirt in the gasoline, can cause engine failure and is avoided by (1) topping off your tanks after each flight, (2) buying gas only from regularly operating FBOs, (3) draining fuel sumps and the strainer before each flight, and (4) straining the gasoline if it is necessary to use fuel of doubtful quality.
4. Engine power is controlled by a throttle on the lower center part of your instrument panel;
    a. when you push the throttle all the way forward, the throttle is open; when you pull it all the way back, it is closed;
    b. there is a friction lock at the base of the throttle, which you turn to make operating the throttle easier, or to lock the throttle so that it can't slip;
5. The mixture control is a red knob mounted on the right corner of the control pedestal;
    a. the full-rich position is full forward and the idle position is back;
    b. the engine is killed by throttling all the way back and then pulling the mixture control all the way back;
    c. you must be *very* careful *never* to pull the mixture control in flight by mistake.
6. The oil pressure gage is located on the subpanel and is operated by oil pressure;
    a. a direct pressure oil line from the engine delivers oil at engine operating pressure to the oil pressure gage;

b. gage markings indicate that idling pressure is 10 PSI (red line), the normal operating range is 30 to 60 PSI (green arc), and the maximum pressure is 100 PSI (red line);
7. Oil temperature is indicated by a gage located on the subpanel;
    a. oil temperature limitations are the normal operating range (green arc) which is 35°C (100°F) to 116°C (240°F) and the maximum (red line) is 116°C (240°F).
8. The carburetor is mounted on the bottom of the engine;
    a. fuel is delivered to the carburetor by gravity flow from the fuel system;
    b. in the carburetor, fuel is atomized, proportionally mixed with intake air, and delivered to the cylinders through intake manifold tubes;
    c. the proportion of atomized fuel to air is controlled, within limits, by the mixture control on the instrument panel, with the richest mixture produced when the mixture control is pushed all the way forward.
9. There is a primer located on the instrument panel to be used for cold weather starting. (Sec. 11.12);
    a. it is a small pump that draws fuel from the fuel strainer when the plunger is pulled out and injects it into the manifold when the plunger is pushed back in;
    b. the plunger knob has a lock and, after being pushed full in, must be rotated either right or left;
    c. always test after using the primer to be sure that the knob cannot be pulled out;
    d. check the primer instantly if you have any engine trouble in flight as it may have worked out.
10. An oil sump on the bottom of the engine supplies 6 quarts to the engine;
    a. the oil filler cap/oil dipstick is located at the rear of the engine on the right side;
    b. the engine must not be operated on less than 4 quarts of oil and should be checked for each flight and whenever you refuel;
    c. to minimize loss of oil through the breather, fill to 5 quarts for normal flights of less than 3 hours and to 6 quarts for extended flight;
    d. use ashless dispersant oil SAE 40 or 50 above 60°F, SAE 40 between 30–90°F, SAE 30 or 40 between 0–70°F and SAE 30 below 10°F.
11. Electrical energy is supplied by a 28 volt direct current system. It is powered by an engine driver 60 amp alternator and a 24 volt, 14 amp hour battery.
12. The master switch is a split-rocker type switch labeled Master and is ON in the up position and OFF in the down position;
    a. the right half of the switch is labeled BAT and controls all electrical power to the airplane;
    b. the left half is labeled ALT and controls the alternator;
    c. normally, both sides of the master switch are used simultaneously;
        (1) the BAT side of the switch can be turned ON separately to check equipment while you are on the ground;

SECTION 7—THE POWERPLANT, FUEL AND ELECTRICAL SYSTEM

    d. when the ALT side is in the OFF position, the alternator is removed from the electrical system and the entire electrical load is placed on the battery.
13. The ammeter indicates the flow of current in amperes, from the alternator to the battery or from the battery to the airplane's electrical system;
    a. when the engine is operating and the master switch is turned on, the ammeter indicates the charging rate applied to the battery;
    b. if the alternator is not functioning or the electrical load exceeds the output of the alternator, the ammeter indicates the battery discharge rate.
14. The automatic over-voltage protection system consists of an over-voltage sensor behind the instrument panel and a red warning light labeled HIGH VOLTAGE, under the ammeter;
    a. when the red light comes on, it indicates that the alternator is not operating and the battery is supplying all electrical power.
15. Normally, your airplane will be equipped with a green position light at the tip of your right wing, a red position light at the tip of your left wing, a white position light at the tail end of the fuselage, and a rotating beacon on top of the rudder;
    a. in addition, you will probably have either a single or dual landing/taxi light in the cowl nose cap;
    b. another valuable safety feature is strobe lights, which give a brilliant intermittent flash, mounted at the end of each wing and greatly improve the ability of other pilots to see you.
16. Your Cessna 152 is also equipped with interior lighting;
    a. there is both flood lighting and integral lighting for the instrument and control panel; the lighting is controlled by rheostat control knobs;
    b. there is also a cabin dome light overhead and a control wheel map light at the bottom of your control wheel;
    c. you should learn the location and operation of all these controls so you can find them in the dark.

Section 8
WEIGHT AND BALANCE

1. Each time before takeoff, it is your responsibility to be sure that you have not overloaded the airplane and that you have distributed the load so that the plane will fly safely;
    a. failure to understand and to compute weight and balance may result in serious—perhaps fatal—accidents.
    b. proper weight and balance calculations differ for each type of airplane, so you must consult the manufacturer's data to be sure that your computations are correct;
    c. if your total weight is excessive or improperly balanced within the airplane, it is absolutely necessary that you either remove some weight, redistribute some weight, or both, before you take off.
2. As a pilot, you are concerned with three kinds of weight in loading your airplane:
    a. *empty weight* is the basic weight of the airplane and includes the structure, the power plant, the fixed equipment, all fixed ballast, the unusable fuel supply, undrainable oil and hydraulic fluid;
    b. *useful load* (sometimes called *payload*) is the weight of pilot, passengers, baggage, usable fuel and drainable oil;
    c. *gross weight* is the empty weight plus the useful load;
        (1) when an airplane is carrying the maximum load for which it is certificated, the takeoff weight is called the *maximum allowable gross weight;*
        (2) you may not take off with the maximum if the length of the runway, taken with the altitude, temperature, etc., indicate that there is insufficient runway. (See Sec. 14.20.)
3. Even though you are under the maximum gross weight, you should not take off if that weight is improperly distributed;
    a. you must always be sure that the airplane and its load are arranged so that they fall within the allowable center of gravity (cg) range, as specified in your airplane's weight and balance data;
    b. the center of gravity (cg) is the point where the airplane will balance;
        (1) you must load your airplane so that the center of gravity is not too far forward or too far aft, that is, within the center of gravity range (cg range);
        (2) this center of gravity range is specified for each type of airplane.

4. Both for safe flying and to pass the private pilot check ride and written examination, you must understand how to compute weight and balance problems, to be sure that you are within the gross maximum weight and so that you can be sure that your airplane is properly balanced.
5. You must be sure that the total weight of your Cessna 152 does not exceed 1,670 pounds (1,600 pounds for a Cessna 150);
    a. refer to the Weight and Balance Data sheet in the airplane to obtain the empty weight of your airplane, which is approximately 1,000 pounds;
    b. with some planes, you add to this the weight of the oil (the 6 quart capacity equals 1½ gallons or 7.5 pounds per *gallon*, not quart); this weight would be 11 pounds; for the Cessna 152, full oil is included in the empty weight;
    c. add to this the weight of the pilot (and passenger, if any);

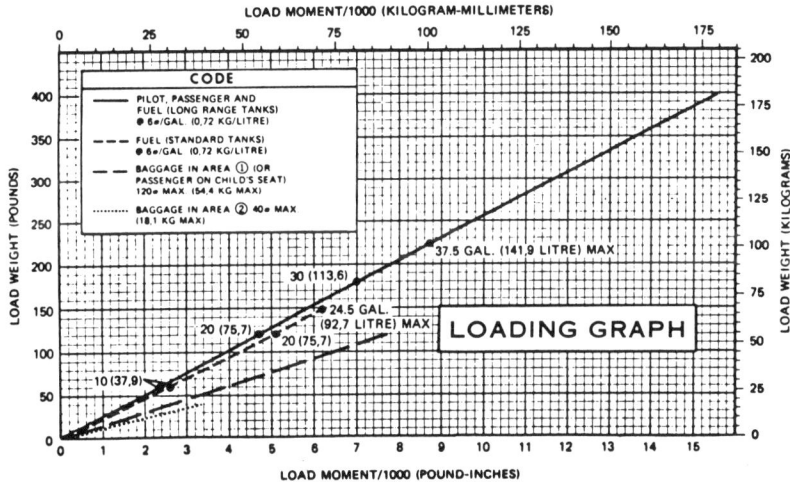

FIG. 8.1—LOADING GRAPH

d. add to this the weight of the fuel, at 6 pounds per gallon; the capacity is 23.5 gallons (The remaining 1.5 gallon of unusable fuel is included in the empty weight of the airplane.);
e. add to this the weight of all baggage;
f. any excess must be corrected by reducing the amount of fuel or baggage, or removing the extra passenger.

6. You use the Loading Graph to determine whether you are properly loaded, that is, whether or not the center of gravity is too far forward or too far back;
    a. for convenience, your Loading Graph shows the moments divided by 1,000 to give more manageable numbers;

A TYPICAL CESSNA 152

	Weight in pounds	Moment (lb-ins) divided by 1000
Basic empty weight—which you take from *your* airplane data	1136	34.0
Usable fuel—24.5 gal with standard tanks	147	6.2
Pilot and passenger	340	13.3
Baggage—Area 1	47	3.0
Baggage—Area 2	—	—
Total Weight and Moment	1670	56.5

FIG. 8.2—COMPUTING WEIGHT AND BALANCE

b. the moment for each item is based upon its distance in front or behind a certain arbitrarily selected point in the airplane;
c. you obtain the basic empty weight and moment from the weight and balance records in your airplane;
d. enter them in the table, Computing Weight and Balance;
e. use the Loading Graph to determine the moment/1000 for each additional item to be carried and list them on the table;
f. total the weight and moments/1000 and plot on the Center of Gravity Moment Envelope to determine whether the point falls within the envelope and the loading is acceptable;
g. if both totals do not fall within the envelope, you must either reduce or redistribute your load, or both.

7. Even though you have not overloaded your airplane, you should be sure that you are not loaded too far forward or your airplane will suffer the following undesirable characteristics:
    a. excessive loads on the nose wheel;
    b. decreased performance;
    c. higher stalling speeds;
    d. higher stick forces.

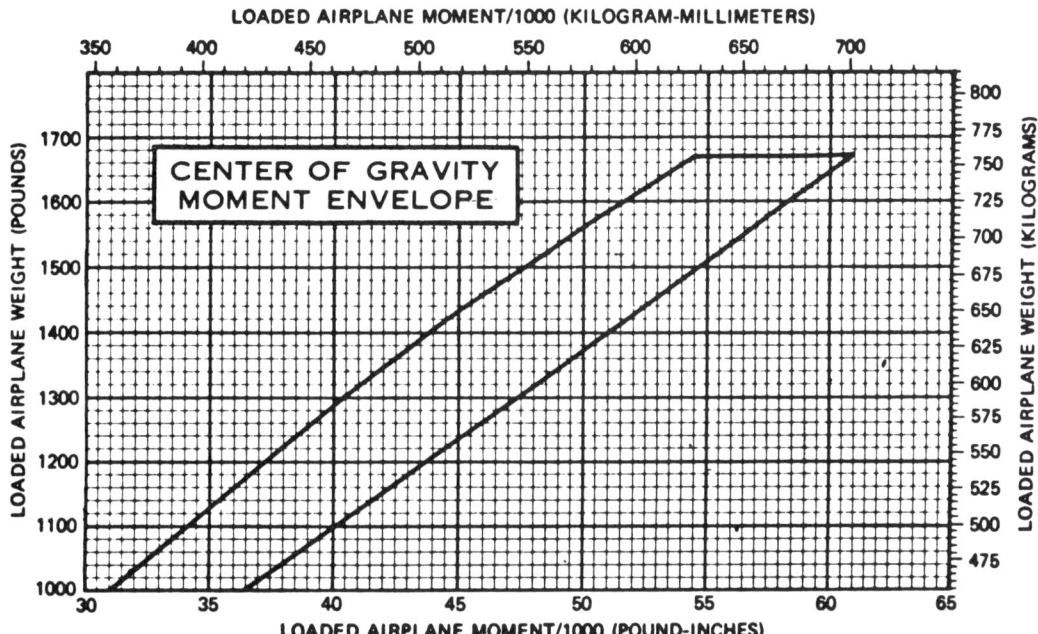

FIG. 8.3—CENTER OF GRAVITY MOMENT ENVELOPE

8. Where your airplane is loaded to the rear of the cg range, it will have these undesirable characteristics:
    a. decreased static and dynamic longitudinal stability, making the airplane very difficult, even impossible, to control;
    b. violent stall characteristics;
    c. very light stick forces, making it easy to overstress the airplane.

SECTION 9—BEFORE YOU GO TO THE AIRPLANE

Section 9
BEFORE YOU GO TO THE AIRPLANE

1. As a student or private pilot who is going to fly from the vicinity of the airport and is serving as pilot in command, you are required to familiarize yourself with all available information about the flight, including:
    a. available weather reports and forecasts (Sec. 39);
        (1) even though you are a student and will be flying with your instructor, you should begin right away to check the weather on your own so that you will become experienced at it;
    b. fuel requirements;
        (1) you may not begin a flight under VFR unless, considering wind and forecast weather conditions, you have enough fuel to fly to your first point of intended landing and, assuming normal cruising fuel consumption, to fly thereafter for at least 30 minutes during the day and 45 minutes at night;
    c. alternatives available if the planned flight cannot be completed;
    d. any known traffic delays of which you have been advised by the ATC.
2. One of the most important factors in every flight is that you will be flying under Visual Flight Rules (VFR) as distinguished from Instrument Flight Rules (IFR) until such time as you receive your instrument rating and are flying on an instrument flight plan;
    a. both for your own safety and to be entirely legal at all times, you must "maintain VFR" at all times while in flight;
    b. this requires that you understand what must be done to maintain VFR and how to check the weather so that it is VFR not only when you take off but for every bit of your flight until you land.
3. For purposes of determining the requirements as to ceiling, visibility and distance from clouds, the airspace is divided into controlled and uncontrolled airspace;
    a. controlled airspace consists of those areas designated as Continental Control Area, Control Area, Control Zones, Terminal Control Areas and Transition Areas;
        (1) when airspace is designated as controlled airspace, it is supported by ground/air communications, navigation aids and air traffic service;
    b. uncontrolled airspace is all other airspace;

SECTION 9—BEFORE YOU GO TO THE AIRPLANE

    c. you should distinguish this kind of control which relates to the existence of VFR conditions from the restrictions and prohibitions on flight which exist in certain areas and are discussed in Sec. 19;

    d. you should also remember that these restrictions are imposed upon you by law and that you are required to comply with them without direction from anyone.

4. A control zone, which is not the same as an airport traffic area (Sec. 31) or an airport advisory area (Sec. 25.10), is controlled airspace that extends from the surface to 14,500 feet mean sea level or higher;

    a. a control zone is normally a circular area within a radius of 5 statute miles of the principal airport within it, but it can contain more than one airport;

    b. it also includes extensions as necessary to include instrument departure and arrival paths;

    c. control zones are shown on sectional charts outlined by a broken blue line;

    d. the chart will also show if a control zone is effective only during certain hours of the day.

5. In *uncontrolled* airspace, you are required to have the following visibility and maintain the following distances from clouds:

    a. 1,200 feet or less above the surface, regardless of MSL altitude—1 statute mile visibility and keep clear of clouds;

    b. more than 1,200 feet above the surface but less than 10,000 feet MSL—1 statute mile visibility and keep 500 feet below, 1,000 feet above and 2,000 feet horizontal from clouds;

    c. more than 1,200 feet above the surface and at or above 10,000 feet MSL—5 statute miles visibility and keep 1,000 feet below, 1,000 feet above and 1 statute mile horizontal from clouds.

6. In *controlled* airspace, you are required to have the following visibility and maintain the following distances from clouds:

    a. 1,200 feet or less above the surface, regardless of MSL altitude—3 statute miles visibility and keep 500 feet below, 1,000 above and 2,000 horizontal from clouds;

    b. more than 1,200 feet above the surface but less than 10,000 MSL—3 statute miles visibility and keep 500 feet below, 1,000 above and 2,000 horizontal from clouds;

    c. more than 1,200 feet above the surface and at or above 10,000 MSL—5 statute miles visibility and keep 1,000 below, 1,000 above and 1 statute mile horizontal from clouds;

    d. in addition, when you are operating within a control zone, the ceiling must be not less than 1,000 feet;

    e. also, if you intend to land or takeoff or enter a traffic pattern within a control zone, the ground visibility must be at least 3 miles at that airport; If ground visibility is not reported at the airport, 3 miles flight visibility is required.

7. Before you taxi out, you should determine the wind direction and velocity;
    a. the wind may be too strong, gusty or both to permit safe flying;
    b. there may be too much crosswind for you to handle as a result of the strength of the wind and alignment of the available runways in relation to the wind;
    c. check with local radio facilities, such as FSS or UNICOM to determine the wind direction and velocity on the field;
    d. visually check by referring to the windsock, wind tee or tetrahedron.
8. Carefully check your weight and balance before each flight. (Sec. 8);
    a. after some experience, you will know whether you are within allowable limits for most loadings, but always check carefully if there is the slightest doubt.
9. Be sure that there is adequate runway, both where you are and at your destination, to take off and land with a comfortable margin of runway left. (Sec. 14.19, 14.20, 14.21, and Sec. 27).
10. As a student, or as a private pilot flying VFR in a single air-cooled engine plane with fixed propeller and non-retractable gear, such as a Cessna 152 or 150, your airplane must be equipped with the following for daytime flight:
    a. airspeed indicator;
    b. altimeter;
    c. magnetic compass;
    d. tachometer;
    e. oil pressure gage;
    f. oil temperature gage;
    g. fuel gage indicating the quantity of fuel in each tank;
    h. an approved safety belt for each occupant two years old or older.

Section 10
HOW TO PREFLIGHT YOUR CESSNA 152 OR 150

1. You are responsible for every airplane you take out to fly. To be sure the airplane is in operating condition and ready to fly, you must make a preflight examination of the airplane before *each* takeoff.
2. No two pilots follow the same identical procedure;
    a. the important thing is to start at the same place every time and to follow a fixed routine so that no step is omitted;
    b. determine to follow the same procedure before *every* flight you make;
    c. sometimes, when you are in a hurry to get going, you will be tempted to skip some of the process but DON'T DO IT!
3. Remove all tie down ropes, gust locks and pitot tube cover, if any.
4. Turn on the master switch;
    a. observe to be sure that both gasoline tanks are FULL; also check the fuel visually;
    b. if both tanks are not full, have them filled;
    c. operate the flaps to full and then retract them;
    d. check landing light, rotating beacon and position lights; turn off the master switch to conserve power.
5. Remove the control wheel lock.
6. Open the engine cowling;
    a. check oil level. The dip stick should show 5 or 6 quarts of oil. (See Sec. 7);
        (1) do not operate with less than 4 quarts of oil;
        (2) be sure the oil cap is locked securely in place;
    b. on the first flight of the day and after each refueling, pull the strainer drain knob and drain for 4 seconds and be sure the strainer drain is closed;
    c. check to be sure there are no connections that are loose or disconnected;
    d. close the cowling securely.
7. Check for bird nests or other foreign objects on the engine and intakes that could cause a fire.
8. Check engine cowling for signs of oil leaks and loose screws.
9. Check the propeller to be sure that it is secure on the shaft.
10. Check the propeller blade for nicks and scratches;
    a. if there is a bad nick in the leading edge, have it filed out by a mechanic as it might be the start of a break in the blade, which is hazardous when it occurs in the air.

11. Check exhaust stacks for cracks.
12. As you walk around the airplane, check the pitot tube, static port, fuel tank vent and stall warning vent opening for stoppage;
    a. remove the pitot tube cover, if any;
    b. be sure there isn't a bug, mud, etc. in the pitot tube and check pitot heat;
13. Check the main landing gear and oleo strut;
    a. look for loose nuts and bolts;
    b. check the oleo strut for proper clearance (2 inches).
14. Check the tires for:
    a. proper inflation;
    b. worn tread, ruptures and other defects.
15. As you walk around, check the metal covering of the wings, fuselage and empennage for wrinkles;
    a. wrinkled skin is good indication of structural damages to the airplane.
16. Test the control surfaces (ailerons, flaps, rudder, elevator) for freedom of movement, and the security of the hinges.
17. Recheck the fuel caps to be sure they are locked in place.
18. Using the sampler cup, drain a sample of fuel from each sump to check for dirt and water. Fuel should be proper color (Sec. 7.2).
19. Check the stall warning signal under the leading edge of the left wing by putting a clean handkerchief over the opening and sucking. The horn should sound.
20. Remove any ice, snow and frost.
21. If a night flight is planned, check the operation of all lights, and flashlight, and check the supply of fuses on hand.

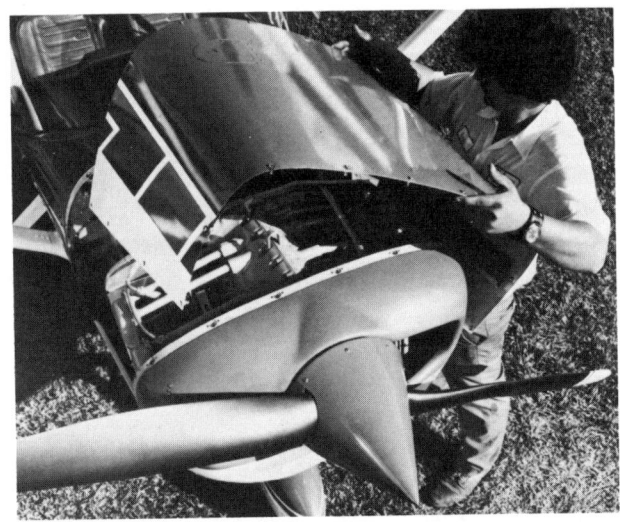

Section 11
STARTING YOUR AIRPLANE

1. When you enter your airplane, it is necessary that you go through a standard series of operations:
    a. use the operating checklist. (Sec. 10). Carelessness in this regard can result in an accident;
    b. be sure your airplane is in a safe place, clear of other airplanes;
    c. avoid starting the airplane in a hangar or on gravel; gravel can cause damage to the airplane, especially to the propeller.
2. Adjust your seat so that you can see well and sit comfortably.
3. Fasten your shoulder harness or seat belt. If, as a private pilot, you are the pilot in command, see that all passengers have their seat belts fastened, and explain the belts' operation.
4. Test the brakes by pushing firmly on the tops of the rudder pedals.
5. Set the parking brake, as follows:
    a. apply the brakes;
    b. pull out on the parking brake knob on the lower left side of your instrument panel;
    c. release the brakes;
    d. release the parking brake knob.
6. To release the parking brake:
    a. apply the release toe pressure on the brake pedals;
    b. be sure the parking brake knob is full in.
7. Turn the master switch ON.
8. Check to be sure that the fuel shutoff valve is in the ON position;
    a. for your Cessna 152, if it is ON, both tanks are on. On some airplanes, the fuel selector can be on the left tank, the right tank or both tanks.
9. The carburetor heat should be in cold position, that is, with the knob pushed all the way forward.
10. The fuel mixture is pushed in all the way, to FULL RICH;
    a. the engine will not start if the fuel mixture is pulled out;
    b. however, it may be pulled out part way, during flight, if operating above 5,000 feet;
    c. if the mixture is not leaned above 5,000 feet, the engine will run rough.

11. Use the primer (Sec. 7.9) as required, by unlocking it (turning it in position so that it can be pulled out);
    a. pull out all the way and wait for several seconds to permit the primer to fill;
    b. if the engine is cold, it may need three full shots of prime;
    c. if the engine is cold but the temperature is not very low, one shot may be enough;
    d. if the engine is hot, no prime is necessary;
    e. in extremely cold weather, it may be necessary to continue priming while cranking;
    f. when priming is completed, push the primer in all the way and turn it sufficiently to be sure it is locked.
12. Open the throttle about ¼ inch.
13. Check the propeller area for people, vehicles, planes and shout, "Clear!"
    a. this may seem unnecessary but *always* do it as a good safety precaution;
    b. it is a constant reminder of the seriousness of a spinning propeller, which can inflict serious, often fatal, injuries.
14. Turn the ignition switch and hold until the engine starts.
15. Adjust the throttle to 800 rpm;
    a. after the engine starts, the oil gage should begin to show pressure within 30 seconds (or twice that long in very cold weather);
        (1) if it does not, stop the engine and have it checked by a mechanic, because lack of oil pressure can cause serious engine damage;
    b. as soon as the oil pressure is in the green arc, you may start to taxi.
16. When the engine is running:
    a. turn on the rotating beacon;
    b. turn on the navigation lights, if at night or if visibility is poor;
    c. turn on the radio(s) and turn up the volume;
    d. tune radio(s) to appropriate frequency;
    e. no special warmup is needed since there is usually sufficient warmup during taxiing and the runup;
    f. every precaution should be taken to avoid overheating the engine on the ground.
17. Taxi to the appropriate runway (Sec. 12).

Section 12
TAXIING YOUR AIRPLANE

1. As a student, you should plan carefully each time before you taxi out to take off:
    a. if there is a control tower in operation, you must contact ground control before you taxi. (See Sec. 31.2);
    b. if there is no control tower but a FSS on or near the field (Aircraft Advisory Area), you do not need their permission to taxi but you should contact them for airport advisories, including the active runway (See Sec. 25.7);
    c. whether you decide which runway to use or it is decided for you by the tower or suggested by the FSS, you should have determined the wind direction so that you can determine the most satisfactory runway;
    d. if the winds are stronger than light and variable, you should select the runway most nearly aligned with the wind so that you take off as nearly into the wind as possible;
    e. be sure that you know where runways and taxiways are located so that you can find your way to the active runway;
    f. most FBOs have a diagram or aerial photo of the airport so that you can study the runways and taxiways and be familiar with them before you taxi out for takeoff;
    g. diagrams of many airports can be found in Jeppesen and NOS approach plates, J-Aids, Sky Prints and in the AOPA Airport Directory.
2. Be sure that you understand the essential facts about runways (Sec. 25.2, & 25.3).
3. Follow these good practices when you taxi your airplane:
    a. avoid excessive speed;
    b. be very careful in taxiing over gravel, cinders, rocks, etc. to avoid damage to the propeller;
    c. use the brakes as little as possible, relying on the steerable nose wheel and rudder for turns as much as possible;
    d. slow down before making turns;
    e. taxi very slowly when going through ice, slush, etc. as it can get into the wheels and pants and freeze solid.
4. When you taxi downwind, push the elevator full forward, lowering the elevator to keep the wind from getting under the elevator and lifting the tail.

5. If there is a crosswind, you should follow these rules:
    a. if the wind is from the right front, raise the right aileron and use a neutral elevator;
    b. if the wind is from the left front, raise the left aileron and use a neutral elevator;
    c. if the wind is from the right rear, lower the right aileron and lower the elevator;
    d. if the wind is from the left rear, lower the left aileron and lower the elevator.
6. The important thing to remember is that if you have a quartering tailwind, you turn the wheel *away* from the wind, with your elevator down (pushed forward).
7. If you have a quartering headwind, turn the wheel *into* the wind with the elevator neutral.
8. Avoid sudden bursts of the throttle and quick stops, particularly if you have a quartering wind.
9. Select a good spot near the end of the active runway to make your runup;
    a. don't cross the yellow restraining line before you are ready to take off;
    b. turn your plane into the wind for better engine cooling;
    c. select a spot so that you can turn around on the runway;
        (1) if there is no tower, you should make a full circle *away* from the runway before entering the runway, to give good opportunity to see aircraft in *all* directions.
10. Your Cessna 152 has a steerable nose wheel which you use by pushing the left rudder pedal to steer left or the right rudder pedal to steer right;
    a. you can increase the degree of turn by applying the left or right brake.

Section 13
THE RUNUP

1. Use your checklist to be sure that nothing is omitted in the runup; it will include the following procedures.
2. Be sure that both doors are closed and securely latched.
3. Be sure that seat belts and shoulder harnesses are securely fastened and that no strap is hanging out of a door.
4. Push the mixture all the way in to RICH, unless you are above 5,000 feet (and there use leaning procedures).
5. Check your elevator, ailerons and rudder, turning each all the way in every direction.
6. Run the flaps all the way down and then back to be sure they are operating properly.
7. Adjust your elevator trim for TAKEOFF.
8. Be sure your fuel shutoff valve is ON.
9. Reduce power to idle with the carburetor heat on to be sure that the engine will idle with heat on, as in landing. It should continue to idle in that condition or repairs are needed.
10. While the engine is idling, the generator light should come on. If it does not, return for repairs.
11. Set your altimeter according to the barometric pressure given by the FSS, ATIS, or tower, or set it to the field elevation;
    a. If there is disagreement between the barometric pressure which is given by the FSS and that indicated by setting the altimeter on the elevation of the airport, note the difference, since you will need this figure to correct any barometric readings given while in flight.
12. Adjust the trim tab so that it is set for takeoff. If there is any question, lift the elevator, look around to see that the trim tab is level with the elevator.
13. Set your directional gyro to agree with your magnetic compass.
14. Carburetor heat—cold.
15. Apply the parking brake.
16. Throttle to 1,700 rpm.
17. Check the magnetos, as follows:
    a. turn from BOTH to LEFT, noting the amount of drop in rpms and then back to BOTH;
    b. turn from BOTH to RIGHT, noting the amount of drop in rpms and then back to BOTH;

      c. if the drop in rpms differs more than 100 in switching to either magneto, taxi back and have the trouble corrected;
      d. if either magneto fails to drop, taxi back and have it repaired;
         (1) you have a hot magneto, which is dangerous, because the engine can start unintentionally.
18. Pull out carburetor heat to check for proper operation. It should drop 75 to 100 rpm and return to the original setting when you remove the heat.
19. Check the suction gage to be sure that it registers between 4.6 and 5.4 inches.
20. Check your engine instruments and ammeter.
21. Set all the proper frequencies in your radio, VOR, and ADF, and set the transponder to ON and squawk 1200, the VFR code.

Section 14
THE TAKEOFF

1. As a student, you should not make an intersection takeoff unless your instructor has specifically authorized it;
    a. as a safety measure, you should get into the habit of using *every* foot of the runway.
2. When you have your Private Pilot Certificate, you should consider intersection takeoffs but only when you are assured of having somewhat more than the minimum takeoff distance, considering the weather and other factors, such as weight. (See Sec. 14.28);
    a. the tower or an FSS on or near the field can advise you the distance from the intersection to the end of the runway.
3. The tower can permit an intersection takeoff, either at its own instance or at your request;
    a. you do not have to accept the intersection takeoff but must advise the tower immediately if you want to use the entire runway;
    b. the tower must enforce a three minute wait before clearing you after large aircraft;
    c. if, after carefully considering the wake turbulence problem, you don't want to wait three minutes, you say REQUEST WAIVER TO 3 MINUTE INTERVAL;
        (1) by doing this, you accept full responsibility for your own wake turbulence separation;
        (2) the waiver will not be given if you are departing behind a heavy jet.
4. Before any takeoff, whether at a controlled or uncontrolled airport, check carefully for heavy aircraft either *landing* or *taking off* on *any* runway, so that you can evaluate the possible impact of wake turbulence. (See Sec. 22.)
5. If there is an operating control tower, switch to tower frequency *before* taking the active runway and announce that you are ready for takeoff.
6. If there is no control tower but an FSS, contact it on 123.6 and announce that you are ready for takeoff. This is not required but is good procedure.
7. If there is no tower or FSS, contact Unicom on 122.8 and announce your intentions.
8. If there is none of these, announce your intentions on 122.9.
9. Upon entering the runway, line up straight with the runway, on the center line;
    a. adjust your directional gyro. It should agree with your magnetic compass and the runway direction.
10. Apply full throttle power by pushing the throttle in *smoothly.*

11. Use your rudder to hold the airplane on the centerline of the runway;
    a. torque and "P" factor (see glossary) will cause the airplane to have a slight tendency to turn to the left during the takeoff roll and the climb out;
    b. this is corrected by a light pressure on the right rudder;
    c. this force becomes great in larger airplanes, requiring a rudder trim to reduce the pressure required in takeoff in such planes.
12. Lift the nose wheel gently off the ground when the airspeed reaches 50 KIAS;
    a. the airplane will take off as soon as the airspeed is sufficient.
13. As soon as the airplane is off the ground, lower the nose gently;
    a. fly level over the runway until the airspeed reaches 65 KIAS;
    b. normal climbs are at 65 to 75 KIAS with flaps up and full throttle.
14. If there are obstacles to clear, you will climb at the best angle-of-climb airspeed (V_x) until the obstacles are cleared;
    a. in your Cessna 152, this is 54 KIAS with flaps up and full throttle;
    b. avoid steep climbs of long duration to avoid engine heating.
15. If you want the best rate-of-climb airspeed (the speed that gives you the greatest gain in altitude in a given horizontal distance) you will climb at 68 KIAS at sea level and 62 KIAS at 10,000 feet.
16. Be constantly ready for the possibility of an engine failure during your takeoff run; if a failure should occur with some runway left, follow this procedure:
    a. pull your throttle all the way back;
    b. apply your brakes sufficiently to avoid running off the runway;
    c. retract your wing flaps;
    d. pull your fuel mixture all the way back;
    e. turn your ignition switch off;
    f. turn your master switch off.
17. If you are airborne and there is no runway left for a landing, be prepared in advance to land as follows:
    a. maintain your airspeed at 60 KIAS;
    b. pull your fuel mixture all the way back;
    c. turn your fuel shutoff valve to OFF;
    d. turn your ignition switch off;
    e. use wing flaps as required;
    f. turn your master switch off;
    g. don't try to turn back but land straight ahead to avoid a fatal stall;
    h. if landing into trees seems inevitable, try to land between two large trees so that the wings absorb the shock.
18. Climb to 400 feet above ground level (AGL), continuing to hold your course straight over the runway.

SECTION 14—THE TAKEOFF

19. When you are within 300 feet of pattern altitude, but not before the end of the runway, lower the nose and get the airspeed to 65–75 KIAS; then make a 90-degree turn to the left (unless a right hand pattern applies to that runway).
20. Look, *really look,* in all directions for the position of all other aircraft in the area.
21. Keep the airspeed up to 70 KIAS during turns in departing from the airport.
22. Throughout the takeoff, constantly check the instruments and traffic;
    a. keep your eyes moving. They should not come to rest on any instrument.
23. It is recommended that you continue straight ahead and that if you intend to remain in the traffic pattern, begin the turn to your crosswind leg when beyond the departure end of the runway, within 300 feet of pattern altitude;
    a. if you are leaving the traffic pattern, continue straight out or exit within a 45-degree turn beyond the departure end of the runway and after reaching pattern altitude. (See Sec. 25.7);
    b. be very careful to watch for other aircraft, particularly those on downwind and those landing on other runways or executing a missed approach.
24. It is permissible to remain in the traffic pattern if you intend to make touch-and-go landings;
    a. if so, rather than making a 45-degree turn to leave the pattern, make a 90-degree turn to the left when within 300 feet of pattern altitude and continue climbing until you reach traffic pattern altitude;
    b. be sure you are cleared to do touch-and-goes if there is an operating control tower;
    c. if there is no control tower but an Aircraft Advisory Service, inform the FSS of your intentions and, from time to time, your position in the traffic pattern.
25. When you reach your desired altitude, level off, throttle back to 2,000–2,750 rpm, and trim your plane so that it will fly level without back or forward pressure on the elevator.
26. SHORT FIELD TAKEOFF—The same procedures are followed in general with the following exceptions:
    a. taxi to the extreme end of the runway;
    b. apply 10 degrees of flaps;
    c. apply your brakes;
    d. smoothly apply full power;
    e. release the brakes;
    f. pull back on elevator to lift off at 54 KIAS;
    g. continue to climb out over obstacles at 54 KIAS;
    h. when past obstacles, lower the nose to gain airspeed to 65 KIAS, and retract the flaps;
    i. be very careful to avoid a stall by keeping your speed up and avoiding banks until you are high and fast.
27. SOFT FIELD TAKEOFF—If the field is soft or there is snow on the runway, the procedures outlined above are followed for takeoff, as in any normal situation, with these exceptions:
    a. taxi to the extreme end of the runway and be prepared to take off without stopping;

b. apply 10 degrees of flaps;
c. apply full power;
d. immediately lift the nose off the ground and hold it off the ground, to avoid the danger of having the airplane nose over;
e. let the plane take off as soon as possible;
f. as soon as the airplane is off the ground, lower the nose to gain airspeed;
g. at 200 feet AGL, raise the flaps. Be prepared for the fact that the plane will drop a little.

28. Before every takeoff, you should carefully consider the following factors in determining whether there is sufficient runway for your takeoff:
    a. *pressure altitude*—this is the elevation as read from your altimeter when the altimeter setting window (Kollsman window) is adjusted to 29.92.
       (1) the *higher* the pressure altitude, the *longer* the takeoff distance required;
    b. *temperature*—the higher the temperature, the more runway required; high temperatures can raise the density altitude by thousands of feet;
    c. *humidity*—humid air is less dense and provides less lift so that the greater the density, the more runway is needed;
    d. *gross weight*—the greater your gross weight, the more runway required;
    e. *runway surface*—long grass, sand, mud or deep snow can double the length of your takeoff run;
    f. *headwind component*—the stronger your headwind, the shorter the takeoff run; a tailwind can greatly increase the runway required;
    g. *ground effect*—this is the ability of your wing to give greater lift when close to the ground, making you think that you are able to take off; as a result, if you lift off at too slow a speed, you will come back down; ground effect can also produce floating when you land;
    h. *flaps*—the use of flaps on takeoff is recommended for some planes but not for others; this can result in a shorter takeoff distance;
    i. *inclined runway*—requires greater or less distance for takeoff; taking off uphill can require a much greater takeoff distance.

29. Use the Takeoff Distance Chart from the Owners Manual for your airplane, particularly noting that:
    a. speed may be given in knots or miles per hour;
    b. temperature may be given in Fahrenheit or Celsius;
    c. altitudes may be given at specific levels and temperatures, or they may be given in pressure altitude;
    d. the chart may be based on flaps up or some specified degree of flaps;
    e. no adjustment has been made for soft field conditions, which you must weigh by multiplying your final figure by a safety factor;
    f. you will be required to adjust your computation for any headwind, in accordance with instructions given with the chart.

SECTION 14—THE TAKEOFF

WEIGHT LBS	TAKEOFF SPEED KIAS		PRESS ALT FT	0°C		10°C		20°C		30°C		40°C	
	LIFT OFF	AT 50 FT		GRND ROLL	TOTAL TO CLEAR 50 FT OBS	GRND ROLL	TOTAL TO CLEAR 50 FT OBS	GRND ROLL	TOTAL TO CLEAR 50 FT OBS	GRND ROLL	TOTAL TO CLEAR 50 FT OBS	GRND ROLL	TOTAL TO CLEAR 50 FT OBS
1670	50	54	S.L.	640	1190	695	1290	755	1390	810	1495	875	1605
			1000	705	1310	765	1420	825	1530	890	1645	960	1770
			2000	775	1445	840	1565	910	1690	980	1820	1055	1960
			3000	855	1600	925	1730	1000	1870	1080	2020	1165	2185
			4000	940	1775	1020	1920	1100	2080	1190	2250	1285	2440
			5000	1040	1970	1125	2140	1215	2320	1315	2525	1420	2750
			6000	1145	2200	1245	2395	1345	2610	1455	2855	1570	3125
			7000	1270	2470	1375	2705	1490	2960	1615	3255	1745	3590
			8000	1405	2800	1525	3080	1655	3395	1795	3765	1940	4195

FIG. 14.1—TAKEOFF DISTANCES OF CESSNA 152

Note: These distances are based upon new equipment in good operating condition, flown by an experienced pilot, with zero wind, 10 degrees of flaps, paved, level, dry runway, with full throttle prior to releasing the brake.

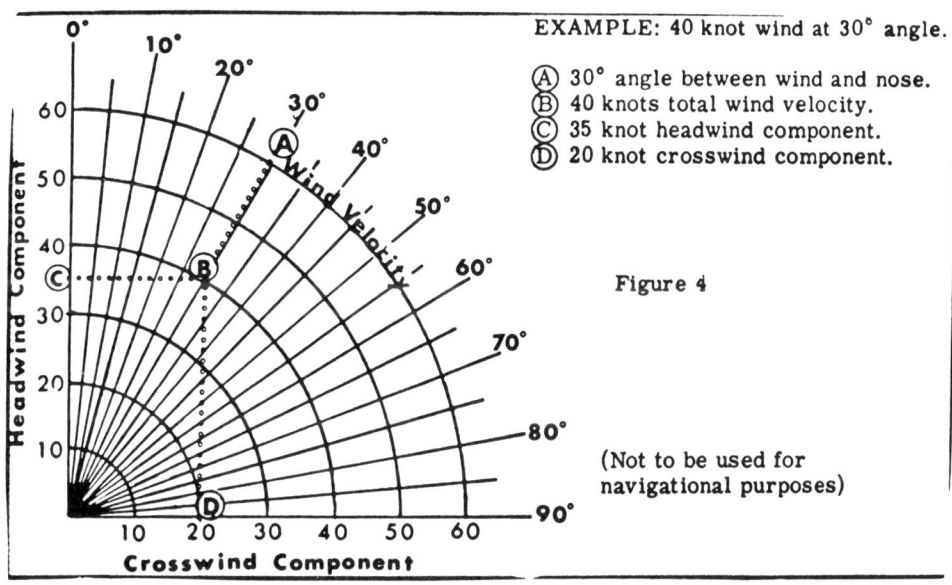

FIG. 14.2—CROSSWIND COMPONENT CHART

30. Use special care in taking off when there is a crosswind;
    a. as a student, avoid any strong crosswind until you are fully capable of dealing with it;
    b. never take off when the crosswind component is more than that recommended for your airplane;
    c. to determine the crosswind component use Fig. 14.2 by going up the line on the left until you reach the wind speed and then going right to the amount of angle there is between the wind and the nose of the airplane on the runway and then come straight down to get the crosswind component;
    d. the maximum demonstrated crosswind velocity for the Cessna 152 is 12 knots, that is, if you had a wind of that speed coming perpendicularly from either your right or left, you should not attempt to take off. As the angle reduces, the component gets less;
    e. do not use any flaps except to the extent required to get off due to the short amount of runway available;
    f. accelerate to a little greater airspeed than normal before lifting off;
    g. lift off fairly abruptly to avoid settling back onto the runway;
    h. just as soon as you are clear of the ground, crab into the wind to keep lined up with the runway.

SECTION 15—NORMAL FLIGHT

Section 15
NORMAL FLIGHT

1. When you have reached your desired altitude, level the plane by checking the airplane's attitude and by reference to the artificial horizon.
2. Continue full throttle until the airspeed reaches 87 KIAS, and then throttle back to 1,900–2,550 rpm.
3. Use your trim tab to trim the airplane, so that it will neither climb nor descend, with no pressure applied to the elevator;
    a. in trimming the airplane, apply the necessary pressure to the elevator so that the plane will fly level and then roll the trim tab wheel sufficiently to remove that pressure;
    b. rolling the trim tab wheel forward will cause the nose to lower;
    c. rolling the trim backward will cause the nose to rise.
4. During normal flight, keep checking the wind direction, both by observation and weather reports, and an eye out for possible emergency landing spots (See Sec. 43 for a discussion of emergency landing procedures.).
5. The wings must be kept level during straight and level flight; this can be done in several ways:
    a. by checking the wingtips to be sure they are both the same distance above the horizon;
    b. by reference to the artificial horizon;
    c. by developing a feel or sense of being level, which comes with experience;
    d. by using some portion of the airplane as a reference point, establishing its relationship to the horizon;
    e. by keeping a light touch on the controls and refraining from excessive use of the controls;
        (1) when properly trimmed, your airplane will normally maintain straight and level flight with little or no assistance.
6. All turns of the airplane should be smoothly *coordinated;*
    a. a turn is coordinated when the aileron and the rudder are both applied in the right amount and at the right time so that the airplane will not *slip* or *skid;*
    b. a *skid* occurs when too much rudder or not enough aileron, is applied;
    c. a *slip* occurs when too much aileron or not enough rudder, is applied;

37

d. you can detect skids and slips immediately by checking the turn-and-bank indicator, as the ball moves to one side or the other;
   e. in a right turn, if the ball moves to the right, the error may be corrected by using more right rudder;
   f. in a right turn, if the ball moves to the left, the error may be corrected by using *less* right rudder (pushing on the *left* rudder);
   g. if the ball is out of center to the right, step on the right rudder; if the ball is out to the left side, step on the left rudder.
7. The bank of a turn is described as shallow, medium or steep;
   a. a shallow bank is any bank up to 20 degrees;
      (1) while in a shallow bank, the airplane tends to right itself, so that a constant pressure on the aileron is needed;
   b. a medium bank is any bank from 20 to 35 degrees;
      (1) while in a medium bank, the airplane tends to hold the same attitude, so that little or no pressure is needed to retain the airplane's attitude;
   c. a steep bank is any bank in excess of 35 degrees;
      (1) while in a steep bank, the tendency of the airplane is to make an even steeper bank, so that some opposite pressure on the aileron is required.
8. There is a natural tendency for the student pilot to sway in his seat during turns, especially if the bank is steep, in order to keep perpendicular to the ground;
   a. it is important that you learn to overcome this tendency as quickly as possible by remaining perpendicular to the floor of the airplane throughout the turn.
9. A normal climb is entered by the application of back pressure on the elevator control and applying full power;
   a. your rate of climb is shown on the vertical speed indicator;
   b. the climb angle is determined by reference to the artificial horizon, as well as the natural horizon.
10. during any extended flight, you should check the directional gyroscope every 15 minutes and re-set, if necessary;
    a. select a heading, and fly the airplane at cruise speed, straight and level, while making the adjustment;
    b. when you have arrived at the heading, adjust the directional gyro so that it agrees with your compass;
    c. as your directional gyro gets older, it will precess faster, requiring repair or replacement.
11. During flights extending to more than brief periods, the altimeter should be reset to the current barometric pressure.
12. As you increase your altitude you will want to lean your fuel mixture for better engine operation and economy;

a. while you may find it advantageous to lean the mixture at lower altitudes, you will definitely want to do so from 5,000 feet and up;
b. if you do not have an Exhaust Gas Temperature (EGT) gage, lean the mixture by pulling out the fuel mixture button very slowly and smoothly until the engine runs rough and then return it just enough for it to run smoothly;
c. you will do this from time to time as you change altitude;
d. don't try to lean the mixture too much as that causes the engine to run too hot and will damage it;
e. don't forget to return your fuel mixture to full rich as you descend for a landing.

Section 16
YOUR ALTITUDE IN FLIGHT

1. One of the most important considerations while you are flying is the determination of your altitude and flying at the proper altitude.
2. Altitude is measured in two ways:
    a. while you are flying, some important concepts are based upon your altitude *above ground level* (AGL);
    b. some of the measurements which are made in comparison to ground level are:
        (1) traffic pattern altitudes;
        (2) the height of cloud bases above the ground;
        (3) the extent of control in control zones and control areas;
    c. other measurements are based upon your altitude above *mean sea level* (MSL), sometimes described as *above sea level* (asl);
        (1) for your practical purposes, mean sea level is the same as sea level;
    c. some of the measurements which are made in comparison with mean sea level are:
        (1) your altitude in flying;
        (2) the elevation of an airport and terrain;
    e. artificial obstacles, such as towers, are depicted on charts both in MSL and AGL.
3. The word altitude is used in several different ways, so that it is important for you to understand each of the terms and their significance to you;
    a. *true altitude* is the actual height of the airplane above sea level;
    b. *indicated altitude* is the altitude that your altimeter indicates, above sea level; this may or may not be the *true altitude,* because:
        (1) the altimeter may not have been adjusted in the first place;
        (2) the altimeter, even though correct at takeoff will be incorrect to the extent that there will be changes in airpressure and temperature which can change the correct altimeter setting;
        (3) the altimeter may be inaccurate;
    c. *pressure altitude* is the altitude reading on your airplane's altimeter if you adjust the barometric window to 29.92;
        (1) this is the altitude which you will use in solving computer problems for density altitude and true airspeed;

SECTION 16—YOUR ALTITUDE IN FLIGHT

    d. *density altitude* is pressure altitude corrected for non-standard temperature.
4. Your altitude is measured in your airplane by the *altimeter;*
    a. the altimeter is part of the pitot static system and is operated by the pressure of the air in that system;
    b. an increase of .1 of an inch of mercury will result in an increase of 100 feet in the altitude reading so that if there is an increase of one inch in the pressure setting, there will be an increase of 1,000 feet in the altitude reading.
    c. decreases of inches in mercury will result in equivalent decreases of altitude reading;
    d. at the same altitude, increases in temperature make the altimeter indicate the airplane is *higher* than it actually is;
    e. at the same altitude, decreases in temperature make the altimeter indicate that the airplane is *lower* than it actually is;
    f. at the same altitude, increases in the actual barometric pressure will indicate that the airplane is *lower* than it actually is;
    g. at the same altitude, decreases in the actual barometric pressure will indicate that the airplane is *higher* than it actually is;
    d. the way to remember these effects to temperature and barometric changes on reading your altimeter, remember the expression: When flying from a high to a low, or hot to cold, look out below, because you are flying *lower* than your altimeter is telling you.
5. Your altimeter consists of three pointers in a dial and a Kollsman window. Each of the pointers has a different meaning;

FIG. 16.1—READING THE ALTIMETER—(1) 7,500', (2) 7,880', (3) 1,380', (4) 8,800', (5) 12,420', (6) 880'.

a. the longest pointer makes one complete revolution for each 1,000 feet of increase in altitude; it indicates hundreds of feet;
b. the short middle sized pointer makes one complete revolution for each 10,000 feet and indicates thousands of feet;
c. the shortest pointer indicates ten thousands of feet;
d. your altimeter is probably equipped with an altimeter setting window which is usually is known as the Kollsman window;
   (1) this permits you to adjust your altimeter to the current altimeter setting.
6. In order to maintain the required altitude during flight, you are required to set your altimeter to the current pressure;
   a. when cruising below 18,000 feet MSL, you set to the current reported altimeter setting of a station along your route and within 100 nautical miles of your airplane;
   b. if there is no such station, or if you have no radio, set your altimeter to the elevation of departure or an appropriate altimeter setting before departure;
   c. bear in mind that the altimeter setting broadcast by the ground station is the station pressure corrected to MSL, but it does not take into account distortions at higher levels and particularly the effect of nonstandard temperature.
7. During normal flight, you are required to maintain certain altitudes above ground level, except during takeoff and landing;
   a. when flying over any congested area of a city, town or settlement, or over any open air assembly of persons, you must maintain an altitude of 1,000 feet above the highest obstacle within a horizontal radius of 2,000 feet of the aircraft;
   b. when flying over an area that is *not* congested, you must maintain an altitude of 500 feet above the surface;
   c. when you are flying over open water or sparsely populated areas, you may fly closer to the surface except that you may not operate your airplane closer than 500 feet to any person, vessel, vehicle or structure; this 500 feet can be either vertical or horizontal separation.
8. When you are more than 3,000 feet AGL, your altitude is governed by your *magnetic* course;
   a. when your *magnetic course* is zero through 179 degrees, you must fly at any odd thousand-foot level above sea level, plus 500 feet;
      (1) that is, if your direction is any portion of the east half of the compass, and you are more than 3,000 feet AGL, your altitude must be 3,500 feet, 5,500 feet, and so on;
   b. if your magnetic course is in any portion of the west half of your compass (180 through 359 degrees), and you are more than 3,000 feet, your altitude must be 4,500, 6,500 feet, and so on;
   c. there are other regulations, but they do not apply to you since they apply to altitudes above the service ceiling of your airplane.

9. During flight, you must not come within 2,000 feet above the surface within 5 statute miles of a *disaster area*:
    a. a disaster area is a place where there has been an aircraft or train accident, forest fire, earthquake, flood, or other disaster of substantial magnitude;
    b. a designation of a disaster area is made in the Notices to Airmen, but can be of such recent happening that it will not be shown there;
    c. under some circumstances, airplanes with a proper purpose may operate in the disaster area, but these are not conditions that will normally apply to the student pilot or most private pilots.
10. There are important restrictions on how high you can fly:
    a. the service ceiling is that altitude at which your airplane's maximum rate of climb is 100 feet per minute or less;
        (1) the service ceiling of your Cessna 152 is 14,700 feet;
    b. you cannot fly higher than 18,000 feet (Positive Control Areas) unless you are instrument rated and are on an IFR flight plan;
    c. you cannot fly higher than 12,500 feet without an encoding altimeter and a transponder;
    d. you must have oxygen at certain altitudes;
        (1) the oxygen must be provided for all crew members when you fly between 12,500 and 14,000 feet for more than 30 minutes;
        (2) you must continuously provide oxygen for all crew members if you fly at more than 14,000 feet;
        (3) you must make oxygen available for all passengers if you fly at more than 15,000 feet.
11. You must always fly sufficiently high to clear all mountains and other obstacles that might be in your path, with some margin to spare.
    a. much information about obstructions is shown on your aeronautical charts.

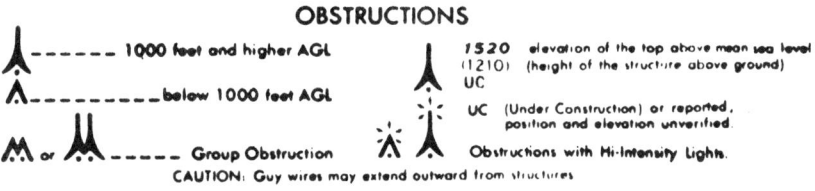

FIG. 16.2—OBSTRUCTION DEPICTION AND AERONAUTICAL CHARTS

12. Your selected altitude may be determined by the forecast winds aloft;
    a. at different altitudes the direction and strength of the wind may vary considerably so

that you would have much more favorable tailwind (or less headwind) at one altitude than another;
   b. all other things being equal, you will select the altitude under 10,000 feet where you get the most help.
13. Clouds will often be an important factor in selecting your altitude:
   a. it is usually smoother, with better visibility, above cumulus clouds;
   b. if you are not instrument rated, you must not risk being caught above a layer of clouds or flying into clouds;
   c. you must plan for altitude changes in cross-country flying where it appears that there is any likelihood of flying into a cloud layer or getting caught above a broken or solid layer of clouds.

Section 17
YOUR SPEED IN FLIGHT

1. It is very important that you understand how your speed in flight is measured;
    a. you are used to measuring speed in miles per hour (mph);
    b. while you may measure speed in flight in miles-per-hour, you must also understand the significance of knots, that is, the speed measured in nautical miles-per-hour;
        (1) to convert from miles-per-hour to knots, you multiply the number of miles-per-hour by .869;
        (2) to convert the knots to miles-per-hour, you divide the number of knots by 1.15;
2. It is necessary that you understand these kinds of airspeed:
    a. *indicated airspeed* (IAS) is the direct instrument reading that you observe on your airspeed indicator, uncorrected for variations in atmospheric density, installation error and instrument error;
        (1) this is known as Knots Indicated Airspeed (KIAS) when shown in knots;
    b. *Calibrated Airspeed* (CAS) is indicated airspeed corrected for installation error and instrument error;
        (1) this error is greatest at lowest speeds and is almost eliminated at high airspeeds;
        (2) this is known as Knots Calibrated Airspeed (KCAS) when expressed in knots;
    c. *true airspeed*—the true speed that the airplane is traveling through the air;
        (1) your airspeed indicator registers true airspeed under standard sea level conditions, that is when the pressure is 29.92 and the temperature is 15°C;
        (2) for a given true airspeed, indicated airspeed decreases as altitude increases, and for a given indicated airspeed, true airspeed increases with an increase in altitude;
        (3) you can make a close approximation for true airspeed by adding to the indicated airspeed 2% of the indicated airspeed for each 1,000 feet of altitude;
    d. *groundspeed* is the speed at which an airplane is traveling over the ground;
        (1) if there is no wind, the groundspeed equals your true airspeed;
        (2) if there is a headwind, your groundspeed is your true airspeed *less* the amount of the headwind;
        (3) if there is a tailwind, your groundspeed is your true airspeed *plus* the amount of the tailwind;

(4) if there is a crosswind, you must use your computer to determine your groundspeed, which then depends on your true airspeed and the direction and speed of the wind.

3. There are various speeds that control your actions in flight and that vary from one type of aircraft to another, some of which may vary for the same airplane, depending on various conditions;

    a. it is very important that you learn what these airspeeds are for your airplane.

Speed Designation	Speed Name	Explanation	KIAS	How Indicated
V_{ne}	Never exceed	Do not exceed in any operation	149	Red line
None	Maximum window open speed	Self-explanatory	143	Not indicated
V_{no}	Maximum structural cruising speed	Exceed only in smooth air, with caution	111	Bottom of yellow & top of green arc
V_a	Maneuvering speed: 1670 pounds 1500 pounds 1350 pounds	Maximum speed for full or abrupt control movements	104 98 93	Not indicated
V_{fe}	Maximum flap extended speed	Do not use flaps when flying faster than this speed	85	Top of white arc
V_y	Best rate of climb airspeed	Gives the most altitude in the least time	67	Not indicated
V_x	Best angle of climb airspeed	Gives the most gain of altitude in the least distance	54	Not indicated
V_s	Stalling speed	Least speed at which a plane is controllable in steady flight	40	Bottom of green arc
V_{so}	Stalling speed	Least speed at which a plane is controllable in landing configuration	35	Bottom of white arc

FIG. 17.1—PERTINENT AIRSPEEDS FOR THE CESSNA 152

Note: Climb speeds vary according to altitude above sea level.

4. *Airspeed indicator markings.* Your airspeed indicator has a standard color-coded marking system;

    a. this permits you to determine at a glance certain airspeeds that are of extreme importance to the safe operation of your airplane;

    b. these airspeeds for the Cessna 152 are indicated in Fig. 17.2.

SECTION 17-YOUR SPEED IN FLIGHT

Marking	Significance	KIAS Value or Range
Red line	Maximum speed for *all* operations	141
Yellow arc	Cautious operations in smooth air only	107–141
Green arc	Normal operating range	47–107
White arc	Full flap operating range	42–85

FIG. 17.2—AIRSPEED INDICATOR MARKINGS FOR THE CESSNA 152

5. You read your indicated airspeed from your *airspeed indicator;*
   a. the airspeed indicator is a sensitive, differential pressure gage that measures and shows fairly promptly the difference between pitot, or impact pressure, and static pressure;
   b. static pressure is the undisturbed atmospheric pressure at your flight level;
   c. the two pressures are equal when the aircraft is parked on the ground in calm air;
   d. when the aircraft moves through the air, the pressure on the pitot line, becomes greater than the pressure in a static line and the difference is registered by the airspeed pointer on the face of the instrument.
6. Some airplanes have a *true airspeed indicator.* It shows the true airspeed and the indicated airspeed in a manner similar to the operation of a flight computer; to compute true airspeed:
   a. obtain the pressure altitude by setting the barometric scale on the altimeter to 29.92 and read the pressure altitude on the altimeter;
      (1) don't forget to return the altimeter barometric scale to the original barometric setting as soon as you have read the pressure altitude;
   b. rotate the ring on the true airspeed indicator until the pressure altitude is aligned with the outside air temperature in degrees Fahrenheit;
   c. read true airspeed on the rotatable ring opposite the airspeed needle.
   d. you can also compute airspeed using your computer:
      (1) set the true air temperature (from your OAT—outside air temperature thermometer) over the pressure altitude (set your altimeter to 29.92 to read);
      (2) read your indicated airspeed on the inside wheel. Opposite it on the outside wheel is your true airspeed.
7. The *vertical speed indicator* shows whether the airplane is climbing, descending, or in level flight;
   a. the rate of climb or descent is indicated in feet per minute;
   b. if the instrument is properly calibrated, the indicator will register zero while the airplane is in level flight;
   c. there is a delay, after the airplane begins any climb or descent, before the vertical speed indicator gives the correct rate indication;
      (1) as a result, smoothness in flight is lost if the pilot tries to "chase the needle;"

(2) you should not try to maintain level flight with the vertical speed indicator, but should use it primarily to establish a determined rate of climb or descent.

PRESSURE ALTITUDE FT	RPM	20°C BELOW STANDARD TEMP			STANDARD TEMPERATURE			20°C ABOVE STANDARD TEMP		
		% BHP	KTAS	GPH	% BHP	KTAS	GPH	% BHP	KTAS	GPH
2000	2400	- - -	- - -	- - -	75	101	6.1	70	101	5.7
	2300	71	97	5.7	66	96	5.4	63	95	5.1
	2200	62	92	5.1	59	91	4.8	56	90	4.6
	2100	55	87	4.5	53	86	4.3	51	85	4.2
	2000	49	81	4.1	47	80	3.9	46	79	3.8
4000	2450	- - -	- - -	- - -	75	103	6.1	70	102	5.7
	2400	76	102	6.1	71	101	5.7	67	100	5.4
	2300	67	96	5.4	63	95	5.1	60	95	4.9
	2200	60	91	4.8	56	90	4.6	54	89	4.4
	2100	53	86	4.4	51	85	4.2	49	84	4.0
	2000	48	81	3.9	46	80	3.8	45	78	3.7
6000	2500	- - -	- - -	- - -	75	105	6.1	71	104	5.7
	2400	72	101	5.8	67	100	5.4	64	99	5.2
	2300	64	96	5.2	60	95	4.9	57	94	4.7
	2200	57	90	4.6	54	89	4.4	52	88	4.3
	2100	51	85	4.2	49	84	4.0	48	83	3.9
	2000	46	80	3.8	45	79	3.7	44	77	3.6
8000	2550	- - -	- - -	- - -	75	107	6.1	71	106	5.7
	2500	76	105	6.2	71	104	5.8	67	103	5.4
	2400	68	100	5.5	64	99	5.2	61	98	4.9
	2300	61	95	5.0	58	94	4.7	55	93	4.5
	2200	55	90	4.5	52	89	4.3	51	87	4.2
	2100	49	84	4.1	48	83	3.9	46	82	3.8
10,000	2500	72	105	5.8	68	103	5.5	64	103	5.2
	2400	65	99	5.3	61	98	5.0	58	97	4.8
	2300	58	94	4.7	56	93	4.5	53	92	4.4
	2200	53	89	4.3	51	88	4.2	49	86	4.0
	2100	48	83	4.0	46	82	3.9	45	81	3.8
12,000	2450	65	101	5.3	62	100	5.0	59	99	4.8
	2400	62	99	5.0	59	97	4.8	56	96	4.6
	2300	56	93	4.6	54	92	4.4	52	91	4.3
	2200	51	88	4.2	49	87	4.1	48	85	4.0
	2100	47	82	3.9	45	81	3.8	44	79	3.7

FIG. 17.3—CRUISE PERFORMANCE OF CESSNA 152

Note: These figures are based upon new equipment in good operating condition, flown by an experienced pilot, at 1670 pounds, using recommended lean mixture, with speed fairings.

8. You have a limited amount of control over the speed at which your airplane will fly, and within those limitations you will determine how fast you want to fly;
    a. since you have a fixed-pitch propeller, you control your speed in level flight and with no flaps by your throttle setting;
        (1) this differs from an airplane with a constant-speed propeller, where the pilot controls the airspeed through using the manifold pressure and the control of the number of propeller revolutions per minute (rpms);
    b. the lower your throttle setting, the better gas mileage you will receive;
    c. normally, an airplane does not get any appreciable increase in speed as it increases the Brake Horse Power (BHP) over 75%;
    d. you should constantly refer to the Cruise Performance chart (Fig. 17.3) to arrive at the best throttle setting to obtain the best combination of speed and fuel economy.

Section 18
YOUR DIRECTION OF FLIGHT

1. One of the most important factors that affect your flights is direction, which you need to understand in order to (1) plan your flights, (2) avoid getting lost and (3) get to your destination by the shortest possible route;
    a. in earlier times, navigation was based upon the Compass Rose, which consists of the 16 points of the compass, from north through southeast, west, north northwest, and back to north;
    b. while we continue to use the points of the compass, aerial navigation is largely based upon the 360-degree circle;
        (1) North is 0 degrees (or 360) while south is 180, west is 270;
    c. directions from one point to another are indicated in terms of degrees measured in a *clockwise* direction from *true north*;
    d. these measurements are based upon meridians that converge at the North Pole;
        (1) the measurements are based upon the prime meridian which passes through Greenwich, England, just outside London, and which gives rise to Greenwich Mean Time (GMT), which is used in aviation.
2. The *magnetic* North Pole is about 1,300 miles from the *true* North Pole;
    a. therefore, your magnetic compass points to the magnetic pole and not to the true North Pole, which requires an adjustment to convert *magnetic* readings to *true* readings;
    b. *variation* is the angle between true north and magnetic north at any given place;
    c. it is expressed as *east variation* or *west variation,* depending on whether magnetic north (MN) is to the east or west of true north (TN);
    d. the compass needle points in the general direction of magnetic north but, since the earth is not uniformly magnetized, it may vary in certain geographical localities by many degrees;
        (1) as a result, sectionals include broken red lines, called *isogonic lines,* that connect points of equal magnetic variation;
        (2) the line that connects points at which there is *no variation* between true north and magnetic north is called the *agonic line;*

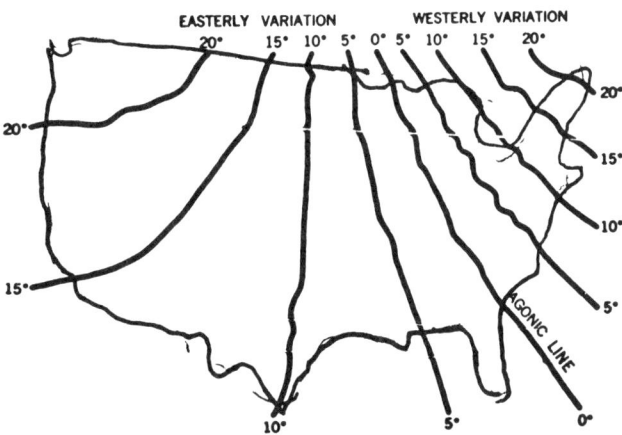

FIG. 18.1—AN ISOGONIC CHART OF THE U. S.

    e. in the Eastern states, there is a westerly variation, while in the Western states there is an easterly variation;

    f. to convert the true to magnetic, you note the variation shown by the nearest isogonic line;

       (1) if the variation is west, add, but if the variation is east, you subtract;

       (2) most pilots remember this with the jingle: East is least (subtract) but West is best (add);

       (3) remember that instrument charts are shown in magnetic directions rather than true so that you reverse the process in converting from magnetic to true.

3. The magnetic compass is a simple instrument composed of two magnetized steel needles mounted on a float around which is a compass card;

    a. the compass card has letters for the 16 cardinal headings, with each 30-degree interval represented by a number the last zero of which is omitted;

       (1) thus, 30 degrees appears as a 3, while 300 degrees appears as 30;

       (2) between the numbers, the card is graduated for each 5 degrees;

    b. in addition to variation, the magnetic compass is subject to other errors, including *deviation;*

       (1) deviation results from magnetic disturbances from magnetic fields produced by the metals and electrical equipment in your airplane;

       (2) because this metal and electrical equipment exists in relation to the compass rather than the direction of the airplane, their influence on the magnetic compass changes as you change direction, so that the deviation is not constant in all directions;

(3) therefore, you have a deviation card in your cockpit to tell you how to maintain any desired magnetic heading. It tells you that to establish a certain magnetic heading, you should steer a particular heading.

4. Your magnetic compass is subject to *oscillation error*, which is the erratic swinging of the compass card as a result of turbulence or rough pilot technique.

5. The compass is also subject to *acceleration error*, which can occur when you change airspeed;
   a. it is most apparent on headings of east to west;
   b. if you accelerate while holding a compass indication of east, either by applying additional power or lowering the nose, the compass card will erroneously indicate a turn to the north;
   c. if you decelerate while holding a compass indication of east, the compass card will erroneously indicate a turn to the south;
   d. a similar result will occur if you accelerate or decelerate while holding a compass indication of west;
   e. remember ANDS (accelerate-North; decelerate-South).

6. The *northerly turn error* is the most pronounced of the magnetic compass in-flight errors;
   a. this error is most apparent when turning to or from headings of north and south;
   b. when your heading is north and you start a turn in either direction, the magnetic compass gives an indication of a turn in the *opposite* direction of the actual turn;
   c. as your turn continues, the compass card will begin to indicate a turn in the correct direction but will lag behind the actual turn;
      (1) you can, while holding a compass indication of north, start a gradual and shallow bank of 3 or 4 degrees, and change the actual heading of the aircraft by 20 degrees or more while still maintaining an indication of north by the compass;
   d. the lag will diminish until you are within a few degrees of east or west;
   e. when your heading is south and you begin a turn in either direction, the compass will give you an indication of a turn in the *correct* direction but at a much *faster* rate than is actually being turned;
      (1) this lead will continue as you approach east or west, but at a diminishing rate until you are within a few degrees of west or east.

7. Your directional gyro (DG) is not subject to the errors that limit the usefulness of your magnetic compass;
   a. therefore, you will normally use it while in flight;
   b. nevertheless, you must check it frequently against your magnetic compass and correct it because of its precession (see glossary).

Section 19
AREAS IN WHICH YOUR FLIGHT MAY BE RESTRICTED

1. Under various conditions, you may be restricted in the *altitude* at which you may fly. These restrictions are described in Sec. 16.
2. Your flight around airports is regulated and restricted as discussed in Sec. 31, 32 and 33.
3. Your flight is regulated or forbidden if there is insufficient ceiling and/or visibility. Sec. 9.
4. A *prohibited area* is one in which the flight of aircraft is not allowed;
    a. such areas are established for security or other reasons associated with the national welfare;
    b. such areas are published in the Federal Register and are depicted on aeronautical charts.
5. A *restricted area* is one in which the flight of aircraft is not wholly prohibited but is subject to limitations;
    a. restricted areas denote the existence of unusual, often invisible, hazards to aircraft or denote security areas such as arsenals;
    b. penetration of restricted areas without authorization from the using or controlling agency may be extremely hazardous to the aircraft and its occupants and is illegal;
    c. such areas are published in the Federal Register and are depicted on aeronautical charts.
6. *Warning areas* are established beyond the 3 mile limit in airspace that may contain hazards to non-participating aircraft in international airspace;
    a. warning areas cannot be legally designated, because they are over international waters;
    b. penetration of warning areas during periods of activity may be hazardous to aircraft;
    c. official descriptions of warning areas may be obtained on request to the FAA, Washington, D.C.
7. *Intensive Student Jet Training Area* (ISJTA) is airspace that contains the intensive training activities of military student jet pilots;
    a. restrictions are imposed in such areas on IFR flight;
    b. information about these training areas may be obtained from any FSS within 200 miles of the area.
8. *Military Operations Areas*—airspace of defined vertical and lateral limits established for the purpose of separating certain military training activities from IFR traffic;

a. if you are flying VFR, you should exercise extreme caution while you are flying within an MOA while military activity is being conducted;
b. MOAs are depicted on Sectional, VFR Terminal and Low Altitude En Route Charts;
c. you may obtain information about activity within an MOA from any FSS within 200 miles of the area.

9. *Alert Area*—an area that may contain a high volume of pilot training or an unusual type of aerial activity;
   a. these are depicted on aeronautical charts;
   b. you should be particularly alert when flying in these areas;
   c. they will be converted to Military Operation Areas (MOA).

10. *VFR Low Altitude Training Routes*—established training routes for use by military;
    a. routes are flown in one direction only, by aircraft with speeds exceeding 250 KIAS;
    b. flights are conducted at or below 1,500 feet AGL;
       (1) You can avoid the traffic by flying well *above* that altitude;
    c. flights are conducted only when forecasts and weather conditions are equal to or better than a 3,000-feet ceiling and 5-mile visibility;
    d. you can assume that the route is continuously active.

11. *All Weather Low Altitude Training Routes* (Olive Branch Route)—similar to VFR Low Altitude Training routes but may extend to higher altitudes and may be operated in both VFR and IFR weather conditions;
    a. Check Part 4 of the AIM for information on these routes.

12. An *Air Defense Identification Zone* is known as ADIZ;
    a. such zones are designated by the Administrator of the FAA;
    b. generally, such zones lie along the Atlantic Coast, the Pacific Coast and the Gulf of Mexico, and the Southern Border;
    c. to penetrate an ADIZ, you must be on a DVFR Flight Plan or an IFR Flight Plan and make frequent reports.

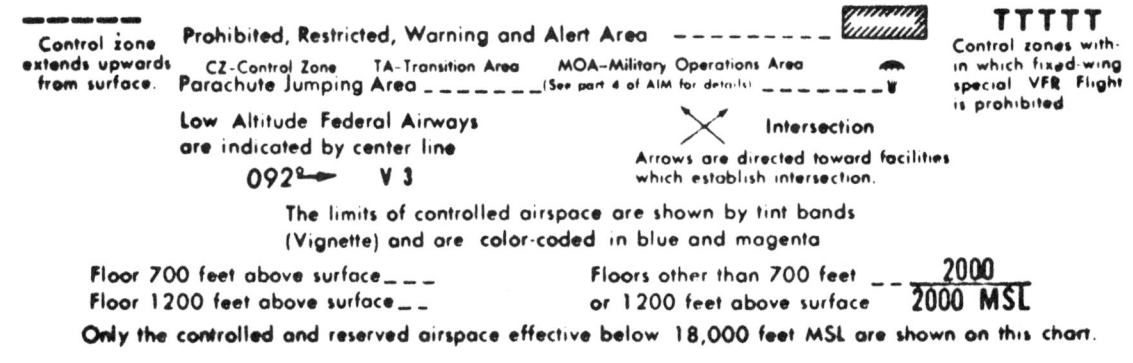

FIG. 19.1—AIRSPACE INFORMATION ON AERONAUTICAL CHARTS

13. You may not operate an aircraft over and in the vicinity of areas to be visited or traveled by the President, contrary to the limitations specified in a NOTAM.
14. Much information about restrictions on your use of airspace is given on your sectional charts.

Section 20
OTHER IMPORTANT FLIGHT RULES

1. In addition to the various rules that are covered throughout this Guide, there are other rules which pertain to various phases of flight.
2. The *pilot-in-command* is directly responsible for and is the final authority as to the operation and safety of the aircraft during the time defined as flight time;
    a. *flight time* is the total time from the moment the aircraft first moves under its own power for the purpose of flight until the moment it comes to rest at the end of the flight.
3. The pilot-in-command, in an emergency requiring immediate action, may deviate from the flight rules to the extent required to meet that emergency;
    a. but any pilot who does so must, upon the request of the Administrator, send a written report of that deviation to the Administrator.
4. No person may operate an aircraft in a careless or reckless manner so as to endanger the life or property of another.
5. You are prohibited from operating your airplane near other aircraft under these circumstances:
    a. you may not operate your aircraft so close to another aircraft as to create a collision hazard;
    b. you may not operate an aircraft in formation flight except by prearrangement with the pilot-in-command of each aircraft in the formation;
    c. no person may operate an aircraft carrying passengers for hire in formation flight, but, as a student, you are not permitted to carry passengers under *any* circumstances.
6. You are required to comply with the following right-of-way rules:
    a. an aircraft in distress has the right-of-way over all other aircraft;
    b. when aircraft of the same category are converging at approximately the same altitude (except head-on, or nearly so) the aircraft to the other's right has the right-of-way. If the aircraft are of different categories:
        (1) a balloon has the right-of-way over any other category of aircraft;
        (2) a glider has the right-of-way over an airship, airplane or rotocraft;
        (3) an airship has the right-of-way over an airplane or rotocraft;
        (4) an aircraft towing or refueling other aircraft has the right-of-way over all other engine-driven aircraft.
    c. when aircraft are approaching each other head on, or nearly so, each pilot of each aircraft shall alter course to the right;

SECTION 20-OTHER IMPORTANT FLIGHT RULES

    d. each aircraft that is being overtaken has the right-of-way and each pilot of an overtaking aircraft shall alter course to the right to pass well clear;

    e. aircraft, while on final approach to land, or while landing have the right-of-way over other aircraft in flight or operating on the surface;

    f. when two or more aircraft are approaching an airport for the purpose of landing, the aircraft at the lower altitude has the right-of-way, but it shall not take advantage of this rule to cut in front of another that is on final approach to land, or to overtake that aircraft.

7. As pilot-in-command, you may not allow any object to be dropped from the aircraft in flight that creates a hazard to person or property;

    a. this provision does not prohibit the dropping of an object if reasonable precautions are taken to avoid injury or damage to persons or property.

8. You are required to keep your seat belt fastened, while soloing or pilot-in-command, during takeoff and landing, *and* while in route.

9. There are certain limitations on the speed of aircraft but they do not apply to your Cessna 152 or 150.

10. You are required to have an operating Emergency Locator Transmitter (ELT) in your airplane, to transmit a signal if you crash;

    a. it is activated either by impact or by an On-Off switch and transmits for several days on 121.5 MHz;

    b. you are required to replace the battery at 50% of normal shelf life as stamped on the battery;

    c. you can test your ELT by tuning your VHF receiver to 121.5 and turning the unit on:

        (1) you should only test it during the first 5 minutes of any hour;

        (2) if you need to test it at any other time, notify the closest control tower or FSS;

    d. if the ELT should be activated by accident, turn it off immediately;

    e. if you should hear an ELT signal, notify the nearest FSS or tower immediately stating your position when you first heard the signal;

    f. after a hard landing, tune to 121.5 to determine whether you have activated your ELT.

11. You may not operate your plane in *acrobatic flight* (1) over any congested area of a city, town or settlement, (2) over an open air assembly of persons, (3) within a control zone or Federal airway, (4) below an altitude of 1,500 agl, or (5) when flight visibility is less than 3 miles;

    a. acrobatic flight, for this purpose, means an intentional maneuver involving an abrupt change in an aircraft's attitude, an abnormal attitude, or abnormal acceleration not necessary for normal flight;

    b. the Cessna 152 (other than the Aerobat) is not approved for any acrobatic maneuver except (1) chandelles, (2) lazy eights, (3) steep turns, (4) spins, and (5) stalls (but not whip stalls);

        (1) as a student pilot, you will not be required to perform any of these except steep turns and stalls.

Section 21
SPECIAL HAZARDS IN FLIGHT

1. A principal cause of engine failure is *carburetor icing;*
    a. when fuel is vaporized and the air velocity is accelerated, there is a sudden cooling of the mixture;
    b. the temperature of the air passing through the carburetor may drop as much as 60°F, causing water vapor to be squeezed out. The moisture will deposit as frost or ice if the carburetor temperature reaches 32°F or below;
    c. carburetor icing can occur at temperatures between 20°F and 70°F if there is visible moisture or high humidity;
    d. the first indication of carburetor icing will be a loss in rpm;
    e. when conditions are favorable for carburetor icing, proper checks must be made:
        (1) apply full carburetor heat;
        (2) leave it in this position until you are sure there is no ice present or, if present, that it has been removed;
        (3) if icing continues, it may be necessary to keep some carburetor heat;
    f. the application of carburetor heat will cause a drop in rpm;
        (1) if there is no carburetor ice, there will be no further change in rpm until the carburetor heat is turned off;
        (2) if carburetor ice is present, there will normally be a drop in rpm (often accompanied by intermittent engine roughness) then a rise in rpm; then, when the carburetor heat is removed, the rpm will rise to a setting greater than that before heat was applied;
    g. carburetor heat should be applied if the throttle is closed or the rpm are reduced below the green line during flight, and should then be left on during the closed or reduced throttle operation;
        (1) the throttle should be opened smoothly for a few seconds, periodically, to keep the engine from loading up;
    h. the use of carburetor heat reduces the output of the engine and allows unfiltered air to enter the carburetor;
        (1) consequently, carburetor heat should not be applied during takeoff, or during normal engine operation except to check for the presence of, or to remove, carburetor ice.

SECTION 21-SPECIAL HAZARDS IN FLIGHT

2. Another serious problem for the pilot is known as *spatial disorientation;*
    a. spatial disorientation is a form of confusion that makes it difficult for a pilot to sense his relationship to things and space around him;
    b. spatial disorientation is often followed by vertigo, which may be manifested by dizziness and nausea;
    c. spatial disorientation often results when the pilot flies into poor weather conditions and is unable to observe the ground or the horizon;
        (1) the best way to prevent this is to check the weather carefully, keep alert for deteriorating weather, and then, if it should still close in on you, perform the most effective of safety maneuvers, that is, the 180-degree turn, and return to your point of departure;
    d. spatial disorientation can be avoided by obtaining a maximum amount of instruction and experience in instrument flying (Sec. 44).
3. *Gusty wind* can present serious problems to the pilot;
    a. if there is a quick drop in the velocity of the wind, the airspeed of the airplane can drop below the stall speed;
    b. this can be serious during landing because the airspeed will already have been reduced, preparatory to landing;
    c. the danger of a stall resulting from gusty wind can be reduced by keeping your approach speed 5 to 10 KIAS faster than normal and by keeping your right hand on the throttle, prepared for immediate use, if necessary.
4. *Turbulence* imposes additional load factors (Sec. 23.6) on the airplane, which can result in moderate to very serious damage to the structure of the airplane, including the loss of a wing;
    a. to avoid this danger, keep the airspeed within the green arc, even in light turbulence. This means not going more than 111 KIAS when the air is turbulent;
    b. avoid turbulence by careful checking of weather in advance and particularly AIRMETS and SIGMETS, (See glossary).
5. *Birds* are another hazard in flight;
    a. study the analysis of the migratory patterns of birds in the AIM;
    b. you are requested to notify your nearest FAA Air Route Traffic Control Center, Flight Service Station, or tower when you observe flocks of birds;
    c. during flight, be constantly alert for flocks of birds and change your course to avoid them.
6. *Hypoxia* - is a condition caused by lack of oxygen, usually as a result of high altitude but it can be caused or accentuated by anemia, smoking, carbon monoxide, alcohol and some drugs;
    a. hypoxia is insidious since it is almost impossible to know when you have it;
    b. it causes a state of well-being (euphoria), slow reactions, impaired thinking ability, fatigue and headache;
    c. it is usually avoided by proper use of oxygen at higher altitudes (Sec. 16.10).
7. *Hyperventilation* - a lack of carbon dioxide in the blood, usually caused by excessive breathing brought on by fright, pain, emotional stress;

SECTION 21-SPECIAL HAZARDS IN FLIGHT

  a. the symptoms are dizziness, hot and cold sensations, tingling hands, legs and feet, nausea, sleepiness and even unconsciousness;
  b. it can be corrected by slower breathing rate, or by breathing a few times in a bag.
8. *Carbon monoxide-* a deadly gas that is colorless, odorless and tasteless; it is produced by a gasoline engine and can filter into the cabin;
  a. you can mount a warning signal in your plane to warn you of its presence;
  b. always keep your plane in good repair to minimize this hazard;
  c. if you smoke, your blood already has a good start toward being saturated with carbon monoxide;
  d. always be alert and take immediate action if you detect any of its symptoms, which are blurred thinking, uneasiness, dizziness and headache.
9. One of the most serious conditions that you can confront is to have ice build up on the surfaces of your airplane;
  a. it is illegal for you to fly into known icing conditions;
  b. every preflight check of the weather should include a check for the possibility of icing, if there is the slightest chance that you could encounter it;
  c. only the most experienced instrument rated pilots, with de-icing equipment, have any business flying when there is even a slight chance of icing;
  d. if you should have any ice form on your plane, immediately turn on the pitot heat and make arrangements to land as quickly as can safely be done.

Section 22
WAKE TURBULENCE

1. While in flight, every airplane generates a wake, which consists of vortices or small whirlwinds, and were formerly thought to be "prop wash";
    a. these vortices become serious when generated by large airplanes, and are generally known as wake turbulence;

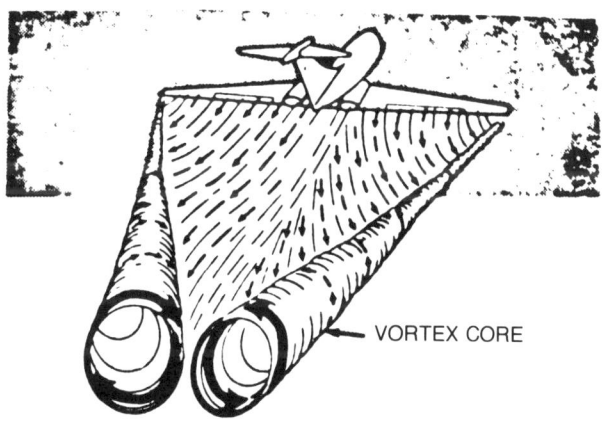

FIG. 22.1—DIAGRAM OF WINGTIP VORTICES

   b. wake turbulence is capable of rolling your airplane over and crashing it into the ground, so that it is extremely important that you understand what it is and how to avoid it.
2. The greatest turbulence is created by a heavy airplane flying slowly;
    a. these trailing vortices are created from the instant the airplane leaves the ground and continue until it lands;
    b. vortices from large aircraft sink at a rate of 400 to 500 feet per minute;

(1) they tend to level off when about 900 feet below the path of the generating airplane;
(2) the strength of a vortex decreases with the passage of time and distance behind the airplane that caused it;
(3) atmospheric turbulence hastens the breakup;

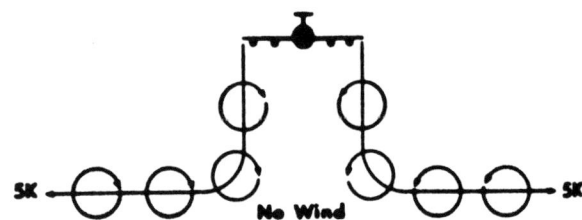

FIG. 22.2—VORTEX MOVEMENT IN GROUND EFFECT—NO WIND

  c. when the vortices of a large airplane sink close to the ground (within about 200 feet) they tend to move laterally over the ground at a speed of about 5 knots;
  d. a crosswind will decrease the lateral movement of the upwind vortex and increase the movement of the downwind vortex;
    (1) this will cause the upwind vortex to hang over the runway for a period of time;
    (2) similarly, a tailwind will tend to push the vortices forward along the runway;
  e. it is important that you constantly visualize the location of these vortices in relation to landing and departing large aircraft and the wind conditions;
  f. airport traffic controllers try to have adequate separation between aircraft to avoid wake turbulence;
    (1) but it always remains your own responsibility to adjust your operations and flight path as necessary to avoid wake turbulence.
3. You should be especially careful to avoid areas below and behind a large aircraft, and particularly in calm wind conditions and situations where the vortices could:
  a. remain in the touchdown area;
  b. drift from aircraft operating on a nearby runway;
  c. sink into the takeoff and landing area from a crossing runway;
  d. sink into the traffic patterns from other airport operations;
  e. sink into your flight path while you are flying below the generating airplane.
4. In addition to visualizing the location of possible wake turbulence, you should memorize certain rules that will help you avoid it:
  a. when you land behind a large aircraft on the same runway, always stay at or above its final approach flight path, carefully note its touchdown point and land *beyond* it;

b. if you are landing behind a large airplane which is landing on a parallel runway within 2,500 feet, you should consider the possible drift to your runway and stay *above* its final approach flight plan;
c. if you are landing behind a large airplane which is landing on a crossing runway, you should cross *above* its flight path;
d. if you are landing behind a departing large airplane on the same runway, you should note its rotation point and land well *before* reaching it;
e. if you are landing behind a departing large airplane on a crossing runway, note its rotation point and land *before* the intersection; if it rotates before reaching the intersection, don't land unless you can be sure of landing well before reaching the intersection;
f. when you are departing behind a large aircraft, note its rotation point and rotate before reaching it and keep *above* its climb path and upwind of its climb path. As you climb out, avoid any heading that will cross *below* or *behind* the large airplane;
g. if you make an intersection takeoff on the same runway, check carefully for large airplanes that may be upwind of your runway, and avoid any subsequent heading that could cross below the large airplane's path;
h. be particularly careful if large aircraft are doing touch-and-goes or missed approaches as the vortices can linger for at least 2 minutes;
i. when you are en route, avoid flying below and behind a large airplane. If you see one above you, move to one side or the other, preferably upwind;
j. there should be at least a 4-mile (and not less than 2 minutes) separation when landing behind a large airplane and 6 miles when landing behind a heavy jet.

Section 23
SLOW FLIGHT AND STALLS

1. Without sufficient airspeed, your airplane will stall, often with disastrous results unless you are prepared to handle the situation;
    a. the best solution to the problem is to avoid stalls;
    b. so that you can recognize an imminent stall and know how to recover if you should stall, you are required to learn *slow flight* and various kinds of *stalls;* this kind of flight is known in government jargon as "flight at critically slow airspeeds";
    c. The stall of an airplane is not to be confused with an automobile engine stall;
    d. your Cessna is equipped with a stall warning signal that produces a steady warning signal 5 to 10 knots above the stall speed, and continues to sound until a greater speed is reached.
2. Slow flight is performed as follows:
    a. apply carburetor heat;
    b. reduce rpm to 1,700;
    c. apply sufficient back pressure on the elevator to maintain the same altitude;
    d. use the trim tab to maintain altitude, with minimum back pressure on the elevator;
    e. apply additional power (about 2,000 rpm) as needed to maintain a constant altitude;
    f. keep your airspeed on 45 KIAS and your heading straight;
    g. during slow flight, your instructor (and later the flight check examiner) may apply flaps;
    h. as flaps are applied:
        (1) lower the nose to maintain a speed of 45 KIAS;
        (2) increase power to maintain a constant altitude;
        (3) with *full* flaps, nearly full power will be required;
    i. as flaps are raised:
        (1) raise the nose of the airplane to reduce speed;
        (2) decrease the power to maintain a constant altitude.
    j. To recover from slow flight:
        (1) return the throttle to cruising power;
        (2) carburetor heat—OFF;
        (3) lower the nose slowly.

SECTION 23—SLOW FLIGHT AND STALLS

3. One of the most serious things that can happen to your airplane is to stall at low altitudes so that it is impossible to recover before hitting the ground;
   a. your Cessna is so well designed that it is extremely difficult to cause it to stall;
   b. consequently, there is *no* reason why it should *ever* stall if you understand what the stall is, what causes it to occur, and how to avoid it.
4. A stall is caused by an excessive angle of attack;
   a. the angle of attack is measured with reference to the relative wind, i.e., the wind as it strikes the airplane, rather than the wind as it blows over the ground;
   b. when there is an excessive angle of attack, the air no longer flows smoothly over the top of the wing;
      (1) instead, the air breaks away from the wing at the leading edge, causing a burble condition;
      (2) this condition causes the wing to lose its lifting ability.
5. Stalls can be avoided best if you understand some pertinent facts about them:
   a. an airplane does not have to be going slow to stall; it can be stalled at *any* airspeed;
      (1) this can be done if the pilot applies abrupt or excessive back pressure on the elevator control;
      (2) a stall that occurs at relatively high speed is called an accelerated or high speed stall;
   b. an airplane can stall in any attitude;
      (1) the nose does not have to be pulled up;
   c. as the weight of the airplane increases, the stall speed increases, that is, the airplane will stall more readily;
      (1) this emphasizes the importance of keeping within the weight and balance limitations (Sec. 8);
      (2) it also emphasizes the need for greater caution in avoiding stalls when the airplane is loaded at or near its maximum;
   d. as you move the center of gravity to the rear, the airplane will stall more readily, due to its nose-high attitude;
   e. the greater the amount of flaps, the *lower* the stall speed;
      (1) a higher indicated airspeed should be maintained when landing without flaps;
      (2) see Sec. 24, for the effect of flaps on the stall speed;
   f. an accumulation of *frost, snow or ice* on the wings, even though slight, can cause an increase in the danger of stalling, because of the increase in stalling speed;
      (1) the accumulation disrupts the smooth flow of air over the wing, thus decreasing the lift it produces;
      (2) because of the loss in lift, a higher angle of attack becomes necessary, or a higher speed must be attained on the takeoff roll;
      (3) the answer is simple—never take off until *all* frost, snow or ice has melted or has been removed from the airplane;

g. an increase in the altitude of the airfield has no effect on the *indicated airspeed* at which an airplane will stall;
   (1) the indicated stall speed remains the same regardless of the altitude;
   (2) the same indicated airspeed should be maintained during the landing approach regardless of the elevation or the density altitude at the airport of landing;
   (3) but remember that if higher than normal approach airspeed is used, a longer landing distance will be required;
h. the greater the angle of bank, the greater the danger of stalling;
   (1) at a 60-degree bank, the stall speed is 40% greater than in straight and level flight;
   (2) at angles of bank above 60 degrees, the stall speed increases very rapidly;
   (3) at 75 degrees, the stall speed is about doubled in comparison with that for straight and level flight.

6. The *load factor* is important to you because an excessive load may damage the structure of the airplane and because the danger of stalling increases rapidly as the load factor increases;
   a. the load factor is the ratio of the load supported by the wings to the actual weight of the airplane and its contents;
      (1) load factors are measured in Gs;
      (2) a load factor of 2 Gs means the plane, occupants and baggage have twice the normal pull of gravity on them, or weigh twice their normal weight;
   b. the *limit load factor* is that load factor an airplane can sustain without taking a permanent bend in the structure;
   c. the load factor increases greatly as the angle of bank increases;
      (1) the load factor in your airplane is two when the airplane is in a 60-degree bank in a coordinated turn;
      (2) the load factor goes up to 6 in an 80-degree bank;
   d. the load factor also increases when the airplane is pulled out of a dive;
   e. turbulence can also produce large load factors;
   f. you can recognize increases in load factors by your feeling of increased body weight, or the feeling that you are being forced down in the seat;
      (1) this is your warning that the airplane will stall at somewhat higher speed than it will in straight and level flight;
   g. speed does not, of itself, increase load factors:
      (1) however, if there is turbulence, the increased speed will have a resulting higher load factor when the gusts strike the airplane;
      (2) you should reduce the airspeed to maneuvering speed during turbulence; (See Sec. 17.4).

7. Airplanes are assigned an operational category, or categories, in which the airplane is certificated, which are:
   a. *normal,* for which no acrobatics or spins are permitted;
   b. *utility,* for which mild acrobatics, including spins, are permitted;

CONDITIONS:
Power Off

NOTE:
KIAS values are approximate and are based on airspeed calibration data with power off.

MOST REARWARD CENTER OF GRAVITY

WEIGHT LBS	FLAP DEFLECTION	ANGLE OF BANK							
		0°		30°		45°		60°	
		KIAS	KCAS	KIAS	KCAS	KIAS	KCAS	KIAS	KCAS
1670	UP	36	46	39	49	43	55	51	65
	10°	36	43	39	46	43	51	51	61
	30°	31	41	33	44	37	49	44	58

MOST FORWARD CENTER OF GRAVITY

WEIGHT LBS	FLAP DEFLECTION	ANGLE OF BANK							
		0°		30°		45°		60°	
		KIAS	KCAS	KIAS	KCAS	KIAS	KCAS	KIAS	KCAS
1670	UP	40	48	43	52	48	57	57	68
	10°	40	46	43	49	48	55	57	65
	30°	35	43	38	46	42	51	49	61

FIG. 23.1—STALL SPEEDS OF CESSNA 152

c. *acrobatic,* for which acrobatic maneuvers are approved;
d. for each of these categories, the FAA has set minimum limit load factors that airplanes in that particular category must have. For airplanes under 4,000 pounds, in weight, these are: Normal: 3.8; Utility: 4.4; and Acrobatic: 6.0;
e. your Cessna 152 or 150 is certified in the Utility category;

(1) it is *not* certified for acrobatics but can perform mild acrobatics, including spins, and can perform all maneuvers required for the private, commercial pilot, instrument pilot and flight instructor certificates.
8. Your plane will stall at the speeds indicated in the Pilot's Operating Handbook;
   a. the stall speed *increases* as the angle of bank *increases;*
   b. the stall speed *decreases* as the amount of flap angle increases;
9. Your flight training emphasizes the different kinds of stalls, and recovery from them, for the following reasons:
   a. so that you will recognize the various ways an airplane can get into a stall;
   b. so that you will recognize the feel of the airplane when it is about to stall and when it stalls;
   c. so that you will learn the technique of recovering from the stall, no matter how it happens, with a minimum loss of altitude;
   d. so that you will learn to recover from a stall without imposing too much strain upon the airplane as a result of increased load factors;
   e. so that you will acquire confidence in your own ability to recover from a stall.
10. Before performing any stall, make a clearing turn to check for traffic.
11. The *departure stall* (sometimes known as the power-on stall) is one that may occur during takeoff if the nose is placed in too high an attitude. To perform this maneuver:
    a. go to an altitude of 2,500 feet AGL;
       (1) all recoveries must be complete at least 1,500 feet AGL;
    b. make clearing turns;
       (1) this is accomplished by making a 90-degree turn to the left and then a 90-degree turn to the right, in a steep bank (at least 30 degrees);
       (2) the purpose is to make sure that there are no aircraft below or in any direction;
       (3) normally, it is considered safe to perform three stalls right in a row before performing additional clearing turns;
    c. apply carburetor heat;
    d. reduce power to 1,700 rpm;
    e. apply back pressure smoothly until your airspeed is reduced to 52 KIAS;
       (1) apply *full* power smoothly;
       (2) carburetor heat—cold;
    f. bring the nose up very smoothly;
    g. when the stall occurs, lower the nose (but not too much) apply full throttle and remove carburetor heat, and then bring the nose up as much as possible without causing a further stall, to prevent loss in altitude;
       (1) this should be done as smoothly as possible and with a minimum of controls;
       (2) when an airplane stalls, one wing may stall before the other;
       (3) if one wing drops first, apply opposite rudder to raise the downed wing;
       (4) ailerons are also useful in the recovery, but rudder is more effective;

SECTION 23—SLOW FLIGHT AND STALLS

   (5) after altitude loss has been regained, lower the nose so that airspeed can build up;
  h. the departure stall may be made straight ahead, to the right or to the left;
   (1) if it is made while in a turn, the angle of bank should be between 20 and 30 degrees.
12. The *arrival stall* (sometimes known as a power-off stall) is the kind that can occur during landing if you let your airspeed get too low, or make too steep a bank, or both; it is performed thus:
  a. go to 2,500 feet AGL;
  b. perform clearing turns;
  c. apply carburetor heat;
  d. throttle all the way back, in idle position;
  e. keep the altitude constant by bringing the elevator back smoothly, but fairly quickly;
  f. when the stall occurs:
   (1) lower the nose a little, but with very smooth motions;
   (2) apply full power;
   (3) carburetor heat—cold;
   (4) return the plane to level flight by using *both* the ailerons and rudder;
   (5) bring the nose up as quickly and smoothly as possible, without causing another stall, to keep the altitude loss to a very minimum;
  g. work to keep the entire loss in altitude in all stalls as small as possible, preferably 100 feet or less;
  h. the arrival stall can be made straight ahead, to the left or right;
   (1) if in a turn, the bank should be 15 degrees.
13. The *accelerated stall* can occur during normal flight if your airspeed is too slow and the angle of bank in a turn is too great. To perform this maneuver:
  a. go to 2,500 feet AGL;
  b. perform clearing turns;
  c. reduce power to 2,000 rpm;
  d. apply carburetor heat;
  e. apply back pressure until airspeed is 57 KIAS;
  f. make a turn to right or left, with 45-degree bank;
  g. maintain your altitude by constantly increasing back pressure on the elevator;
  h. when a stall occurs, recover as indicated above for the arrival stall.

Section 24
USING YOUR FLAPS

1. Flaps are the movable sections of the trailing edge of the wings, on the inside portion of the wing.
2. While they look somewhat like the ailerons, they differ in that they can only be moved down and returned, but cannot be moved up; both move together, rather than in opposite directions.
3. Your flaps are extended by pushing down on the wing flap switch lever;
   a. in some airplanes, the flaps are manually operated; if so, they are extended by pushing the release button and lifting the flap handle;
   b. flaps are raised by lifting up the wing flap switch, or by pushing the release button and lowering the flap handle.
4. The amount of such extension is measured in degrees;
   a. it is normal to use 10, 20, or 30 degrees of flap;
   b. the more the flaps are extended, the greater the camber of the wings.
5. Because flaps increase lift, 10 degrees of flap (but no more) are recommended for a soft field takeoff (Sec. 14.27) and short field takeoff (Sec. 14.26);
   a. lift the flaps after all obstacles are cleared and 60 KIAS is attained.
6. Flaps are used primarily in landing, especially on the short field (Sec. 27.24) and soft field landings (Sec. 27.25).
7. The Cessna 152 should never be flown with any flaps extended when its airspeed exceeds 85 KIAS.
8. On takeoffs, touch-and-go landings, and go-arounds, great care must be exercised in raising the flaps.
9. The airplane should not be slipped with the flaps extended, as that creates too much drag and makes the airplane difficult to control.
10. Avoid the use of flaps when the wind is strong or gusty or there is a considerable crosswind.

Section 25
AIRPORTS

1. Although an airport does not look much different from any other piece of cleared land, there are *many* special features that you must know and understand in order to be a good, safe pilot;
    a. military airports are not available to you except in a case of a real emergency;
    b. many small airports are restricted so that they are not available to you except in an emergency or with permission of the owner;
    c. but *all* airports are important to you, both as landmarks in determining your location and to use in emergencies, so that you should constantly check for their location as you fly cross-country;
    d. you should memorize and frequently review the symbols used on sectional charts to depict airports and data concerning them.

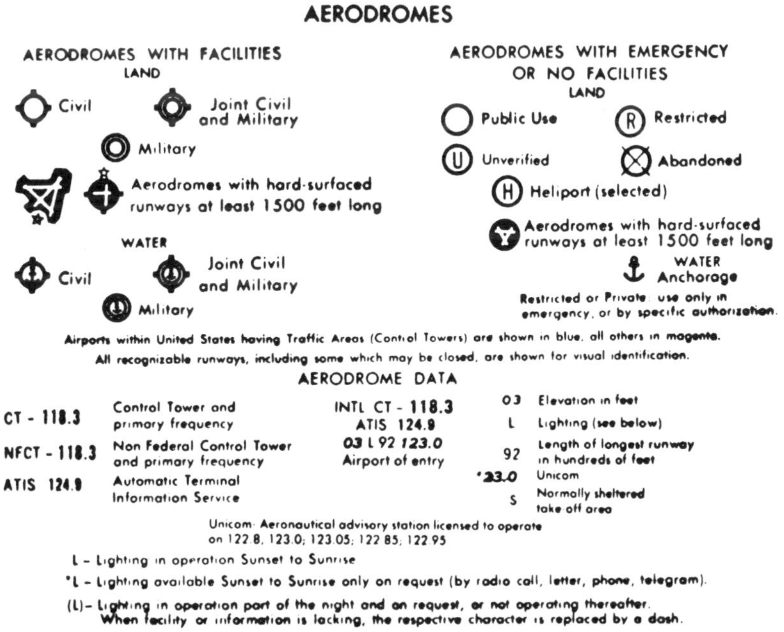

AERODROMES

AERODROMES WITH FACILITIES
LAND
- Civil
- Joint Civil and Military
- Military
- Aerodromes with hard-surfaced runways at least 1500 feet long

WATER
- Civil
- Joint Civil and Military
- Military

AERODROMES WITH EMERGENCY OR NO FACILITIES
LAND
- Public Use
- Restricted
- Unverified
- Abandoned
- Heliport (selected)
- Aerodromes with hard-surfaced runways at least 1500 feet long

WATER
- Anchorage

Restricted or Private use only in emergency, or by specific authorization.

Airports within United States having Traffic Areas (Control Towers) are shown in blue, all others in magenta. All recognizable runways, including some which may be closed, are shown for visual identification.

AERODROME DATA

- CT - 118.3 — Control Tower and primary frequency
- NFCT - 118.3 — Non Federal Control Tower and primary frequency
- ATIS 124.9 — Automatic Terminal Information Service
- INTL CT - 118.3
- ATIS 124.9
- 03 L 92 123.0 — Airport of entry
- 03 — Elevation in feet
- L — Lighting (see below)
- 92 — Length of longest runway in hundreds of feet
- *123.0 — Unicom
- S — Normally sheltered take off area

Unicom: Aeronautical advisory station licensed to operate on 122.8, 123.0; 123.05; 122.85; 122.95

L - Lighting in operation Sunset to Sunrise
*L - Lighting available Sunset to Sunrise only on request (by radio call, letter, phone, telegram).
(L) - Lighting in operation part of the night and on request, or not operating thereafter.
When facility or information is lacking, the respective character is replaced by a dash.

FIG. 25.1—AIRPORT SYMBOLS AND DATA ON AERONAUTICAL CHARTS

2. You should become familiar with the pattern of runways and taxiways for every airport you will be using, even if only to land there to refuel;
    a. most FBOs have a diagram or aerial photo of their airport, so that you can study the runways and taxiways and thereby be familiar with them before you taxi out for takeoff;
    b. descriptions of the runways of many airports are given in the *AIM*;
    c. diagrams of many airports are also given in such publications as *Sky Prints*, the *AOPA Airport Directory*, instrument approach plates and J-Aids;
    d. paved runways are depicted in the diagrams of airports on sectional charts.
3. Runways may be sod or paved;
    a. a good sod runway is very satisfactory, except when it is wet and soft, but many of them drain well and are usable most of the year;
    b. airports with paved runways at least 1,500 feet long are shown by a pattern on sectional charts;
        (1) all recognizable runways, including closed runways, are shown for visual identification;
    c. the sectional chart shows the altitude and length of the runway next to the airport; thus "768 L 60" means that the 768 is the field elevation in feet, the L is for lights, and the 60 denotes that the longest runway (given in hundreds of feet) is 6,000 feet long.
4. Runway numbers and letters are determined from the approach direction;
    a. you will visualize this best if you imagine yourself at the runway, ready to take off;
    b. runways are numbered according to their *magnetic* direction;
    c. a runway is given the number closest to its magnetic direction but the last digit is omitted;
        (1) a runway with a magnetic direction of 30 degrees is designated Runway 3; that with a magnetic direction of 340 degrees is Runway 34;
    d. each runway runs in two directions and therefore is treated as *two* runways;
        (1) Runway 18 is also Runway 36; Runway 13 is also Runway 31; Runway 9 is also Runway 27;
        (2) to obtain the runway number when approaching from the opposite direction, just take the reciprocal, that is, add or subtract 180 degrees;
    e. if there are two parallel runways, they are given the same number but the one on the left, as you approach, is number L, such as 35L, and that on the right is designated R, such as 12R.
5. Runways may be marked to give you important information such as their number, centerline, hold line and other information;
    a. a runway or taxiway that is closed is marked with an X;
    b. a threshold is the beginning of the portion of a runway usable for landing;
    c. when a portion of the runway is not usable for landing, there is a *displaced* threshold which is marked to tell you the location of the threshold;

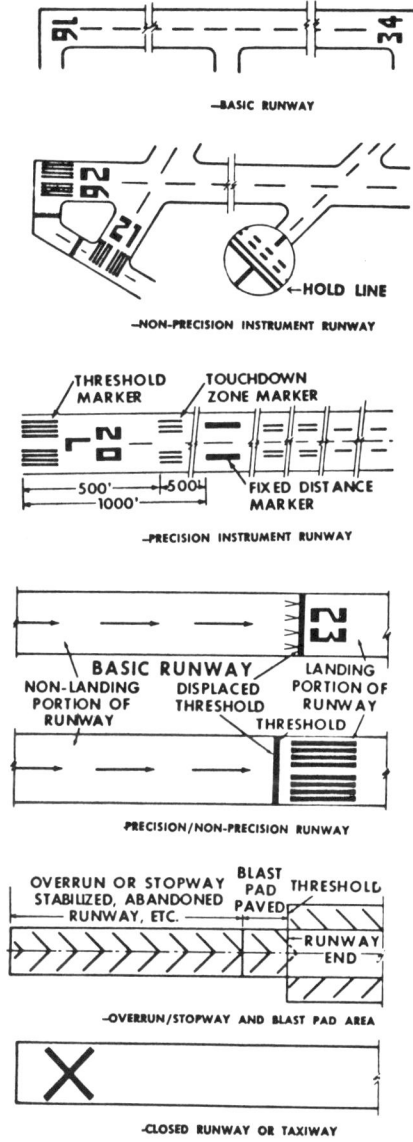

FIG. 25.2—RUNWAY MARKING

d. taxiway centerlines may be marked with a continuous yellow line, and the edge may be marked with two continuous yellow lines 6 inches apart;
e. taxiway holding lines consist of two continuous and two dashed lines, spaced 6 inches between the lines, perpendicular to the centerline;
   (1) when you are instructed by ground control to HOLD SHORT of a runway, you should stop so that no part of your plane extends beyond the holding line;
   (2) you should hold short of the holding line while making your runup;
f. when you land and turn off the runway, you are not clear until your whole plane has crossed the holding line.

6. The segmented circle system is designed to provide traffic pattern information at airports without operating control towers. It consists of:
   a. a *segmented circle* is located in a position that affords maximum visibility to pilots in the air and on the ground; it provides a centralized location for other elements of the system;
   b. a *wind direction indicator* is a windsock installed at the center of the circle and is used to indicate the wind direction and velocity;
      (1) a windsock is a cloth sleeve which gives the wind direction with the large end pointing *into* the wind;
   c. a *landing direction indicator,* which may be either a tetrahedron or wind tee, located at the center of the circle;
      (1) a wind tee looks like an airplane and points *into* the wind;
      (2) the tetrahedron is a four-sided diamond shaped object that points *into* the wind;
      (3) it is used to indicate the direction in which landings and takeoffs should be made;
   d. *l-shaped indicators* located at various positions around the indicator, or at the end of the runway. They consist of two parts:
      (1) the *landing strip indicators,* installed in pairs and used to show the alignment of landing strips;
      (2) *traffic pattern indicators* are arranged in pairs, at right angles to the landing strip indicators, and making up the other section of the L;
   e. the traffic pattern indicators are used to indicate the direction of turns when there is a variation from the normal left traffic pattern;
   f. if there is no segmented circle installed at the airport, traffic pattern indicators may be installed on or near the end of the runway;
   g. a *flashing amber light* near the center of the segmented circle, or on top of a nearby building which indicates that a right traffic pattern is in effect at the time.

7. Each airport has a designated traffic pattern which is the path that is to be followed by planes landing and taking off there;

a. when there is an operating control tower, the pattern to be flown will be designated by the controller;
b. the pattern that is used in the absence of unusual local conditions is shown in Fig. 25.3;

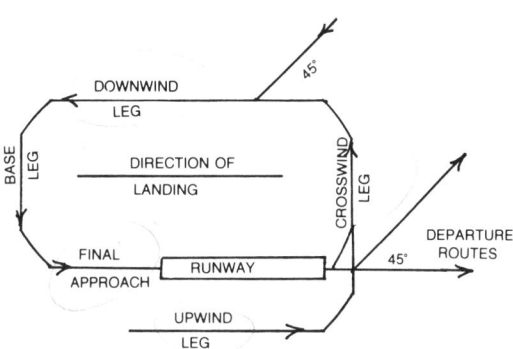

FIG. 25.3—LANDING PATTERN

c. because of the terrain, populous areas, other airports and similar conditions, a different pattern may be in effect for the airport or for one or more of its runways;
  (1) for some runways, there may be a left approach but a right departure.
8. Before landing at an airport without a control tower, or when the tower is not in operation, you should carefully check the indicator for the approach end of the runway to be used;
   a. when approaching for landing, all turns must be to the left unless a light signal *or* traffic pattern indicator indicates that turns should be made to the right.
9. *CONTROL ZONES* may exist around airports whether or not there is a control tower at that airport;
   a. the control zone usually extends in a 5-mile radius from the center of the airport, and may also include legs or extensions for ILS approaches and departures;
   b. the control zone extends upward for an unlimited distance above the ground;
   c. the importance of the control zone, as distinguished from the airport traffic area, is the fact that certain conditions of visibility, ceiling and clouds must exist within that area to fly, take off or land in VFR conditions. (See Sec. 9.2);
   d. the existence of a control zone does not, of itself, mean that there is a control tower;
     (1) there is a control zone if there is a control tower but not necessarily vice versa;
     (2) an FSS on a field where there is no control tower does not exercise control over taxiing, takeoffs and landings.
10. *AIRPORT ADVISORY AREA*—This is the area within 5 statute miles of an airport where there is a FSS but no control tower is operating;
    a. at these airports, the FSS provides advisory service to arriving and departing aircraft;
      (1) you are not required to contact the FSS for this service but you are strongly urged to do so;

(2) not only will you be well informed on wind and weather conditions, but you will learn about known aircraft in the area and other aircraft will be informed of your whereabouts;
   b. you should call in when you are 20 to 25 miles out, advise the FSS as to your location and intentions and request airport advisories: QUINCY RADIO, CESSNA 2151 SIERRA, TWENTY EAST, LANDING QUINCY, REQUEST AIRPORT ADVISORIES;
      (1) you will normally contact them on 123.6 for this service;
      (2) other frequencies can be found on your aeronautical chart, *AIM,* and *Sky Prints;*
         (a) the *AIM* suggests that the initial call be made when you are from 5 to 15 miles but that may not be enough if the FSS is busy with numerous other calls. You could be there before you have contacted them;
   c. you should also advise them your position when you enter the pattern: QUINCY RADIO, FIVE ONE SIERRA ON DOWNWIND FOR RUNWAY THREE ONE;
   d. you should also advise them when you are down clear of the runway: QUINCY RADIO, FIVE ONE SIERRA DOWN AND CLEAR;
   e. also, when you are departing and ready to taxi, you obtain the airport advisories thus: QUINCY RADIO, CESSNA 2151 SIERRA, PARKED ON THE RAMP, READY TO TAXI, REQUEST AIRPORT ADVISORIES;
   f. advise the FSS when you take the active runway and give your direction of flight so it can alert other aircraft as to your presence: QUINCY RADIO, 51 SIERRA TAKING THE ACTIVE, DEPARTING TO THE WEST;
   g. advisories provide wind direction and velocity, favored or designated runway, altimeter setting, *known* traffic, notices to airmen, airport taxi routes, airport traffic patterns and instrument approach procedures;
      (1) they only advise of *known* traffic and not of all traffic since some aircraft do not have two way radios or the pilots are too stupid to take advantage of this important, life-saving service;
   h. continue to guard 123.6 at all times while you are in the vicinity of the airport to learn of additional traffic;
   i. the FSS does not exercise any control over aircraft in the area;
      (1) however, they are in an excellent position to observe and report any violations of the FARs;
   j. airport advisory areas exist at airports with FSS and with part-time control towers during the hours the towers are not in operation;
   k. airports that have airport advisory areas are shown in magenta on sectional charts.
11. *AIRPORT TRAFFIC AREA*—This is the airspace within a horizontal radius of 5 statute miles from the geographical center of any airport at which a control tower is operating, and extends from the surface to 3,000 feet above the elevation of the airport;
   a. no person may operate an aircraft within an airport traffic area except for the purpose of taking off from or landing at an airport within that area;

b. airports that have airport traffic areas are shown in *blue* on sectional charts;
c. you are required to maintain radio contact with the tower and to have a clearance to enter an airport traffic area, but you may use light signals under some circumstances. (See Sec. 31.8);
d. the procedures to be followed while in the airport traffic area are explained in Sec. 31.

12. *SPECIAL VFR CLEARANCES*—Even though the weather conditions within a control zone are below VFR minimums, it may be possible to obtain a special VFR clearance to take off from, land at or fly through a control zone;
    a. you *must* obtain an ATC clearance before operating within a control zone when the weather is less than that required for VFR flight;
    b. a VFR pilot may request and be given a clearance to enter, leave or operate within most control zones in special VFR conditions, traffic permitting and provided such flight will not delay IFR operations;
    c. such clearance may be obtained at any control zone which is not circled with TTTTTTTT on the sectional chart;
    d. the visibility requirements are: 1-mile flight visibility for operations within the control zone and 1-mile ground visibility if taking off or landing;
    e. all special VFR flights must remain clear of clouds;
    f. if there is an operating control tower in the control zone, you direct your request to that tower; otherwise, you request it from the nearest tower, FSS or center;
    g. you do not need to file a complete flight plan with your request for a clearance but you should state your intentions in sufficient detail to permit air traffic control to fit your flight into the traffic flow;
    h. your clearance will not contain a specific altitude as you must remain clear of clouds;
    i. the controller may require you to fly at or below a certain altitude due to other traffic but the altitude specified will permit flight at or above the minimum safe altitude;
    j. at radar locations you may be vectored if necessary for control purposes or if you request such vectors;
    k. ATC provides separation between special VFR flights and between them and other IFR flights;
    l. you cannot obtain a special VFR clearance between sunset and sunrise unless you are instrument rated and the aircraft is IFR equipped;
    m. have pencil and paper ready to copy the clearance as it may be too complex to remember.

Section 26
AIRPORT LIGHTING AND NAVIGATION AIDS

1. There are a number of lighting aids that assist you in making safe landings either at night or when visibility becomes greatly reduced;
    a. as a student, or a private pilot without an instrument rating, you should not be concerned about landing when visibility is low during the daytime, but weather conditions can deteriorate quickly and you may need all the help you can get;
    b. the sectional chart shows whether an airport has lights, which are indicated by the L between the altitude and runway length;
    c. you can obtain a more detailed list of lighting aids at any airport by consulting your *AIM,* or instrument approach plates.
2. *ROTATING BEACON*—A beacon located on the airport that rotates in a clockwise direction, when viewed from above, and produces the visual effect of flashes at regular intervals;
    a. the flashes may be in one or two colors alternately;
    b. the flashes occur at the rate of 12 to 20 per minute for beacons that mark airports, landmarks, and points of Federal airways, 30 to 60 per minute for beacons that mark heliports, and 12 to 60 per minute for hazard beacons;
    c. when the rotating beacon is operating within a control zone during daytime, it indicates that the ground visibility is less than 3 miles and/or the ceiling is less than 1,000 feet, but never rely solely on the rotating beacon to tell you whether VFR weather conditions exist.
3. *AUXILIARY LIGHTS* are of two general kinds;
    a. *code beacons,* which can be seen from all directions, are used to identify land airports (green) and hazards (red);
    b. *course lights,* which can be seen clearly from only one direction, and are used with rotating beacons of the Federal Airway System.
4. *OBSTRUCTION LIGHTING* is used to mark light obstructions to warn airmen of their presence, and consist of various kinds of aviation red obstruction lights, orange and white paint for daytime use, and high intensity white obstruction lights.
5. *RUNWAY AND TAXIWAY LIGHTING*—Runway edge lights are used to outline the edges of runways during periods of darkness and restricted visibility;
    a. these light systems are classified according to their intensity or brightness;

b. they are High Intensity Runway Lights (HIRL), Medium Intensity Runway Lights (MIRL), and Low Intensity Runway Lights (LIRL);

c. runway edge lights are white except that on instrument runways aviation yellow replaces white on the last 2,000 feet or half of the runway, as a caution zone;

d. taxiway lights are blue;

e. lighting that is in operation from sunset to sunrise is indicated on your chart by an L, while that which is available from sunset to sunrise only by prior request by radio call, letter, phone or telegram is indicated by *L, and lighting which is in operation part of the night and on request, or not operating thereafter is indicated by (L).

6. *CONTROL OF LIGHTING SYSTEMS*—Lighting systems are controlled in different ways at different airports;

    a. at some airports without a tower, the FSS operates the lighting;

    b. where there is an operating control tower, the tower operates approach and runway lighting;

    c. you may request that lights be turned off, on, up or down;

        (1) don't hesitate to ask that they be turned all the way up during periods of low visibility;

    d. where there is no FSS or tower, some airports have equipment which permits you to operate the runway lights simply by keying your mike, which is known as pilot-controlled lighting (PCL) and is indicated on the sectional chart by a circle around the L.

7. *VISUAL APPROACH SLOPE INDICATOR* (VASI)—one of the most useful facilities available to all pilots is VASI. It greatly increases your ability to bring your airplane down to a safe landing at night or during poor visibility;

    a. VASI is a system of lights so arranged as to provide visual descent guidance information during the approach to the runway;

    b. these lights are visible from 3 to 5 miles during the day and up to 20 miles or more at night;

    c. the visual guide path provides safe obstruction clearance within ±10 degrees of the extended runway center line and to 4 nautical miles from the runway threshold;

    d. you should not begin your descent using the VASI until you are visually aligned with the runway;

    e. the VASI may consist of two bars (near and far) or three bars (near, middle and far);

    f. the two bar VASI provides just one glide path while the three bar VASI provides two visual glide paths, the lower provided by the near and middle bars and the upper glide path is provided by the middle and far bars;

        (1) the higher glide path is for high cockpit airplanes; you will use the lower path;

    g. the indications of the two types of VASI are depicted in Fig. 26.1;

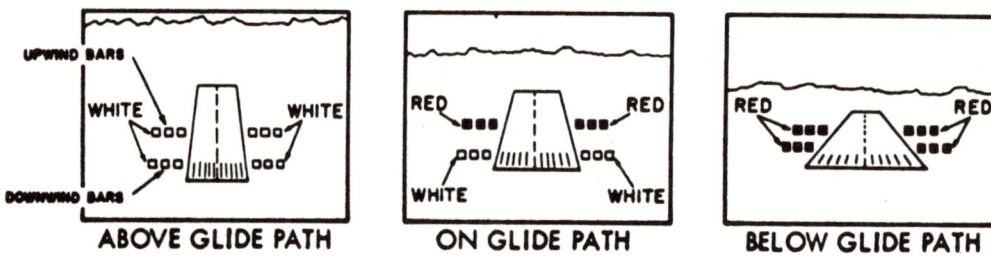

FIG 26.1—THE VISUAL APPROACH SLOPE INDICATOR (VASI)

  h. white over white indicates you are above the glide slope; red over white indicates that you are on the glide slope, red over red means that you are too low and should hold your altitude or climb until you are back on the glide slope;
    (1) but don't panic and pull it up too fast without increasing your throttle or you could stall;
  i. just remember that "red over red, you're dead" and "red over white, you're all right," if you have any trouble remembering this code;
  j. as you descend, the far bar appears to be above the near bar;
  k. the white lights may appear yellowish in haze or dust, or at night when the VASI is operated at low intensity, or may appear orange or brownish during certain atmospheric conditions;
  l. when you are approaching to land at a runway served by VASI, you must maintain an altitude at or above the glide slope until a lower altitude is necessary, for a safe landing.

Section 27
LANDING YOUR AIRPLANE

1. It is recommended that you enter the traffic pattern at pattern altitude at a 45-degree angle to the downwind leg, abeam the midpoint of the active runway;
    a. 1,000 feet AGL is the recommended pattern altitude unless it is established otherwise;
    b. the legs of the traffic pattern and the recommended traffic patterns are shown at Sec. 25.7;
    c. at most airports, which have left patterns, your downwind leg will be parallel to the active runway, with the runway on your left;
    d. see Sec. 25.6 for the ways to determine the traffic pattern;
    e. many airports have right traffic patterns to keep aircraft away from cities;
    f. where two or more airports are close to each other, as at Wichita, there may be unusual traffic patterns or pattern altitudes to avoid collisions.
2. When you are opposite the end of the active runway:
    a. apply full carburetor heat;
        (1) you always apply carburetor heat when you reduce the rpm below the green line;
    b. reduce the throttle to 1,500 rpm;
    c. be sure that fuel mixture is full rich.
3. Apply back pressure to the elevator to reduce the airspeed to 60 KIAS (70 KIAS if the wind is strong or gusty);
    a. use the trim tab as necessary to hold the nose up without excessive back pressure on the elevator;
    b. your Cessna 152 or 150 is so responsive that the proper attitude can be maintained using little or no back pressure and little elevator trim;
    c. with full flaps, your airspeed will be from 55 to 65 KIAS;
    d. if you are landing following a long glide, you should "clear the engine" at intervals by smoothly applying power for several seconds.
4. Approximately one-fourth to one-half mile past the end of the runway, make a 90-degree turn to the left, thereby turning onto "base leg";
    a. after leveling out on base leg, check traffic carefully in all directions;

      b. check especially carefully to your right for any airplane coming in on a long final approach; failure to do so could result in having another airplane move in with you;

      c. keep the airspeed up to 60 KIAS (55 KIAS with flaps) until ready to touch down.

5. Begin the next 90-degree turn in time to line up as straight as possible with the active runway;

      a. when you are lined up with the runway, you are on *final approach.*

6. If you are too low to reach the end of the runway, apply more power as needed;

      a. keep your hand on the throttle so that you are ready instantly to increase the power if the stall warning signal sounds when you are more than a foot or two off the runway.

7. If you are too high, reduce power;

      a. if necessary, apply flaps as needed to set the airplane down at the intended spot;

      b. with 40-degree flaps, the airspeed should be 54 KIAS but never *below* that.

8. If you are too high to get down with flaps or by using a slip do not hesitate to go around, following the traffic pattern and landing again. (See Sec.27.22 for go-around procedures.)

9. As your airplane approaches the ground:

      a. throttle all the way back;

      b. keep your hand on the throttle at all times, prepared to apply power if needed to reach the runway, or full power if there is *any* need to go around.

10. Begin your initial flare when you are about 10 feet above the runway;

      a. this is done by applying back pressure on the elevator;

         (1) this will slow you down and stop your descent and you will be flying almost level down the runway;

         (2) by this time, you will be about 2 feet off the ground;

      b. as you see the airplane start to settle closer to the runway, apply more back pressure in an attempt to keep the airplane from landing;

         (1) don't do this until you are very close to the runway or you will stall several feet above the runway and bounce it in;

      c. continue to hold the airplane off the runway as long as possible;

         (1) as you do, the airspeed will drop to stall speed;

         (2) by so doing, you will cause the airplane to set down smoothly;

      d. by the time you lose your airspeed, you should be just inches above the ground, effecting a smooth landing and avoiding structural damage to the airplane.

11. Be careful to keep your feet on the rudder pedals only and not the brakes, or the brakes will be locked on touchdown.

12. Throughout the landing, keep your eyes moving to detect other airplanes in the vicinity;

      a. particularly, look for other airplanes that may be using a different landing pattern, to land on a different runway from the one you are using;

    b. if there is an instrument approach, it is always possible that another aircraft, making an instrument approach, will be circling to land, thus coming in from an entirely unexpected direction.
13. One of the hazards in landing is the *ground loop* which is an abrupt, uncontrolled 180-degree turn on the ground;
    a. the ground loop is avoided by (1) keeping the airplane lined up with the direction of the runway, (2) turning your wheel into the wind, and (3) avoiding excessive crosswinds.
14. In all landings, you should land on the main wheels first;
    a. keep your nose wheel high until the landing is completed and then lower it slowly.
15. It is probably inevitable for student pilots to flare out too high with the result that they bounce when landing. If that happens to you, either:
    a. apply full power and go around; *or*
    b. if there is sufficient runway, apply power and then reduce slowly, and settle down for another landing.
16. Immediately upon landing:
    a. remove flaps, if any;
    b. turn carburetor heat to cold.
17. Reduce speed to normal taxi speed.
18. Get off the runway in use as quickly and safely as possible.
19. Use the regular taxi procedures discussed in Sec. 12.
20. If there is a control tower, upon leaving the active runway, switch to ground control for taxi instructions.
21. If there is a FSS on the field, report when you are down and off the runway: CESSNA 27 JULIET; DOWN AND CLEAR.
22. If there is any doubt about your ability to land, follow the *go-around* procedure, which includes the following steps:
    a. apply full power;
    b. carburetor heat OFF;
    c. retract wing flaps to 20 degrees;
    d. if the airplane is trimmed for landing, keep the nose from rising too quickly by use of forward pressure on the elevator and retrimming the airplane as quickly as possible;
    e. climb out at 55 KIAS;
    f. raise flaps slowly to prevent sinking;
    g. go around, following the regular traffic pattern.
23. If you are practicing touch-and-go landings, promptly take the following steps after touching down:
    a. raise flaps;
    b. adjust trim tab for takeoff;

c. apply full throttle;
d. carburetor heat to cold;
e. proceed with normal takeoff procedures.
24. If the field is short, you will use the *short field landing* techniques, which are the same as the normal landing procedures outlined above, with the following exceptions:
    a. follow the usual landing pattern, at normal pattern elevation, applying carburetor heat when on your downwind leg opposite the end of the active runway;
    b. apply 10 degrees of flaps while still on the downwind leg but below 85 KIAS;
    c. reduce your airspeed to 60–70 KIAS as you turn onto the base leg;
    d. while on the base leg, apply 10 degrees more of flaps, or a total at this point of 20 degrees of flaps;
    e. be very sure to keep the airspeed at 54 KIAS during the rest of the landing, until ready to touch down;
        (1) failure to do so will produce severe danger of a stall;
    f. on final approach, apply 10 degrees more of flaps, so that they are all the way down;
    g. do not apply any power, except as necessary to reach the field; all power must be off before touching down;
    h. immediately after touching down, lower the nose;
    i. apply the brakes firmly;
    j. apply back pressure on the elevator during braking to keep the nose strut from compressing.
25. If the field is soft, because of mud or snow or being freshly plowed, it is necessary to make a *soft field landing*. This consists of the following procedure:
    a. the procedure is the same as for the short field landing, until you make your final approach;
    b. as the airplane starts to flare, add enough power to hold the nose wheel off the ground;
        (1) this will prevent the airplane from nosing over;
        (2) 200–300 rpm is normally sufficient power;
    c. keep the nose off the ground as long as possible by adjusting power and by constantly maintaining back pressure on the elevator.
26. If the wind is more than 5 knots and is not straight down the runway, it is necessary to make a *crosswind landing*. The techniques are the same as in any normal landing, with the following exceptions:
    a. before landing, get an update on the wind direction and velocity from UNICOM, FSS, ATIS or the tower;
    b. cross check this information by noting the tetrahedron or windsock to determine from which side the wind will strike the airplane;
    c. if the winds are strong or gusty, use your radio to determine whether there is some

airport that could be reached where the winds would not be as dangerous or where they might be more in line with one of their runways;
    d. while on final approach, lower the windward wing into the wind by use of your ailerons;
    e. use the *opposite* rudder as much as necessary to keep the airplane lined up with the runway;
    f. if the airplane is drifting toward the wind, use *less* aileron, but if it is drifting with the wind, use *more* aileron;
    g. if the nose is not straight down the runway, correct with the rudder;
    h. in a crosswind landing, it may be necessary to use enough aileron at touchdown so that the airplane lands on one wheel;
    i. after landing in a strong crosswind, keep the aileron pressure on, to keep the windward wing low *after* landing;
        (1) as your airspeed slows, you will have to use *more* aileron pressure;
    j. remember to use aileron to stop the airplane from drifting and rudder to keep the nose straight.
27. If, on final approach, it appears that you are too high, you can get down quickly and safely without increasing your speed by using a *slip;*
    a. flaps should not be used if the wind is strong or gusty.
28. In the slip, you use regular landing procedures with the exception of the following procedures:
    a. after the airplane is lined up with the runway, use your ailerons to lower the windward wing;
    b. as the plane tends to turn, apply a sufficient amount of *opposite* rudder so that the airplane continues to be lined up with the runway;
    c. the more aileron and opposite rudder that you apply, the steeper will be the angle of descent;
        (1) to obtain the maximum angle of descent, use *full* rudder and *enough* opposite aileron to stay lined up with the runway;
    d. be extremely careful to maintain sufficient airspeed, by lowering the nose;
        (1) the airspeed should never be less than 60 KIAS until you are ready to touch down;
    e. the instant before touchdown, level the wings and straighten the airplane;
    f. if there is any doubt about your ability to land safely, never hesitate to go around and try again.
29. Before landing at any airport, you must be sure that, under the existing conditions, there is enough runway;
    a. this is particularly important if the temperature or humidity is high, the elevation of the airport is high, the runway is inclined, or its surface is short grass, or there are obstacles at the end of the runway (See Sec. 14.26 & 14.27);
    b. use the Landing Distance Performance chart in the Pilot's Operation Handbook for your airplane.

WEIGHT LBS	SPEED AT 50 FT KIAS	PRESS ALT FT	0°C		10°C		20°C		30°C		40°C	
			GRND ROLL	TOTAL TO CLEAR 50 FT OBS	GRND ROLL	TOTAL TO CLEAR 50 FT OBS	GRND ROLL	TOTAL TO CLEAR 50 FT OBS	GRND ROLL	TOTAL TO CLEAR 50 FT OBS	GRND ROLL	TOTAL TO CLEAR 50 FT OBS
1670	54	S.L.	450	1160	465	1185	485	1215	500	1240	515	1265
		1000	465	1185	485	1215	500	1240	520	1270	535	1295
		2000	485	1215	500	1240	520	1270	535	1300	555	1330
		3000	500	1240	520	1275	540	1305	560	1335	575	1360
		4000	520	1275	540	1305	560	1335	580	1370	600	1400
		5000	540	1305	560	1335	580	1370	600	1400	620	1435
		6000	560	1340	580	1370	605	1410	625	1440	645	1475
		7000	585	1375	605	1410	625	1440	650	1480	670	1515
		8000	605	1410	630	1450	650	1480	675	1520	695	1555

FIG. 27.1—LANDING DISTANCES FOR THE CESSNA 152

Note: These figures are based upon new aircraft, in good operating condition, flown by an experienced pilot, zero wind, power off, 30 degrees of flaps, maximum braking on a paved, level, dry runway.

30. If you have a hard landing, tune your radio to 121.5 to see if you have activated your ELT.

Section 28
PROCEDURES AFTER LANDING

1. Once off the runway, proceed to your destination;
    a. if there is a control tower, be sure to obtain a clearance from ground control after you are off the active runway.
2. If you are low on gasoline or will not use the airplane any more that day, proceed to the fuel pump to have the tanks filled, or "topped off";
    a. this will prevent moisture from accumulating in the tanks.
3. When at your desired location, set the throttle at 1,000 rpm;
    a. kill the engine by pulling out the mixture control;
    b. try to park on a level surface so that fuel will not leak out of full tanks.
4. Turn off:
    a. all radios, VOR, ADF, transponder;
    b. rotating beacon, navigation and landing lights;
    c. master switch and ignition.
5. Set the parking brake and lock;
    a. this is optional, depending on the wind and probable weather conditions;
    b. don't set the brakes and lock the door if your plane may have to be moved.
6. Install the control lock.
7. If the winds are brisk or the airplane will remain outside, unattended, for more than a brief period of time:
    a. tie sufficiently strong rope or chains (700 pounds tensile strength) to the wing and tail tiedown fittings, and secure each rope to the ramp tiedown;
    b. install a surface control lock, if available, over the fin and rudder;
    c. install a pitot tube cover;
    d. put chocks around the wheels.

Section 29
RADIO FACILITIES

1. Your radio is an essential method of transmitting and receiving information, as well as an instrument for determining your precise location.
2. Your VOR operates on *very high frequencies* (VHF);
    a. VHF is from 30 to 300 MHz;
    b. VHF transmissions follow an approximate line-of-sight course, that is, your reception *distance* increases as the *altitude* of your airplane above ground level increases, as follows:

Feet above Ground Stations	Reception Distance in Statute Miles
500	30
1000	45
3000	80
5000	100
10000	140

FIG. 29.1—RECEPTION DISTANCES FOR VHF RADIO SIGNALS

    c. these figures assume that there are no intervening physical obstructions, such as buildings or mountains;
    d. VHF has the advantage of giving relatively static-free radio communications.
3. Your Flight Service Station (FSS) performs many services for you;
    a. before you take off, they will brief you on the existing weather and forecasts that pertain to your route;
        (1) during your flight, you may request information, such as weather, airport conditions, and navigation aids;
        (2) it is not required that you identify yourself as a student, but you should do so in order to alert the FSS personnel and enable them to provide you with extra assistance or consideration you may need;
    b. your Flight Plan is filed with the FSS (See Sec. 48);
    c. at certain airports where there is no control tower, the FSS will furnish you with *airport advisories:*

(1) airport advisories provide wind direction and velocity, favored runway, altimeter setting, pertinent *known* traffic, Notices to Airmen, airport taxi routes, airport patterns, and instrument approach procedures;

(2) but the FSS furnishes no airport control;

d. Even when you are not on a flight plan, it is a good idea, when contacting the FSS, to give them your position and altitude;

(1) this information is recorded and can serve as a method of expediting search and rescue procedures if you should meet with trouble;

e. when you are ready to taxi out, notify the FSS of your intentions, including the aircraft identification, type, location, and type of flight planned (VFR or IFR) and destination;

(1) report your takeoff time to the FSS as soon as practicable;

f. when you are approaching an airport with FSS on the field but no control tower, you should contact the FSS from 10 to 25 miles of the airport;

(1) give your position, and advise you are landing;

(2) it is not required that you contact the FSS, but is good operating practice.

4. You can contact the FSS on several frequencies;

a. normally you can transmit and receive on 122.6 and 123.6;

b. you can also transmit on 122.1 and receive on 122.2;

(1) however, if the simplex system has been adopted, you can both transmit *and* receive on 122.2;

c. you can transmit to FSS on 122.1 and listen on a VOR frequency;

d. in case of emergency, you can transmit and receive on 121.5;

e. always remember to tell the FSS the frequency you are listening on.

5. The FSS is prepared to give other assistance to you in flight:

a. they are trained to assist you if you become lost; some can give you a DF steer (See Sec. 41);

b. if there is no UNICOM at the airport, and the FSS is not too busy with more important matters, it may give information about fuel, repairs, transportation, lodging, etc.

6. If there is a control tower, traffic within the air traffic control area is under the jurisdiction of the tower, with control divided between approach control, tower control and ground control. (See Sec. 31, 32 and 33.)

7. One of the most useful of the radio facilities available to you is Unicom;

a. Unicom is a private aeronautical station;

(1) at small airports, the service may not be consistent, so it may be possible to call in and receive no reply;

b. Unicom provides communication for many airports *without* control towers;

(1) if there is no control tower, you will transmit and receive on 122.8, which is identified on your aeronautical chart as U1;

c. Unicom also serves many airports *with* control towers;

(1) if there is a control tower at that airport, you will transmit and receive on 123.0, which is identified on your aeronautical chart as U2;

SECTION 29—RADIO FACILITIES

    d. new frequencies are being assigned, with 122.8, 123.0 and 122.75 being assigned to landing areas *without* ATC or FSS, 122.95 being assigned to landing areas with ATC or FSS, and 122.85 being assigned to Multicom;

    e. you can determine whether or not there is Unicom at an airport by referring to:

        (1) the sectional chart which will indicate the presence of Unicom by the letter U in the airport information box;

        (2) the Airport Directory Section of the *AIM;*

    f. Unicom may be used for communications with ground facilities concerning runway and wind conditions, types of fuel available, availability of ground transportation, food and lodging;

    g. Unicom at an airport where there is a control tower is used in the same way, except that runway, wind conditions, weather, etc., are furnished by the tower;

    h. Unicom is often useful in emergencies, both to communicate important messages to and from the airplane, and to advise of emergencies that have arisen in flight;

    i. Unicom is never used for air traffic control purposes.

8. Follow these suggestions in using Unicom:

    a. do *not* use the Unicom frequencies to chat from aircraft to aircraft. The higher your altitude, the more you inconvenience others when you tie up the frequency;

    b. be brief;

    c. limit your use to the transmission of *essential* messages;

    d. always remember that *anyone* can answer your call to Unicom for information about the wind, runway, etc., including a visitor with nothing better to do, so, do *not* rely too heavily upon their advice, but, in addition you should make your own check of the wind sock or wind tee before landing.

9. The frequency of 122.9 has been designated for Multicom, but 122.85 is being assigned to it;

    a. this frequency is used to provide communication facilities essential to the conduct of activities being performed by or directed from private aircraft;

    b. such ground/air communications include those pertaining to agriculture, ranching, conservation activities, aerial advertising and parachute jumping;

    c. the frequency is also used for essential air-to-air communications between aircraft;

        (1) as such, it takes some of the pressure off Unicom, which should not be used for this purpose;

        (2) this use should be limited to essential communications and should not include idle chatter;

    d. Multicom is not used for the purpose of traffic control.

10. The radio beacon is a non-directional facility operation on low and medium frequencies, which you will use if you have an ADF. (See Sec. 37.)

11. There are numerous facilities of the Air Traffic Control (ATC) system that primarily serve IFR traffic but also perform many services to VFR traffic. (See Sec. 33.)

12. Much information about radio aids to navigation and communications is contained on your sectional chart.

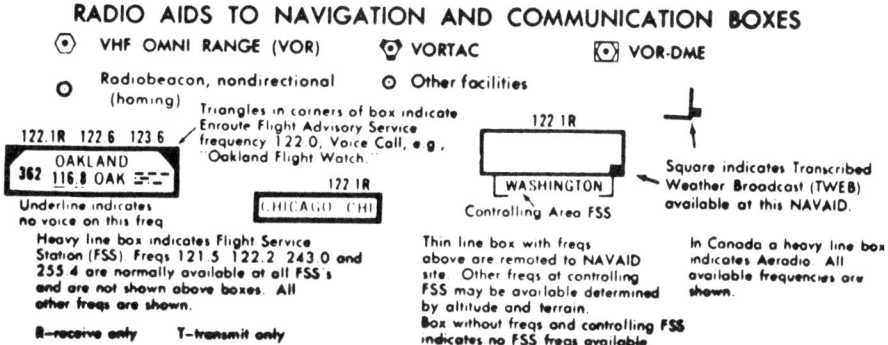

Section 30
TECHNIQUE IN USING YOUR RADIO

1. Never hesitate to use your radio;
    a. while brevity is important, it is more important that each party to the conversation understand the other;
    b. since concise phraseology is not always adequate, you should use whatever words are necessary to get your message across;
    c. try to memorize all the standard terminology and procedures, to make yourself a safer, more professional pilot;
    d. slang, profanity, and CB talk have no place in your radio communications;
    e. there is no place on the frequencies for anything but essential communications, so avoid idle conversations, banter and frivolous talk.
2. Always follow these rules when you use your radio:
    a. listen for 10 or 15 seconds before you transmit. Be sure someone else is not using the frequency;
    b. think before you transmit. Decide what you want to say, how you will say it and how you will respond, depending on the reply you get;
    c. be alert for sounds and lack of sounds in your receiver. Always be sure that you have the right frequency, that you are using the right radio, if you have more than one, and that your volume is turned up;
    d. be sure that you are within range of the station before you try to communicate with it, since you are limited to "line of sight";
    e. don't panic right away if you don't get an immediate response. The controller or FSS specialist may be talking on another frequency or be otherwise occupied;
    f. fly your airplane first. Don't let your preoccupation with your radio make you forget to fly your plane safely.
3. To communicate accurately and quickly, you need to know the special language that is used in aeronautical radio communications. This includes knowing the phonetic alphabet, but you do not need to memorize the Morse code;
    a. this is used throughout the world and will help you even when you are flying outside the U.S.;
    b. you should use the phonetic alphabet when identifying your aircraft, as during your initial radio contact with a controller or FSS specialist.

SECTION 30—TECHNIQUE IN USING YOUR RADIO

Letter	Morse	Word	Pronunciation
A	▪━	Alfa	(AL-FAH)
B	━▪▪▪	Bravo	(BRAH-VOH)
C	━▪━▪	Charlie	(CHAR-LEE)
D	━▪▪	Delta	(DELL-TAH)
E	▪	Echo	(ECK-OH)
F	▪▪━▪	Foxtrot	(FOKS-TROT)
G	━━▪	Golf	(GOLF)
H	▪▪▪▪	Hotel	(HOH-TEL)
I	▪▪	India	(IN-DEE-AH)
J	▪━━━	Juliett	(JEW-LEE-ETT)
K	━▪━	Kilo	(KEY-LOH)
L	▪━▪▪	Lima	(LEE-MAH)
M	━━	Mike	(MIKE)
N	━▪	November	(NO-VEM-BER)
O	━━━	Oscar	(OSS-CAH)
P	▪━━▪	Papa	(PAH-PAH)
Q	━━▪━	Quebec	(KEH-BECK)
R	▪━▪	Romeo	(ROW-ME-OH)
S	▪▪▪	Sierra	(SEE-AIR-RAH)
T	━	Tango	(TANG-GO)
U	▪▪━	Uniform	YOU-NEE-FORM)
V	▪▪▪━	Victor	(VIK-TAH)
W	▪━━	Whiskey	(WISS-KEY)
X	━▪▪━	Xray	(ECKS-RAY)
Y	━▪━━	Yankee	(YANG-KEY)
Z	━━▪▪	Zulu	(ZOO-LOO)
1	▪━━━━	One	(WUN)
2	▪▪━━━	Two	(TOO)
3	▪▪▪━━	Three	(TREE)
4	▪▪▪▪━	Four	(FOW-ER)
5	▪▪▪▪▪	Five	(FIFE)
6	━▪▪▪▪	Six	(SIX)
7	━━▪▪▪	Seven	(SEV-EN)
8	━━━▪▪	Eight	(AIT)
9	━━━━▪	Nine	(NIN-ER)
0	━━━━━	Zero	(ZEE-RO)

FIG. 30.1—THE PHONETIC ALPHABET

4. All times used in aircraft radio communication are based on the 24 hour clock and Greenwich Mean Time (GMT). (See Sec. 48.3.);
    a. the hour is indicated by the first two figures and the minutes by the last two figures, thus: 0000 is stated ZERO ZERO ZERO ZERO, and 0920 is stated ZERO NINER TWO ZERO.

5. Where figures are used to indicate such things as ceiling heights, upper wind levels, etc., up to 9,900 they are expressed as follows: 500 is said FIVE HUNDRED, and 4,500 is said FOUR THOUSAND FIVE HUNDRED:

a. numbers above 9,900 are spoken by separating the digits preceding the word "thousand," thus: 10,000 is expressed ONE ZERO THOUSAND and 13,500 is expressed ONE THREE THOUSAND FIVE HUNDRED.
6. Airways are transmitted thus: V12 is expressed VICTOR TWELVE.
7. All other numbers are transmitted by pronouncing each digit. 10 is expressed ONE ZERO.
8. When you state a radio frequency that contains a decimal point, you state it as POINT, that is, 122.1 is expressed ONE TWO TWO POINT ONE.

Word or Phrase	Meaning
Acknowledge	Let me know that you have received and understood this message;
Roger	I have received all of your last transmission (Used to acknowledge receipt, should be used for no other purpose);
Affirmative	Yes; (or, affirm
Negative	That is not correct;
Correction	An error has been made in the transmission (or message indicated). The correct version is. . . . ;
I say again	(Self-explanatory);
Say again	(Self-explanatory);
Repeat back	Repeat all this message back to me;
Stand by	If used by itself means "I must pause for a few seconds." If the pause is longer than a few seconds, or if "Stand by" is used to prevent another station from transmitting, it must be followed by the ending, "Out;"
Verify	Check with originator;
Over	My transmission is ended and I expect a response from you;
Out	This conversation is ended. I do *not* expect a response from you;
Words twice	(a) As a request: "Communication is difficult. Please say every phrase twice;" (b) As information: "Since communication is difficult, every phrase in this message will be spoken twice."

FIG. 30.2—THE VOCABULARY OF RADIO COMMUNICATION

9. When you are expressing altitudes you state the separate digits of the thousands, plus the hundreds if appropriate, up to 18,000 feet MSL; thus: 12,000 is expressed ONE TWO THOUSAND, and 12,500 is expressed ONE TWO THOUSAND FIVE HUNDRED;
    a. altitudes above 18,000 are termed "flight levels," which do not apply to the student or to most private pilots.
10. Whenever course bearing, heading or wind direction is given, it is magnetic with *all three digits* given;
    a. all three digits are given; thus: 5 degrees is expressed ZERO ZERO FIVE, 50 degrees is expressed ZERO FIVE ZERO, 360 degrees is expressed THREE SIX ZERO, 100 degrees is expressed ONE ZERO ZERO, and 220 degrees is expressed TWO TWO ZERO;

b. the word "true" must be added when it applies.
11. Each digit of a speed is expressed, followed by the word "knots;"
    a. 250 knots is expressed TWO FIVE ZERO KNOTS, 185 knots is expressed ONE EIGHT FIVE KNOTS, and 95 knots is expressed NINER FIVE KNOTS.
12. The other terms you will use in radio communications are defined in Fig. 30.2.
13. Each radio contact generally comprises four parts:
    a. the *callup:* this consists of the call sign of the station being called, the words "This is," the call sign of the caller;
    b. the *reply:* this consists of the call sign of the station being called, the words "This is," the call sign of the caller;
    c. the *message:* this is the portion of the contact that conveys information or requests information;
    d. the *acknowledgement* and *ending:* this consists of the aircraft's call sign (regardless of whether the acknowledgement is being made by an aircraft or ground station), and the word "roger."
14. In contacts with the tower, it is unnecessary that you respond when it is apparent that no response is needed, such as when:
    a. the tower can see you and can see your airplane respond to their direction;
    b. the tower is busy and begins immediately to talk to another pilot.
15. When a message is short or when it is probable that the callup will be heard without difficulty, the message may be transmitted following the callup without waiting for a reply or invitation to go ahead.
16. After contact has been definitely established, it may be continued without further callup or identification.
17. During your initial contact with a ground station, use your *complete aircraft call sign;*
    a. this consists of the make of your aircraft (or model, such as Skyhawk), followed by the complete certification number, thus: CESSNA NOVEMBER 8424 JULIET.
    b. if there is no danger of confusion, it is customary to omit November.
18. The ground station call sign consists of the name of the location or airport, followed by the appropriate indication of the type of station, thus:
    a. Oakland Tower (airport traffic control tower);
    b. Miami Ground Control (ground control position in the tower);
    c. Kennedy Approach Control (tower radar or non-radar approach control position);
    d. St. Louis Departure Control (tower radar departure control position);
    e. Washington Radio (FAA Flight Service Station);
    f. New York Center (FAA Air Route Traffic Control Center).
19. When using your radio, follow these steps:
    a. turn on your radio and turn up volume and then turn squelch knob to the right until you get static and then turn squelch to the left until clear;
    b. tune it to the frequency of the facility you wish to contact;
    c. most radios in use today do not require warming up;

d. be sure no one else is using the frequency;
e. determine what you are going to say or ask;
f. hold the microphone very close to your mouth;
g. push the button firmly;
h. make your callup and complete your communication;
i. release the button promptly and decisively;

20. When you are communicating with a Flight Service Station, the following procedures are followed:
    a. flight service stations are identified by the name of the station, followed by the word RADIO;
       (1) for instance, you will begin by saying: QUINCY RADIO; THIS IS . . . ;
    b. your aircraft is identified by the make of the aircraft followed by all digits of the certificate number and letter suffix:
       (1) for example: THIS IS CESSNA, NOVEMBER EIGHT FOUR TWO FOUR JULIET;
    c. to call a flight service station, you might say: QUINCY RADIO, THIS IS CESSNA EIGHT FOUR TWO FOUR JULIET. LISTENING ONE TWO THREE POINT SIX OVER;
    d. the flight service station will normally answer on 123.6;
    e. if you desire a reply on another frequency, you should indicate the frequency, such as the VOR frequency, on which the station reply is expected;
    f. after you have established contact, you may use an abbreviated form of identification, using only the last three units of the certificate number, thus: TWO FOUR JULIET;
    g. after the station has answered your call, proceed with your message without further callup other than preceding the message with the aircraft identification.

Section 31
TOWER CONTROLLED AIRPORTS

1. There is a separate set of rules that govern your flight at and near an airport where traffic control is being exercised by a control tower; that area is known as an Airport Traffic Area and is shown in blue on your sectional chart;

   AIRPORT TRAFFIC AREAS

   Federally operated control tower
   FSS
   DAYTON CT - 119.9
   1008 L 70

   Non-Federal control tower
   MARTIN NFCT - 119.2
   556 L 70

   Other Airport (no traffic area)
   SOMERSET
   1540 L 37

   Hours of operation of tower, if not continuous, are included with tower frequencies.

   FIG. 31.1—AIRPORT TRAFFIC AREAS ON AERONAUTICAL CHARTS

   a. the busier the airport, the more the functions are divided and the more controllers you will have to contact to taxi, take off, land or fly through the airport traffic area;
   b. while the airport traffic area only extends outward for 5 statute miles and upward only 3,000 feet, you should contact Radar Traffic Information or Approach Control whenever you fly within 25 miles of the busy airport so that you can learn of other traffic and they can know your presence;
   c. the separate services provided at and near any tower controlled airport may include ground control, tower, approach and departure control and radar traffic information;
      (1) these are all important to you, both as a student and as a private pilot and whether or not you are instrument rated;
      (2) at busier airports there may also be Clearance Delivery but that is only of interest to pilots who are filing IFR unless ground control asks you to switch to clearance delivery for your clearance to take off;
   d. two or more of these functions may be handled by the same controller, even though you talk to him on more than one frequency.
2. *Ground Control* has control over all aircraft at a controlled airport that are on the ground, other than those that are taking off or landing;
   a. the ground controller is in the tower and usually has a view of all the runways and taxiways;

b. you must contact ground control before you begin to taxi and after turning off the runway upon landing;
   (1) you will contact ground control on the appropriate frequency.
   (2) you can determine the ground control frequency by referring to *AIM,* instrument approach charts, *Sky Prints* or by calling the tower, whose frequency is shown on your sectional chart;
   (3) if there is ATIS, be sure that you have "gotten the numbers" *before* you contact ground control to ask for a clearance to taxi for takeoff;
c. if the airport is in a TCA, you will also contact ground control for your clearance out of the TCA (see Sec. 32);
   (1) be sure you have pencil and paper ready to copy your clearance out of the TCA, as it may be complicated;
   (2) read the clearance back until it is absolutely correct; don't be afraid to ask for explanations or a slower reading;
d. tell the controller you are a student; he will then be much more patient and will be more attentive in watching you;
   (1) even if you are an experienced pilot, ask for help, directions along taxiways, etc., if you are not acquainted with the airport;
e. always state your position on the airport when calling ground control for taxi instructions;
   (1) authorization to taxi "to" a runway is authorization to cross runways that intersect the taxi route unless you receive instructions to the contrary;
   (2) authorization to taxi "to" a runway does not constitute a clearance to taxi *onto* that runway;
f. a typical callup to ground control would be: SPRINGFIELD GROUND CONTROL, CESSNA 2151 SIERRA, PARKED IN FRONT OF THE TERMINAL BUILDING, READY TO TAXI, VFR TO PEORIA. WITH BRAVO (The current ATIS), OVER;
g. it is very important that you understand your clearance or instructions since ATC clearances and instructions pertaining to taxiing are based on known traffic and known physical airport conditions;
h. it is your responsibility to avoid collision with other aircraft, even though you are operating pursuant to an ATC clearance;
i. when you have reached the runup area, you perform your regular runup, *then* transfer to the tower frequency and proceed;
j. similarly, you will contact ground control just *after* turning off the active runway after landing;
   (1) when you are given instructions to turn off the runway by the tower, they will tell you the ground control frequency;
   (2) if you have two radios, you should have the ground control frequency set in the other radio so you can switch automatically;

SECTION 31—TOWER CONTROLLED AIRPORTS

    k. as soon as you are completely clear (not partially) off the runway, stop, change to ground control frequency, and advise ground control your intentions (they know you are there). PEORIA GROUND CONTROL. CESSNA 2151 SIERRA, JUST OFF RUNWAY TWO TWO. WANT TO TAXI TO TERMINAL BUILDING (or other destination).

3. After you have completed your runup, you switch to the *tower* frequency and obtain clearance to take off;
    a. your request for permission: SPRINGFIELD TOWER, CESSNA 8424 JULIET, READY FOR TAKEOFF;
    b. permission to take off: CESSNA 8424 JULIET, CLEARED FOR TAKEOFF or other instructions;
    c. you acknowledge: 24 JULIET, ROGER. If they are busy, your taking the active runway is enough;
    d. if the tower has not been informed of the direction of your departure, you should request permission to make a departure in any direction that is not a standard departure;
       (1) you may make this request when you switch to the tower to request clearance for departure or you may do it as you are taking off;
    e. you may request a straight out departure, a right or left departure, or a downwind departure;
       (1) unless traffic conditions make your request impractical, you will normally be cleared to depart in any direction convenient for your flight.

4. About the time you have lifted off, the tower may direct that you contact *departure control* on a specified frequency;
    a. acknowledge the request by repeating the frequency and then switching to the new frequency;
    b. after you have the plane well under control, comply with the direction to contact departure control;
    c. unless there is considerable air traffic in the area, or unless you are receiving radar vectors, etc., you will not normally have to communicate with departure control.

5. When you are approaching an airport with an operating control tower, you will normally contact approach control;
    a. tune your radio to the approach control frequency 25 or 30 miles out so that you can be monitoring the frequency as you get near the airport;
       (1) you can find the proper frequency in *AIM, Sky Prints* or IFR approach plates;
       (2) if you can't find the frequency any other way, check the sectional chart for the tower frequency, contact the tower and it will advise you the frequency of approach control;
       (3) you should monitor ATIS, where available, *before* contacting approach control;
    b. depending on how busy the tower is, call it up when directed by approach control;

Color and Type of Signal	On the Ground	In Flight
STEADY GREEN	Cleared for take-off	Cleared to land
FLASHING GREEN	Cleared to taxi	Return for landing (to be followed by steady green at proper time)
STEADY RED	Stop	Give way to other aircraft and continue circling
FLASHING RED	Taxi clear of landing area (runway) in use	Airport unsafe—do not land
FLASHING WHITE	Return to starting point on airport	
ALTERNATING RED & GREEN	General Warning Signal—Exercise Extreme Caution	

FIG. 31.2—TRAFFIC CONTROL LIGHT SIGNALS

  c. you will be given instructions and particularly at what point you are to switch to the tower frequency.
6. At the point indicated by approach control, you will switch to the tower frequency and give your position (giving your position is not necessary if the tower has radar);
  a. the tower will give you instructions as to landing and, if you are behind other traffic, whom you are to follow;
  b. you may *not* land until the tower has advised you that you are CLEARED TO LAND;
    (1) this may come when you are several miles from the airport if there is no other traffic ahead of you;
    (2) at busier airports, you will normally be cleared to land when you are some place in the landing pattern, but not until the aircraft ahead of you is down (and clear of the active runway unless you are still some distance from touchdown);
  c. the tower will normally give you instructions, consistent with your speed and point of touchdown, as to turning off the active runway;

SECTION 31—TOWER CONTROLLED AIRPORTS

   (1) if you are still going too fast to turn off where directed, so advise the tower;
  d. you will be advised the frequency to contact ground control (see Sec. 31.2).
7. You can take off and land at tower controlled airports (other than TCAs) even though you do not have two-way radio or yours is not operating;
  a. this is done through the use of a signal that emits an intense red, white or green beam;
  b. you should not use this procedure except in emergencies;
   (1) normally, you will be much better off to go to a non-controlled airport if you do not have an operating two-way radio;
  c. the lights have different meanings, depending on whether you are in the air or on the ground;
  d. you will acknowledge these directions (1) at night by blinking your navigation or landing lights, and (2) during the day by moving your ailerons or rudder.

Section 32
TERMINAL CONTROL AREAS

1. Terminal control areas (TCAs) have been established at the busiest airports in the United States;
    a. their purpose is to separate the large, fast aircraft from smaller aircraft;
    b. this is primarily done by keeping the big aircraft high as long as possible before landing and by keeping the small aircraft outside the area, except on the very strictest of conditions;
    c. TCAs are described as upside-down wedding cakes that extend from ground level to a fixed altitude MSL at the airport and permit low flying at the edges of the cake. The farther from the center of the TCA, the higher you can fly even though you are under the TCA;
    d. every pilot is required to have a clearance to enter any TCA, regardless how good the weather conditions are;
    e. you contact approach control before entering the TCA to obtain a clearance;
        (1) contact approach control on its frequency, which you can find in the *A/M,* instrument approach plates or *Sky Prints;*
        (2) have pencil and paper ready so you can copy the clearance, since you can proceed into the TCA only by conforming with that clearance;
        (3) you are supposed to contact approach control at geographical fixes shown on local charts;
    f. when you are departing from an airport within a TCA, you should contact ground control to obtain your clearance out of the TCA;
        (1) advise the ground controller of your intended altitude and route of flight to depart the TCA;
    g. even though you may not be entering the TCA, you should study it carefully any time you are flying near it, to avoid entering it by accident;
        (1) you can determine the existence (but not all the details) of a TCA by the series of concentric circles on your sectional chart surrounding major airports;
        (2) you can get a detailed chart of TCAs from your *A/M,* local chart, instrument approach charts or *Sky Prints.*

2. *Group-I-TCAs* are found around the busiest airports. To be able to enter one, you must meet these requirements:
    a. have two-way radio capable of communicating with ATC on appropriate frequencies;
    b. have a VOR or TACAN;
    c. have a 4096 code transponder with encoding altimeter (capable of registering your altitude on the controller's radar screen);
        (1) you can get a waiver of this but it requires a prior request;
    d. a private pilot certificate or better to land or takeoff from an airport within the TCA (but not necessarily to fly through it with ATC permission);
    e. other requirements that do not apply to you.
3. *Group II TCAs* are the same as Group I TCAs except that they are found at large airports that are not quite as busy;
    a. the requirements to fly into a Group II TCA are the same as those listed above for a Group I TCA except that a student may land and takeoff at airports within the TCA and an encoder is not required;
    b. obviously, you should not fly into a TCA, either as a student or an inexperienced private pilot, until you have received adequate instructions and flight experience to be a safe pilot in the midst of heavy, fast traffic, dealing with *very* busy controllers.
4. When you are flying in a TCA you must operate your airplane in accordance with current IFR procedures;
    a. but if you are not instrument rated and on an IFR flight plan, it is your continuous duty to maintain VFR conditions.
5. If you are not landing or departing the primary airport within the TCA, you may obtain an ATC clearance to fly through the TCA when traffic conditions permit, but you must meet the requirements set forth above.

Section 33
RADAR SERVICES FOR VFR PILOTS

1. One of the greatest services for pilots is radar assistance and information that is provided by air traffic controllers:
    a. many of these services are available to you, the student pilot, or private pilot;
    b. you do not have to be instrument rated and do not have to be on either an IFR or VFR flight plan to use these services;
       (1) however, some such services are available to VFR flights on a time-permitting basis, so that your request for assistance may be refused (or even ignored) if the controller is too busy;
    c. radar equipped ATC facilities provide radar assistance and navigation service (vectors) to VFR aircraft provided (1) your aircraft can communicate with the facility, (2) you are within radar range, and (3) you can be radar identified.
    d. you should clearly understand that authorization to proceed in accordance with radar navigational assistance does not give you the right to violate the FARs;
       (1) this service is advisory in nature. You continue to be responsible for flying your airplane safely;
    e. the controller may be unable to know whether his instructions will cause you to fly into IFR conditions;
       (1) therefore, you must keep the controller advised of the weather conditions where you are and where you are heading.
2. The controller will give you vectors if:
    a. he suggests them and you agree;
    b. the service is advertised at that location;
    c. the controller believes the vectors are necessary for air safety; or,
    d. you request them.
3. The controller has complete discretion, based upon his work load, in determining if he is able to provide the service in any particular case, and his decision is not subject to question.
4. ATC will issue a radar safety advisory to pilots of radar identified aircraft if the controller observes aircraft to be at an altitude which, in his judgment, puts the aircraft too close to terrain, obstructions or other aircraft;
    a. he cannot know your altitude unless you report it to him or you have an encoding altimeter that is functioning.

5. You are more likely to obtain radar services if you are transponder equipped (See Sec. 38) since the controller can communicate much more quickly with you;
   a. when you communicate with an air traffic controller for any form of assistance, his reply will normally include the instruction to Squawk (Number);
   b. if you are not transponder equipped, you will reply NEGATIVE TRANSPONDER and he will otherwise identify you if he has time; otherwise, he may decline to give service;
   c. follow his instructions. If he says to SQUAWK 4013, dial that code. If he adds AND INDENT, push the Ident button, but *not* unless he asks you to.
6. Radar assistance may be given by any of several different kinds of traffic controllers;
   a. at most larger controlled airports, the controllers have radar but you cannot assume that every airport with a tower has radar;
      (1) the tower controller will use his radar to determine your position around the airport and to vector you and other aircraft to your destinations and to avoid collisions;
   b. approach and departure control will use radar, where available, to provide radar assistance and radar vectors where necessary;
      (1) you can learn the frequency of these facilities by consulting the *AIM*, instrument approach plates and *Sky Prints;*
   c. around some busy airports, there is a frequency available to you on which only radar advisory information is given to VFR aircraft to relieve the load on controllers; it can be found in the *AIM* Part 3.
7. *Radar Traffic Information Service.* When you are given this information, you are advised of any radar target observed on the radar display which may be so close to your position or intended route that it warrants your attention;
   a. this service does not relieve you of your responsibility to be constantly vigilant to see and avoid other aircraft;
   b. it is not unusual for the controller to get too busy to tell you about aircraft that could collide with you.
8. When the other aircraft is radar identified, the traffic information given to you will include:
   a. azimuth from your airplane in terms of the 12-hour clock;
   b. distance from your airplane in nautical miles (add about a tenth to arrive at statute miles);
   c. direction in which the target is proceeding; and,
   d. type of aircraft and altitude if known (he will not know the altitude unless the aircraft is in communication with him or has an operating encoding altimeter.
9. When the other aircraft is not radar identified, the traffic information given to you will include the following:
   a. distance and direction with respect to a fix;
   b. direction in which the target is proceeding; and,
   c. type of aircraft and altitude if known.
10. If you are crabbing into a crosswind, advice about the location of other aircraft in relation to your airplane will be misleading;

a. error can also result when you change your course during the time that the radar traffic information is being given;
b. in Fig. 33.1, if you were the pilot of plane A, the traffic information would be issued to you as 12 o'clock, but the actual position would be one o'clock. The pilot of plane B would be advised of traffic at 12 o'clock, but he would see the traffic at 11 o'clock;

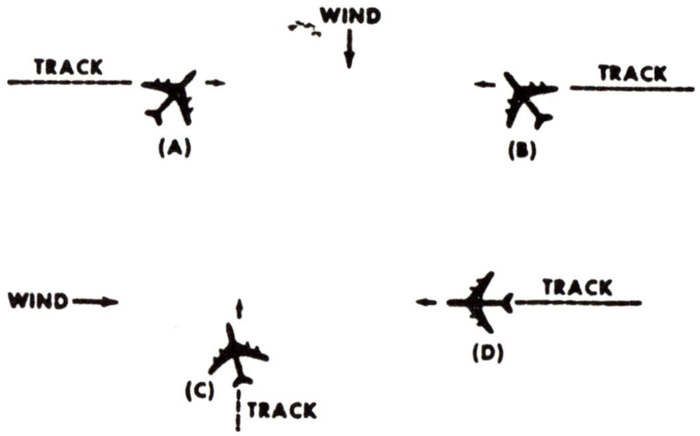

FIG. 33.1—AIRCRAFT RECEIVING RADAR TRAFFIC INFORMATION

c. similarly, the pilot of plane C would be advised of traffic at two o'clock but he would see it at three o'clock. The pilot of plane D would be advised of traffic at 11 o'clock which would be the correct position for him since he has not had to crab into the wind.

11. *Radar service for VFR aircraft in difficulty.* Radar equipped ATC facilities provide navigation service (vectors) to VFR aircraft in difficulty provided the aircraft can communicate with the facility, are within radar coverage and can be radar identified;
    a. many pilots who are not instrument rated cannot maintain control of their aircraft when in clouds or encountering reduced visibility conditions;
    b. the controller cannot know whether his instructions will take you into IFR conditions;
    c. keep the controller apprised of the weather conditions where you are and where you are headed;
    d. if you have an alternative course of action that will permit flight in VFR conditions, you should choose the alternative rather than requesting a vector or approach into IFR conditions, or, if no alternative course of action is available, you should so advise the controller and declare an emergency.
12. Some DOs and DON'Ts: when having difficulty:

a. DON'T wait until the situation becomes an emergency;
b. DO let ATC know of your difficulty immediately;
c. DO have pencil and paper ready to write down frequencies and other instructions because you won't remember them when you are under great stress;
d. DO give as much information as possible on your initial contact with ATC, including (1) the nature of the difficulty, (2) your position, preferably in relation to a navaid, (3) altitude, (4) radar beacon code, if transponder equipped, (5) weather conditions, (6) that you are a student (or not instrument rated, if you are a private pilot), (7) your destination, and (8) the service you are requesting;
e. DON'T change your radio frequency without informing the controller;
f. DO adhere to ATC instructions or information and, if that is impossible, advise the ATC immediately that you cannot comply.

Section 34
TERMINAL RADAR PROGRAMS FOR VFR AIRCRAFT

1. Busier airports that are served by approach and departure, but those that are not busy enough to have terminal control areas (TCAs), have terminal control programs for VFR aircraft;
    a. these programs are known as Stage I Service, Stage II Service and Stage III Service;
    b. you can determine which service is offered at any particular airport by checking the *AIM.*
2. *Stage I Service* provides radar advisory service for VFR aircraft;
    a. this includes traffic information and limited vectoring to VFR traffic on a work-permitting basis;
    b. vectoring may be provided when you request it or with your concurrence when suggested by ATC;
    c. when arriving you should contact approach control on the frequency published on your sectional chart, *AIM,* instrument approach plate, or *Sky Prints;*
    d. give your position, altitude, what you are squawking (if transponder equipped), your destination, and *request* traffic information;
    e. approach control will give you the wind and runway unless you say HAVE NUMBERS or that information is in the ATIS broadcast and you say you have the ATIS information;
    f. traffic information is also given on a workload permitting basis;
    g. approach control will specify the time or place at which you are to contact the tower on the local frequency for further landing instructions;
    h. radar service is automatically terminated when you are told to contact the tower.
3. *Stage II Service* provides *both* radar *and* sequencing for VFR aircraft;
    a. the purpose of the service is to adjust the flow of arriving VFR and IFR aircraft into the traffic pattern in a safe and orderly manner and to provide radar traffic information to departing VFR aircraft;
    b. pilot participation is urged but is not mandatory;
    c. when you arrive VFR, you should contact approach control about 25 miles out;
    d. on initial contact by VFR aircraft, approach control will assume that STAGE II service is requested. If not, say NEGATIVE STAGE II;
    e. advise whether you have the ATIS numbers;

SECTION 34—TERMINAL RADAR PROGRAMS FOR VFR AIRCRAFT

   f. after you have established radar contact, you may navigate on your own into the traffic pattern or, depending on traffic conditions, you may be directed to fly specific headings behind a preceding aircraft in the approach sequence;
   g. when you have been positioned behind a preceding aircraft and report that you have it in sight, you will be directed to follow it;
   h. with Stage II service, standard radar separation between VFR or between VFR and IFR aircraft is *not* provided;
   i. when you are *departing* VFR you are encouraged to ask for radar traffic information by notifying *ground control* on your initial contact: XRAY GROUND CONTROL, CESSNA 2151 SIERRA AT HANGAR 6, READY TO TAXI, VFR SOUTHBOUND, WITH BRAVO, REQUEST RADAR TRAFFIC INFORMATION;
   j. after you have taken off, the tower will advise you when to contact departure control;
   k. when you are transiting the area and in radar contact or communication with approach control, you will receive traffic information on a controller workload basis;
   l. when you contact approach control for radar advisories, you should give your position, altitude, transponder code (if so equipped), destination and/or route of flight.
4. *Stage III Service* provides *radar sequencing* and *separation* service for VFR aircraft;
   a. you can find these locations in your *AIM* or *Sky Prints;*
   b. the purpose of the service is to provide separation for all participating VFR aircraft and all IFR aircraft operating within the airspace defined as the Terminal Radar Service Area (TRSA);
   c. your participation is urged but is not mandatory;
   d. if you do not want the service, you should state NEGATIVE STAGE III when you make your initial contact with approach or ground control, as appropriate;
   e. when your VFR flight is positioned behind preceding traffic and you report having the aircraft in sight, you will be directed to follow it;
   f. when you are departing VFR, you may be asked if you can visually follow a preceding departure out of the TRSA;
      (1) if you agree, you will be directed to follow it until leaving the TRSA;
   g. when you operate VFR in a TRSA, you must maintain an altitude when assigned by ATC;
   h. while you are in the TRSA you will be given traffic information on observed but unidentified targets, to the extent possible;
   i. if you request it, you will be vectored to avoid the observed traffic, insofar as possible, as long as you are within the jurisdiction of the controller;
   j. on departing, you should inform ATC of your intended destination and/or route of flight and proposed cruising altitude.

Section 35
AUTOMATIC TERMINAL INFORMATION SERVICE

1. *AUTOMATIC TERMINAL INFORMATION SERVICE* (ATIS) is a continuous broadcast of recorded noncontrol information;
    a. this service is available at selected terminal areas where there is high activity;
    b. because of it, controllers don't have to keep repeating the same information;
    c. where ATIS is operating, you should turn it on when you start your engines;
    d. when approaching an airport with ATIS, you should contact it as far out as possible (usually 20 to 25 miles) so you can digest the information and prepare for your landing;
    e. you can get the ATIS frequency from your sectional chart, the *AIM,* instrument approach plates or *Sky Prints.*
2. Information that is included in ATIS:
    a. time of the latest weather sequence, ceiling, visibility (sky conditions will be broadcast if the ceiling is below 5,000 feet and visibility is less than 5 miles, but will be omitted if better than that);
    b. obstructions to visibility, temperature and wind direction (magnetic) and velocity, altimeter and other pertinent remarks;
    c. instrument approach and runway in use;
    d. where VFR arrival aircraft is expected to make initial contact with approach control, this fact and the appropriate frequencies may be given;
        (1) there may be more than one frequency to contact approach control at busier airports;
        (2) if more than one frequency is in use, the one for you to use will depend on your direction from the airport.
3. Each recording is given a letter from the phonetic alphabet;
    a. the first is Alpha, then Bravo, etc.;
    b. a new recording is made each time there is a change in pertinent data, such as a runway change.
4. Sample ATIS broadcast: DULLES INTERNATIONAL INFORMATION SIERRA. 1300 GREENWICH. WEATHER MEASURED CEILING THREE THOUSAND OVERCAST. VISIBILITY THREE. SMOKE. TEMPERATURE SIX EIGHT. WIND THREE FIVE ZERO AT EIGHT. ALTIM-

ETER TWO NINER NINER TWO. ILS RUNWAY ONE RIGHT APPROACH IN USE. LANDING RUNWAY ONE RIGHT AND LEFT. DEPARTURE RUNWAY THREE ZERO. ARMEL VORTAC OUT OF SERVICE. ADVISE YOU HAVE SIERRA.
- a. you will let the controller know that you have received the information by saying WITH SIERRA, or HAVE INFORMATION SIERRA;
- b. if you say WITH THE NUMBERS, you only indicate that you have the wind and runway information and the tower will not repeat *that* information but it does not indicate that you have received ATIS.

5. When you acknowledge that you have received ATIS, the controller will omit those items contained on the broadcast if they are current;
   - a. if conditions are changing rapidly, the new information may be given by the tower or approach control;
   - b. controllers may issue pertinent information to pilots who do not acknowledge receipt of a broadcast or who acknowledge receipt of a broadcast that is not current.

Section 36
USING YOUR VOR

1. Your plane is probably equipped with equipment designed to receive very high frequency omni-directional range (VOR);
    a. VOR stations are located throughout the U.S. They enable equipped airplanes to:
        (1) fly to or from such stations;
        (2) obtain a *fix*, by taking bearings on two or more stations;
    b. VOR stations transmit on frequencies from 108.2 through 117.9 MHz;
        (1) the frequency of any particular VOR can be determined by referring to an aeronautical chart, the *AIM*, by calling the nearest Flight Service Station, or from instrument en route or approach charts;
    c. VOR signals, like other VHF transmissions, are line-of-sight transmissions so that the higher you are the greater your reception distance;
    d. VOR is sometimes designated as VORTAC, to signify that the station is equipped to supply properly equipped airplanes (having distance measuring equipment—DME) with the distance of the airplane from the station.
2. The word "omni" means *all;*
    a. an omnirange is a VHF (very high frequency) radio range that projects courses in all directions from the station, like spokes from the hub of a wheel;
    b. each of these spokes is known as a *radial;*
        (1) a radial is defined as a line of magnetic bearing extending *outbound* from a VOR;
        (2) there is a radial for each degree of the compass, or a total of 360 radials;
        (3) each of these spokes, or radials, is denoted by the *outbound* magnetic direction of that radial.
3. Some of the advantages of flying omniranges are:
    a. flight may be made *to* a VOR from any direction, by flying the course *to* the station;
    b. a flight may be made in any direction *from* the station by selecting the proper radial. Always remember that VOR radials, as shown on the charts, are always numbered *from* the station, *never toward;*
    c. when you are within the range of two or more VORs you may obtain a "fix" on your position quickly and easily;
    d. the operation of your VOR is simple in comparison with other orientation procedures;
    e. you obtain static-free reception.

SECTION 36—USING YOUR VOR

4. Where you are within range of two VORS, you can obtain your exact position by following this procedure:
    a. tune to one VOR;
        (1) center the needle with a FROM indication and read the omnibearing selector to determine what radial you are on;
        (2) draw the radial on your chart;
    b. tune to the other VOR;
        (1) again, center the needle with a FROM indication and read the omnibearing selector to determine what radial you are on;
        (2) draw the radial on the chart;
    c. the point where the two radials cross is your present position;
    d. with some practice, you will be able to use this procedure to obtain your position without actually drawing the lines.
5. VOR frequencies are also used by FSS personnel for:
    a. for weather broadcasts at 15 minutes after the hour;
    b. to communicate, you can transmit on 122.1 and receive on the VOR frequency.
6. VOR stations are assigned three letter identifications;
    a. these identifications appear on the chart in the VOR frequency box;
    b. at some stations, these identification letters are broadcast continuously in Morse Code every five seconds;
    c. other stations are identified by a voice recording alternating with the usual Morse Code identification.
7. Your VOR receiver consists of three basic components:
    a. the *omnibearing selector* enables you to select the course you want to fly;
    b. the *"TO-FROM"* indicator shows you whether your course is TO or FROM the station;
        (1) it is also known as the *ambiguity meter* or *sense indicator;*
    c. the *course deviation indicator* tells you whether you are on course, or to the left or right of course;
        (1) it is also known as the LEFT-RIGHT indicator or CDI;
    d. the indication on the TO-FROM indicator is not dependent on the heading of the aircraft;
        (1) the indication is dependent only on the setting of the course selector (CS) and the direction of the aircraft from the station;
    e. the TO-FROM indicator will give a neutral indication:
        (1) when an unreliable signal is being received, either because you are too far from the station or at too low an altitude, or the station is not properly tuned in;
        (2) when you pass directly over the station; *and,*
        (3) when you cross the radials perpendicular to the course selected on the course selector (CS).
8. If you wish to fly directly to a VOR facility:
    a. tune the frequency of the desired VOR;

b. positively identify the station either by code or by voice recording;
   (1) if you cannot identify the station, do *not* use that station for navigation;
c. there should be a TO or FROM reading on the TO-FROM indicator;
   (1) if this indicates neither TO nor FROM, or just partially indicates TO or FROM, or there is an oscillation, the signal is not usable;
d. manually rotate the omnibearing selector until you have a TO indication;
   (1) continue to rotate the omnibearing selector until the needle is centered;
e. turn the airplane to the heading that is shown on the omnibearing selector;
   (1) some correction is needed for any crosswind to keep the airplane on the desired radial;
f. if the needle moves away from the center, turn the airplane toward the needle.

9. The following example will illustrate your procedure for getting on and staying on the desired radial:
   a. for example, if the needle moves to the right, turn the airplane to the right 10 degrees;
   b. allow enough time for the airplane to fly back on course;
   c. when the needle centers, take out one-half of your wind correction, that is, turn left 5 degrees;
   d. this will leave a 5-degree right wind correction to allow for the wind drift;
   e. if the 10-degree turn does not center the needle within four or five minutes, make a second 10-degree turn to get on course;
   f. then, as before, when the needle centers, take one-half the correction out by turning left 10 degrees;
   g. if your corrections are too large, you will find yourself crossing back and forth over the selected radial course.

10. If you wish to fly *from* the VOR to a selected point or destination:
    a. on a chart, draw a line from the VOR station to the desired point or destination;
    b. determine the magnetic course from the VOR to the destination by using the azimuth around the station;
    c. follow the procedures set forth in ¶¶a, b, and c of No. 8 above;
    d. manually rotate the omnibearing selector until you have a FROM indication and the needle is centered;
    e. fly *toward* the needle to remain on the course;
    f. as always, the important thing to remember in flying VOR is to keep your heading and the omnibearing selector in substantial agreement, which gives *proper sensing;*
    g. if the heading and the course selected are approximately reciprocals, the needle will give *reverse* or *opposite* sensing.

11. More and more airplanes are being equipped with a very useful device known as Distance Measuring Equipment (DME), which measures the slant distance of the airplane from a VORTAC in nautical miles;

a. only those VORs that are designated as VORTACS on your sectional chart can provide this information;
b. some DMEs are also capable of providing you with your groundspeed and the time in minutes to the station.

Section 37
USING YOUR ADF

1. One of the most useful of your navigation instruments is the Automatic Direction Finder (ADF);
   a. even though you may not have one in your plane during your preparation for the Private Pilot Certificate, you should learn to operate this useful equipment;
   b. if there is ADF in your airplane, your examiner may ask you to demonstrate your understanding of its operation.
2. The ADF has numerous advantages:
   a. it provides a backup if you should have a failure in your other navigation equipment;
   b. it aids you in cross-country flight by providing additional data to determine your exact location;
   c. because the ADF signals are not limited to line-of-sight, you can home to a radio station many miles away in a direct line;
   d. when you obtain your instrument rating, there will be many approaches that require the use of ADF, either as the sole instrument or as one of the instruments;
      (1) there are countless airports where you can make an instrument landing *only* if you have an ADF. There are no other instrument approaches;
   e. you can even listen to sports, news and music on your ADF.
3. Your ADF receiver can be tuned to any station that transmits between 150 and 1,750 KHz;
   a. this includes all AM radio transmitters, some of which can be received hundreds of miles away;
   b. it also includes "H" facilities which are shown on Low Altitude En Route Charts, and are listed in instrument approach plates and *Sky Prints;*
   c. many of these are near airports so that you can home in to your destination in bad weather, thus giving an additional margin of safety.
4. The ADF has some basic limitations:
   a. it is not static-free like your VHF radio, which can be disconcerting (but informative) when there are thunderstorms in the area;
   b. the "H" facilities cannot be received very far from the station;
   c. the commercial stations do not identify themselves very often and usually do not operate 24 hours a day;
   d. the needle is subject to certain vagaries such as night effect and reflection of sky waves which can cause it to fluctuate.

5. To operate the ADF:
    a. turn it on;
    b. select the frequency to which you want to tune;
    c. turn the function switch to ADF;
    d. if you are receiving a sufficiently strong signal, the needle will point to the station;
    e. then turn to TEST and hold it there for a moment. The needle will continue to turn and then, when you release the TEST, the pointer will return to the original bearing position, if the bearing is reliable. Otherwise, it will continue to wander about, indicating that you cannot rely on that signal.
6. The three basic purposes of the ADF are (1) to *home* to a station; (2) to take a heading *away* from a station; (3) to determine your present position in relation to a station, for navigation purposes.
7. Unlike your VOR receiver, which indicates your magnetic bearing TO or FROM the station, regardless of the heading of your airplane, the ADF needle points TO the station, regardless of the heading or position of the airplane;
    a. the relative bearing indicated is thus the angular relationship between the heading of the airplane and the station, measured clockwise from the nose of the airplane;
    b. a bearing is simply the direction of a straight line between the airplane and the station, or vice versa;
    c. the bearing line measured clockwise from the nose of the airplane is a *relative bearing;*
        (1) measured clockwise from true north, it is a *true bearing;*
        (2) measured clockwise from magnetic north, it is a *magnetic bearing.*
8. You home to a station by determining the direction of the station, turning to that direction so that the needle points straight up and continuing that direction until you cross the station, which is indicated by having the needle turn around and point to the tail of the plane;
    a. if there is a crosswind and you do not crab into it sufficiently, your path to the station will wander from one side to the other;
    b. you avoid this by crabbing into the wind just enough to hold a straight line to the station;
    c. when you find you have drifted to one side or the other, you will turn back onto course, overcorrecting enough to get back on the course and then, when on course, changing your crab angle enough to avoid further drifting from the course.
9. You fly outbound in a no-wind condition by crossing the station and establishing yourself on your selected heading;
    a. if there is a crosswind, you will attempt in advance to estimate the amount of crab needed to maintain your selected heading;
    b. if the needle starts to drift off to one side, you have to get back on your selected heading by crabbing more into the wind and then, when you are on your selected heading from the station, correct your heading enough to compensate for the wind.

Section 38
USING YOUR TRANSPONDER

1. The transponder is equipment in your airplane capable of communicating with a ground radar beacon antenna, known as an interrogator;
    a. while this equipment is not required and may not be available to you during your training period, you should learn its operation so you can understand and use it when it is available;
    b. you may use your transponder on either VFR or IFR flights and whether or not you are in communication with an air traffic controller;
        (1) during VFR flights, you will "squawk" 1200, that is, you will dial your transponder to 1200;
        (2) when you are in communication with an air traffic controller, you will "squawk" a "designated code," that is, some other number assigned to you by the controller;
    c. when your transponder is operating, either on 1200 or the code assigned to you by a controller, he can identify you much quicker than if you do not have a transponder;
    d. if he has any doubt as to which of the blips on his screen is your airplane, he will ask you to "Squawk Ident," that is, push the Ident button which lights up your blip much brighter;
    e. if you do not have a transponder, the only way he can tell which is your airplane is to have you take different headings, which slows you down and takes time he may not have;
    f. the transponder operates on line-of-sight so you cannot be "seen" unless you are sufficiently high and close to his antenna;
        (1) controllers have antennas scattered about the country but they cannot "see" all the aircraft in the sky.
2. There are six basic "modes" of transponders presently available;
    a. modes 1 and 2 are used by the military;
    b. mode A in the civil system is the same as military mode 3 and both are used exclusively for air traffic control;
    c. mode C is used for automatic altitude reporting;
        (1) this requires an encoding altimeter in the airplane;
        (2) this encoding altimeter is one of the requirements if you want to penetrate a TCA I (see Sec. 32);
        (3) this keeps the controller constantly informed as to your altitude.

SECTION 38—USING YOUR TRANSPONDER

3. You are governed by certain rules in using and changing codes;
   a. never use Code 0000 (for military use only);
   b. use 1200 for VFR flight below 10,000 feet;
   c. use 7500 if being hijacked;
   d. if you have lost radio capability, squawk 7700 for 1 minute, 7600 for 15 minutes, and repeat;
   e. use 7700 to declare an emergency;
   f. be very careful never to run through 0000, 7500, 7600 or 7700 in changing from one code to another as they will signal an emergency to the controller.
4. You should learn to use the terminology in Fig. 38.1;

> SQUAWK (number)—Operate radar beacon transponder on designated code in Mode A/3;
> IDENT—Engage the "IDENT" feature of the transponder;
> SQUAWK (number) AND IDENT—Operate transponder on specified code in Mode A/3 and engage the IDENT feature;
> SQUAWK STANDBY—Switch transponder to standby position;
> SQUAWK LOW/NORMAL—Operate transponder on low or normal sensitivity as specified;
> SQUAWK ALTITUDE—Active Mode C with automatic altitude reporting;
> STOP ALTITUDE SQUAWK—Turn off altitude reporting switch and continue transmitting Mode C framing pulses. If your equipment does not have this capability, turn off Mode C;
> STOP SQUAWK—Switch off transponder;
> SQUAWK MAYDAY—Operate transponder in emergency position (7700);
> SQUAWK VFR—Operate transponder on code 1200 regardless of altitude.

FIG. 38.1—TRANSPONDER PHRASEOLOGY

   a. when you are about ready for takeoff, you will switch to "standby;"
   b. as you take the active runway, you switch to ON;
   c. while you are in contact with a controller, he will issue various instructions, including what code to squawk, when to ident, and when to squawk VFR (1200) when you are on a VFR flight and out of his area;
   d. without being told, you will turn your transponder off immediately upon landing unless a controller has already directed you to change to standby.
5. Many general aviation aircraft are being equipped with encoding altimeters which work in conjunction with their transponders to give the radar facility on the ground a readout on their radar screens the altitude of the airplane;
   a. this greatly facilitates the work of the air traffic controller;
   b. the encoding altimeter is required for flight into a Group I TCA and for flight above 12,500 feet MSL.

Section 39
THE WEATHER

1. Despite all the improvements in aircraft, equipment, and communications, the weather is always of supreme importance to the pilot;
    a. it is absolutely essential that you understand as much as possible about the weather;
    b. it is equally important that you understand the effects of the weather on flying, and particularly, how to obtain as much information as possible about the weather;
    c. every pilot should own the FAA publications *Aviation Weather* (AC00-6A) and *Aviation Weather Services* (AC00-45A) and read them frequently;
    d. there is a strong movement toward automatic weather briefings so you must become increasingly self-reliant in getting your weather information.
2. The wind is of utmost importance to the pilot for a number of reasons:
    a. a very strong wind can make takeoff, flying and landing dangerous;
    b. the amount and direction of wind affects the runway to be used, the ground speed and the true course of the airplane;
    c. a wind that is not straight down the runway requires the use of crosswind takeoff (Sec. 14) and crosswind landing techniques (Sec. 27);
    d. the wind can be particularly treacherous when it is blowing around buildings or other obstructions around the landing field;
        (1) when the wind blows around an obstruction, it breaks up into eddies (gusts with sudden changes in velocity and direction) that may be carried along some distance from the obstruction;
        (2) this turbulence is dangerous because it can cause the airplane to "drop in" when landing, or to fail to gain the necessary altitude to clear obstructions during takeoff;
        (3) where gusty conditions exist, approaches and landings should be made at higher speeds to maintain adequate control.
3. Convection currents, sometimes known as thermals, or updrafts and downdrafts, are caused by the uneven heating of the air;
    a. thermals are nothing more than vertical columns of air moving at different velocities;
    b. ploughed ground, sand, rocks and barren ground give off heat, causing the air over them to rise;
    c. on the other hand, vegetation and bodies of water absorb and retain heat, contributing to the bumpiness of the air;

d. convection currents are strongest close to the ground and can be avoided by flying over the clouds, provided they are sufficiently scattered to permit return to low altitudes.
5. Within cumulonimbus clouds and beneath them are strong updrafts and downdrafts which can be sufficiently turbulent to cause damage to an airplane.
6. The clouds can close in and cause a ceiling so that the VFR pilot cannot fly through them.
7. Clouds can become storms, bringing rain and other forms of precipitation, as well as high winds and poor visibility;
   a. cumulus clouds can build into thunderheads, sometimes very rapidly;
   b. under some conditions, it is very easy to fly into clouds, causing disorientation.
8. The height above the ground of the lowest layer of clouds is called the *ceiling;*
   a. the ceiling is determined by the lowest layer of clouds and/or an obscuring phenomenon that is reported as "broken," "overcast," or "obscuration," and not classified as "thin," "partial," or "scattered";
   b. clouds are classified as *broken* when they cover $6/10$ to $9/10$ of the sky and as *overcast* when they cover more than $9/10$ of the sky;
   c. for practical purposes, ceiling is the lowest height above the surface at which the total cloudiness between that level and the surface (as seen by a ground observer) covers more than half of the sky;
   d. the ceiling is unlimited if the sky is cloudless or less than $6/10$ covered as seen from the ground;
   e. the height of the lowest cloudlayer is shown by a code figure directly below the station circle on a weather map;
   f. ceilings are reported in feet above ground level (AGL) but the top of a cloud layer is reported with reference to MSL (Mean Sea Level) since such altitudes are determined by a pilot by referring to his altimeter.
6. *Visibility* is the greatest surface distance at which prominent objects can be seen and identified;
   a. visibility is plotted at the left of the station circle between the temperature and the dew point;
   b. when visibility is more than 10 miles, it is omitted from the station model on the map;
   c. visibility is not the same in all directions;
      (1) therefore, the value for *prevailing visibility* is based on surface observations and is measured in statute miles;
      (2) prevailing visibility is ground visibility only;
      (3) prevailing visibility is stated in hourly sequence reports;
      (4) prevailing visibility is always reported in statute miles;
      (5) prevailing visibility is the greatest surface visibility attained or surpassed throughout at least one-half of the horizon circle but not necessarily continuous or for all of the horizon circle.
7. Precipitation is important to the pilot because of damage that can be caused by hail, the dangers of icing, resulting low ceilings and, at times, the reduction of visibility to zero.

8. Weather information is collected at weather stations throughout the United States;
    a. this information is assembled and plotted on weather maps each 6 hours.
9. *Area forecasts* forecast general weather conditions over an area the size of several states and are issued every 6 hours;
    a. they cover the weather for an 18 hour period for each of the 23 areas of the United States;
    b. they also give the outlook for the following 12 hours;
    c. they describe such conditions as the location of areas of low clouds, heights of cloud bases and cloud tops;
    d. they also describe surface visibilities and the movement of major weather disturbances such as thunderstorms and squall lines;
    e. they also contain information on the height of the freezing level and zones of expected icing and turbulence.
10. *Terminal forecasts* are issued 3 times daily, generally for a 12-hour period, giving detailed forecasts for the busier air terminals in the United States;
    a. they state specifically the *expected* ceiling, visibility, and wind conditions at each particular location;
    b. if a change is expected during the forecast period, this change, and the expected time of change, will be given;
    c. if the surface wind is expected to be less than 10 knots, it will be omitted from the forecast;
    d. if the visibility is expected to be greater than 6 miles, it will be omitted.
11. A SIGMET (WS) identifies weather phenomena of particular significance to all aircraft, regardless of size;
    a. this advisory covers tornadoes, lines of thunderstorms (squall lines), embedded thunderstorms, hail of ¾ inches or more, severe and extreme turbulence, heavy icing, and widespread duststorms, sandstorms lowering visibility to less than 3 miles.
    b. Flight Service Stations broadcast SIGMETS on navigation aid voice channels upon receipt and also at quarter hour intervals during the valid period;
    c. FSS and control towers make announcements on en route voice frequencies when a SIGMET is to be issued, by advising pilots to monitor a VOR voice frequency.
12. An AIRMET (WA) identifies weather phenomena less severe than those covered by a SIGMET but still important to light aircraft safety;
    a. this kind of advisory covers moderate icing, moderate turbulence, the onset of extensive areas of visibilities of less than 3 miles or ceilings less than 1,000 feet including mountain ridges and passes, and sustained winds of 30 knots or more within 2,000 feet of the surface;
    b. you will be advised, during preflight briefings by FSS and Weather Bureau stations of both SIGMETS and AIRMETS that may be valid at the time;

SECTION 39—THE WEATHER

    c. continuing AIRMETS (WAC) are issued for continued moderate turbulence over mountainous terrain and for continued ceilings below 1,000 feet and/or visibility of less than 3 miles over an extensive area.

13. The very latest weather information is available in hourly aviation weather teletype sequence reports transmitted by weather stations;
    a. they are known as Surface Aviation Weather Reports;
    b. changes in weather can be so rapid that conditions at the time of flight are quite different from those shown on a weather map issued several hours previously;
    c. the sequence report is your most reliable source of information, as it is an *actual* report of existing weather rather than a *forecast*.

14. The *winds-aloft forecast* forecasts the winds at selected altitudes for a 12-hour period and is issued every 6 hours;
    a. winds are normally forecast for Mean Sea Level (MSL), altitudes of 3,000, 6,000, 9,000, 12,000 feet and thereafter for each 6,000 foot interval;
    b. because of terrain effect, no winds-aloft forecasts are made for levels within 1,500 feet of station elevation;
    c. the winds-aloft forecasts also contain temperature forecasts for all wind-reporting levels except for 3,000 feet or for a level within 2,500 feet of station elevation.

15. Weather information can be obtained in the following ways:
    a. visit the Weather Bureau (WS) or Flight Service Station;
        (1) identify yourself as a pilot and give your aircraft identification and type;
        (2) state your intended route, destination, proposed departure time, and estimated time en route;
        (3) advise them that you are *not* prepared to fly IFR;
    b. telephone for information by calling Weather Bureau stations (WS) Flight Service Stations, and Combined Station/Towers (CS/T) found in the *AIM* and *Sky Prints;*
    c. in some areas you can call the Pilots' Automatic Telephone Answering Service (PATWAS), a transcribed aviation weather report;
    d. you may also receive continuous broadcasts of weather information, known as Transcribed Weather Briefing, over certain VORs, and many of the low and medium frequency navigational aids;
    e. at some airports there is a direct line (DL) from the FBO to the FSS or WS;
    f. at other airports there is a toll free line (known as Foreign Exchange Telephone Service) from the FBO to the FSS or WS.

16. An important source of weather information is the En Route Flight Advisory Service, which is designed to provide you with timely weather information that is pertinent to your type of flight, route and altitude;
    a. this system is presently being implemented so that it will be available from selected FSSs controlling one or more remote communications outlets;

b. it will be available throughout the 48 contiguous states along prominent and heavily traveled flyways, so that it can be received at 5,000 feet and above a distance of 80 miles;

c. you contact this service on 122.0 MHz, saying ST. LOUIS RADIO, FLIGHT WATCH, and your call sign and position in relation to the nearest VOR;

d. they will provide you with the routine weather information, current reports on the location of thunderstorms and other hazardous weather as observed and reported by pilots or observed on weather radar;

e. altimeter settings are not routinely furnished but will be given if requested;

f. this service is not intended for flight plans, routine position reporting or preflight weather briefings;

g. you are encouraged to report weather that you encounter.

17. FAA stations are required to solicit and collect PIREPS (Pilot Weather Reports) whenever the ceiling is at or below 5,000 feet, the visibility is at or below 5 miles, or thunderstorms are reported;

a. along with other pilots, you are urged to cooperate by volunteering reports of cloud tops, upper cloud layers, thunderstorms, ice, turbulence, strong winds and other significant flight condition information;

b. if you are unable to make PIREPS by radio, then call them in to the FSS, or WS, upon landing.

18. Despite every precaution that you take, it is possible to fly into unsatisfactory weather conditions. One such condition arises if you get caught on top of an overcast;

a. you have absolutely no business on top of an overcast unless you have an instrument rating, your airplane is fully equipped for instrument flying, and you have the required instrument experience;

(1) as a student, or a private pilot without an instrument rating, you must *never* get caught on top of an overcast;

b. take the following precautions to avoid getting caught on top of an overcast;

(1) obtain a thorough weather briefing, as outlined above, for your entire route;

(2) select an altitude for your flight that will be compatible with the terrain and the cloud separation requirements;

(3) don't push your luck when weather conditions are close to the VFR minimums;

(4) always remember that a low overcast can form under you within minutes when weather conditions are right (or wrong, as far as you are concerned);

(5) always allow yourself a margin of safety, having in mind the weather, the terrain you are flying over, and your own level of experience.

19. This does *not* mean that you *cannot* fly over clouds under any circumstances;

a. it may often be both practical and desirable to select a cross-country cruising altitude above a *scattered* cloud condition to take advantage of smoother air, improved visibility, more favorable winds, or provide for more terrain and obstacle clearance;

b. however, you must have *legal cloud separation* for climb, cruise and destination descent;

c. weather conditions must be stable or improving;

d. you *must* stay alert and take immediate action if the clouds beneath you increase and the holes start to shrink.

20. If you find that you are above the clouds, or about to get caught there, take the following steps:

    a. if it is not too late, descend before the clouds have closed in too much to permit legal cloud separation;

    b. make a 180-degree turn, one of the oldest and best of aviation's safety devices;

    c. establish communications with a FSS or other ground station and confess your predicament (Sec.40);

    d. have the FSS advise you the closest airport where the condition does not exist; determine whether you have sufficient fuel and, if so, plot a course toward that airport. If not, prepare to let down through the overcast;

    e. if the cloud layer is spread over a wide area, constantly look for any break in the clouds to let yourself down below the clouds. Rarely are cloud layers solid for many miles, particularly if you have been given the direction of better conditions.

21. A major cause of VFR fatal accidents is flight into unfavorable weather. Pilots fly into unfavorable weather because:

    a. they lack an adequate understanding of weather information;

    b. they are too anxious to "get there" (get-home-itis) without careful consideration of the problems involved;

    c. they fail to keep abreast of weather changes;

    d. they ignore or minimize the significance of the weather ahead of them;

    e. they don't know and understand all the weather information available to them.

22. You can avoid flight into unfavorable weather if you will:

    a. make a concentrated study of weather, both while you are studying for your Private Pilot Certificate and continuously thereafter, as long as you fly;

    b. be extremely careful in interpreting the weather information that is given to you. If in doubt, ask for an explanation;

    c. keep abreast of weather changes while en route by listening to the inflight advisories and the scheduled broadcasts;

    d. learn the signs of deteriorating weather (see below) and constantly be alert to observe them;

    e. exercise sound reasoning and judgment, so that you are capable of rejecting the natural impatience to get where you are going if there is the slightest danger that you will fly into unfavorable weather.

23. Learn the signs of approaching unfavorable weather and the meaning of each of the signs;

a. blowing dust signifies turbulence, poor visibility at low levels, particularly when you are flying into the sun;
b. low layer of haze signifies fog or stratus cloud in the early morning or late evening; poor visibility, particularly into the sun;
c. light puffs of clouds at low levels signify fog or stratus clouds, particularly in the early morning or late evening;
d. a ragged cloud base signifies turbulence, erratic visibility and possible precipitation;
e. bulbous cloud base signifies turbulence, erratic visibility, conducive to *tornadoes;*
f. roll-type clouds signify *dangerous* turbulence, dust and poor visibility, hazardous landing conditions and subsequent precipitation;
g. a line of heavy dark clouds signifies *severe* turbulence, dust and poor visibility, hazardous landing conditions, precipitation and hail;
h. an opening in a wall of dark clouds (also known as a sucker hole) signifies *dangerous* turbulence, and possible precipitation and poor visibility as the hole is entered;
i. a gradual lowering and thickening of the ceiling signifies inadequate clearance of the terrain, possible widespread precipitation and fog;
j. a near-freezing temperature signifies poor visibility in precipitation with ice forming on the windshield as well as the aircraft structure.

24. Despite all precautions, the student or non-instrument rated private pilot can find himself in unanticipated adverse weather. If you do, you should:
    a. make a 180-degree turn to get back into good weather, land and reassess your trip;
    b. establish immediate radio contact with a FSS and if unable to, proceed with the other "if-lost" procedures listed in Sec. 40;
    c. make maximum use of your VOR (Sec. 36), ADF (Sec. 37) and transponder (Sec. 38);
    d. if the conditions, such as clouds, poor visibility, storms, etc. are deteriorating rapidly, take immediate steps for an emergency landing (Sec. 43);
    e. if the emergency condition is ground fog, have the FSS inform you of the closest place where the condition does not exist; determine whether you have sufficient fuel to reach it, and plot your course to it.

25. If you should find it absolutely necessary to let yourself down through the clouds, but are not instrument rated, you should:
    a. determine from the FSS the altitude of the cloud bases to be sure about how high off the ground you will be when you break out of the clouds;
    b. determine your location as well as possible, using your VOR and ADF, or through radar advisories or a DF steer;
    c. determine the conditions on the ground where you will break out of the clouds, to avoid cities, mountains, lakes, forests, obstructions.
    d. if you are in radio contact, request an emergency clearance for your descent through the clouds;
    e. check and reset your directional gyro (DG);

f. have the FSS give you the current altimeter setting and reset your altimeter;
g. apply pitot heat;
h. apply full rich mixture;
i. apply full carburetor heat;
j. begin your descent by reducing your power to permit a descent of 500 feet per minute;
k. adjust your trim tab to maintain your descent at 70 KIAS;
l. check your heading and maintain it by using your rudder but little or no pressure on the control wheel;
m. constantly check your attitude indicator and rely on what it tells you even though you think it is wrong.

26. There are certain facts about the weather that you should constantly bear in mind:
    a. remember the significance of the dew point: when the dew point value is relatively close (2°–5°F) to the air temperature, there is a strong probability of fog, low clouds or precipitation;
    b. reported visibility is visibility on the surface only, so that visibility aloft may be better or worse than reported;
    c. cockpit visibility in precipitation is further reduced by rain, drizzle or snow spreading over the windshield;
    d. forward visibility in light snowfall may be zero due to relative horizontal movement of the snow;
    e. sunlight reflecting off haze or dust aloft reduces the visibility considerably.

Section 40
PROCEDURES WHEN LOST

1. There is no need to panic when you suddenly realize that you don't really know exactly where you are. There are many ways for you to find yourself;
    a. use your VOR to home in to a station near you (Sec. 36);
    b. use your ADF to home to an airport or a radio station near a city you are seeking (Sec. 37);
    c. contact the closest FSS for assistance;
        (1) if it has DF, it can steer you to an airport for landing (Sec. 41);
        (2) even if it does not have DF, it can help you determine where you are and how to get where you want to go;
    d. obtain radar assistance through ATC such as center, approach control, or tower (Sec. 34);
    e. if you wish to declare an emergency and have a transponder, squawk 7700 to advise the ATC ground facilities you are in trouble and where you are;
2. Even if there is no assistance available to you, there are techniques, discussed below, for finding yourself and getting home safely;
    a. as you are seeking to find where you are, also be thinking calmly and coolly about where you could make an emergency landing, and review in your mind the proper procedures for an emergency landing (Sec. 43);
    b. keep watching for any airport and land there immediately (after dragging it to be sure it is safe, if there is the slightest doubt) so that you can find where you are and make a fresh start for your destination;
    c. check your VOR against your magnetic compass; you could be getting negative sensing because the VOR is set on the reciprocal of your direction;
    d. check your directional gyro (DG) against your magnetic compass, as it may have precessed (slipped off) enough to have you going in the wrong direction, or, you may have forgotten to set it when you took off.
3. You should memorize the Four Cs now so that, if you suddenly think you are lost, you will not panic and do something stupid;
    a. CONFESS your predicament. Call any available ground station. Don't wait too long. Give Search and Rescue (SAR) a chance to find you if you should have to make an emergency landing;

b. COMMUNICATE with any ground station and give them as much of your distress message as possible on the first transmission;
c. CLIMB, if at all possible, to obtain better communication with ground facilities, such as VOR, FSS, and ATC;
  (1) the higher you are, the farther you can glide if you should also develop engine trouble;
  (2) remember that it is not legal to climb through clouds while you are flying VFR but an exception might be made during an emergency;
d. COMPLY with the advice and instructions given to you.

4. Always remember that before you acquire a lot of experience in solo flight, there is always a chance that you will become lost, at least temporarily. If so, your first job is to assess just how serious it is by checking these facts:
  a. check your fuel and fuel consumption rate to determine how long you have to get onto the ground;
    (1) use the reduced speed that gives the best performance;
    (2) taking into consideration the wind, determine the radius that gives you a chance to find a landing field of some kind;
    (3) leave plenty of margin, just in case;
  b. analyze the weather as to whether it is good, bad or deteriorating;
    (1) if it is bad or deteriorating, the first thing you will want to know after establishing radio contact is the general direction of the best VFR weather;
  c. check to be sure that everything is functioning properly. If so, you have until your gas runs out to get down. Otherwise, make plans accordingly to get onto the ground soon;
  d. check the time to see if you have plenty of time to land during daylight. Plan to make a forced landing before sundown;
  e. check the terrain where you are and within your practical range to be sure that you have a selection of safe landing places in case you can't reach an airfield.

5. Just as soon as you feel that you don't know exactly where you are, use your radio;
  a. if you don't have any special problem, such as being in clouds, engine trouble, icing, etc., don't be in a hurry to declare an emergency;
  b. even though an emergency has not really developed, feel free to ask for assistance and guidance;
  c. in most situations, the closest FSS will be able to help you learn exactly where you are;
  d. don't be embarrassed; this happens to many of us while we are learning.

5. If the situation is beginning to look serious but is not really an emergency, you can announce PAN, PAN, PAN which *alerts* the ground radio facility to the fact that you have a problem;
  a. if you are actually in *distress,* announce MAYDAY, MAYDAY, MAYDAY (French for "help me");

b. when you announce either the alert or the distress call, transmit as much of this information as possible: (1) your aircraft identification three times; (2) the type of your aircraft; (3) your position or estimated position; (4) your true or magnetic heading (stating which you are giving); (5) your true airspeed or estimated true airspeed (stating which you are giving); (6) your altitude (MSL); (7) your remaining fuel in hours and minutes; (8) the nature of your distress; (9) your intentions (whether you intend to bail out, ditch, crash land, etc.); and (10) what assistance you desire (such as a fix, a steer, a bearing, etc.).
6. As long as you do not have a real emergency, contact the FSS on the usual frequencies;
   a. if you require special assistance, you will probably be assigned another frequency so that you can communicate with them without interruption.
7. If you have been unable to reach assistance using your frequencies, transmit and receive on 121.5;
   a. this frequency is guarded (listened to) by all control towers, VHF direction finding (DF) stations, radar facilities and flight service stations;
   b. any station hearing you will either assist you or advise you the frequency that you should use to obtain help.
8. Even if you are unable, for any reason, to get ground assistance, there is no reason to panic;
   a. be sure that you are high enough to avoid all obstacles on the ground for many miles around;
   b. continue on your established heading and keep watching for prominent landmarks;
   c. don't alter your course until you are sure where you are unless there are obstacles, mountains, large bodies of water ahead, etc.;
      (1) if you see these, a careful study of your chart should tell you about where you are;
   d. constantly watch for bodies of water, cities, railroad tracks, roads and particularly superhighways and then check with other landmarks to locate your position;
      (1) when you finally recognize a landmark, don't accept it until you confirm what it is by locating other landmarks;
   e. when you find yourself, measure carefully the direction and distance to your destination, making any necessary corrections for the wind so that you don't get lost again.
   f. keep using your VOR (and ADF, if available) to get a fix on your location, and your radio to contact someone on 121.5.
9. You can avoid this whole problem by careful planning *in advance;*
   a. don't fly solo outside the practice area until you have been checked out for cross-country flight;
   b. never leave the area of your airport without your sectional chart or charts for your area;
   c. understand the use of your VOR (and all other instruments you have) before leaving the area of your airport;

a. this type of approach will not be given in IFR conditions unless you have declared an emergency;
   (1) if you are receiving this assistance, don't be in a hurry to declare the emergency unless they demand that you do so;
   (2) if you really need help, don't hesitate to declare the emergency if the weather conditions are IFR. Getting home alive is the *only* important consideration;
b. you should become familiar with this procedure early in your flight training and before you solo;
   (1) you are encouraged to request practice guidance and approaches during VFR weather conditions;
   (2) DF specialists will be glad to have the practice, if they aren't too busy.

SECTION 42—EMERGENCY OPERATIONS

Section 42
EMERGENCY OPERATIONS

1. If you experience *partial loss of power* or a rough running engine in flight:
    a. take immediate steps to prepare for a forced landing (Sec. 43);
    b. maintain your altitude and reduce power to 2,000 rpm;
    c. trim your airplane, as you do in slow flight, to maintain altitude;
    d. apply carburetor heat to check for icing and remove carburetor ice, and continue enough heat to avoid further icing (Sec. 21.1);
    e. check engine heat. If above red line, it is too hot and prepare to land;
    f. spark plug fouling can cause roughness, which can be verified by turning your ignition switch from BOTH to either L or R;
        (1) an obvious power loss in single engine operation is evidence of spark plug or magneto trouble;
        (2) if this appears to be the trouble, lean your mixture to the recommended setting for cruising flight;
        (3) if the trouble has not cleared up in several minutes, use a full rich mixture to see if that will produce smoother operation;
        (4) if still running rough or with loss of power, land for repairs as soon as possible;
    g. if your magneto check shows that one magneto is not working properly, switch to the other magneto and land for repairs as soon as possible;
    h. if you have both low oil pressure and normal oil temperature, the oil pressure gage or relief valve may be malfunctioning and you should prepare to land for repairs as soon as possible;
    i. if you have both low oil pressure and high oil temperature, an engine failure is imminent and you should immediately prepare for an emergency landing.
2. If you should experience a *complete power failure* in flight:
    a. prepare for an immediate forced landing (Sec. 43);
    b. reduce your airspeed to 60 KIAS;
    c. apply full carburetor heat (you may have carburetor icing);
    d. check your primer to be sure that it is IN and LOCKED (it could have worked OUT);
    e. check your dual shutoff valve to be sure that it is ON (someone could have turned it by mistake);

      f. FULL RICH with your mixture (you may have pulled it out by mistake);
      g. be sure that your ignition switch is on BOTH;
      h. try to restart the engine while you are gliding to land;
      i. use all other available time in checking the landing area and setting up for a safe landing;
      j. see Sec. 14.17 for procedures if it occurs just after takeoff.
3. *Fuel starvation* results from running out of gas or failing to have the fuel shutoff valve turned to a tank with fuel in it;
      a. you can avoid running out of gas by:
         (1) topping off your tanks every time you land unless it was a very short flight;
         (2) planning your flight carefully and providing enough fuel to get there with a good margin to spare;
         (3) stopping for fuel any time you have less than a comfortable amount in both tanks;
      b. one of the many reasons your Cessna 152 (or 150) is so safe is that the tanks are above the engine, so that no fuel pump is required, and because you can't crash (as so *many* pilots have) with the fuel valve turned to an empty tank while you have plenty of gas in the other tank;
      c. as you fly, check your fuel consumption and your remaining fuel frequently.
4. If you should have an *engine fire in flight,*
      a. pull your fuel mixture all the way out;
      b. turn your fuel shutoff valve to OFF;
      c. turn your master switch OFF;
      d. turn your cabin heat and cabin air OFF, but leave the wing root vents open;
      e. reduce your airspeed to 85 KIAS. If the fire is not extinguished, you should then increase your glide speed to find an airspeed that will provide an incombustible mixture;
      f. throughout this operation, keep going over your forced landing checklist.
5. If your generator, alternator, battery or circuit breaker should malfunction, you could have an *inoperative electrical system;*
      a. if the over-voltage light turns on, you should:
         (1) turn off both sides of the master switch;
         (2) then, turn the master switch ON;
         (3) if this results in turning the over-voltage light off, continue your flight and have it checked upon landing;
         (4) if the over-voltage light turns on again, prepare to land as soon as possible for repairs;
      b. if your ammeter shows a discharge:
         (1) turn your alternator off;
         (2) turn off all but the most essential electrical equipment;
         (3) prepare to land as soon as possible for repairs.

6. If you have an *electrical fire or smoke in your cockpit,* you should:
    a. turn the master switch OFF;
    turn off all your other electrical switches *except* your ignition switch;
    c. close all your vents, cabin air and cabin heat;
    d. use your fire extinguisher;
    e. be sure to ventilate your cabin after using the extinguisher;
    f. if the fire appears to be out and you need electrical power to finish your flight, you should:
        (1) turn the master switch ON;
        (2) check your circuit breakers, but do not reset a faulty circuit;
        (3) turn your radio and electrical switches on one at a time, pausing after each one until you locate the short circuit;
        (4) open your vents, cabin air and cabin heat after you are sure that the fire is completely extinguished.
7. Since you have a fixed landing gear, you avoid the problems that confront the pilot who has malfunctions in the operation of retractable gear.
8. Since your Cessna 150 or 152 does not *usually* need flaps for normal landings, it is not serious when your flaps fail to extend;
    a. however, if you find that such is the case, be careful to have enough runway for landing without any extension of flaps;
    b. if you are unable to retract your flaps after a takeoff, return to land for repairs.
9. If you have a *door open in flight,* you should:
    a. slow your airplane to 70 KIAS;
    b. trim your airplane for straight and level flight;
    c. open the left window if right door is open;
    d. slam the door firmly.
10. If you experience an inoperative elevator trim tab, you should:
    a. arrange to land as soon as possible for repairs;
    b. to the extent that you cannot control the pitch attitude of the airplane with the elevator, use power settings to control the attitude of the plane.

Section 43
FORCED LANDINGS

1. During every flight, you must constantly be alert to the fact that your engine could quit without any warning, forcing you to land immediately. This demands that you give constant attention to:
    a. *the wind direction*—so that, if possible, you can take advantage of the wind by landing into it;
        (1) you can always know the wind direction by constantly monitoring the radio, hearing weather reports, ATIS at nearby airports, contacting a FSS and Unicom;
        (2) it can also be determined by observing blowing smoke and dust, the shadows of clouds, waves on water or grain, etc.;
    b. *possible landing sites*—The more rugged the terrain, the more alert you must be so that you always know where you could land if you had to;
        (1) the lower you are flying, the more important that you select a landing spot *before* you need it;
    c. *your altitude*—since the higher you are if your engine quits, the more time you have to get it going again, the more good sites you will be able to reach and the more time you will have to set up a safe landing.
2. See Sec. 14.16 and 14.17 for the procedures where there is an engine failure during, or shortly after, takeoff.
3. When your engine fails, or loses most of its power, you must very calmly but as quickly as possible (1) establish your glide, (2) select a place to land, and (3) eliminate the cause of the trouble, if possible;

Height above terrain	Ground distance
12,000 ft.	19 miles
10,000 ft.	16 miles
8,000 ft.	13 miles
6,000 ft.	10 miles
4,000 ft.	6 miles
2,000 ft.	3 miles

FIG. 43.1—APPROXIMATE GLIDE DISTANCE OF CESSNA 152/150

a. the best glide speed for your airplane is 60 KIAS;
b. trim the plane so it will maintain that speed without any further effort on your part;
c. the distance you can glide in your airplane is shown in Fig. 43.1;
d. obviously, you can glide farther and reach more suitable landing places if you glide with the wind rather than into it.

4. As quickly and calmly as possible, survey all the terrain within reach and select the best possible landing site;
    a. be sure that it is the most suitable terrain available;
    b. of course, if there is any kind of airport, landing strip, etc. within reach, that will be the best choice but be sure it is within reach or you may stall trying to stretch out your final approach;
    c. a level pasture with short grass or with small grains, particularly if recently harvested, is normally the next best choice;
    d. a cornfield is good if the corn is still short but tall corn can be a dangerous place to land;
    e. freshly plowed ground can be very dangerous. If plowed ground is your only choice, be sure to land parallel to the furrows;
    f. if there is nothing but timber within your gliding range, find the longest and smoothest open patch, land into the wind, let down as close as possible to one end and, if you run out of clearing, arrange to hit the trees with your wings and not your propeller;
    g. check the area of the chosen spot for dangers such as telephone poles, trees, power lines, fences, buildings, auto traffic, ditches, etc;
    h. while a road should not normally be your first choice, it may be the only place you can land safety;
        (1) in landing on a road, do everything in your power to avoid traffic;
        (2) most country roads look enticing for this purpose but can be very dangerous since there may be wires parallel to the road and, even more dangerous, crossing the road;
    i. if there is any choice, land as close to a road as possible to lessen the problem of getting back to civilization and to assure your being found as quickly as possible;
    k. in making a simulated forced landing, be sure that you do *not* do so in populous areas and that you never come within 500 feet of people or buildings.

5. If you are in contact with a FSS when your engine fails, tell them your problem. If that is not practical, immediately get on the radio and call MAYDAY on 121.5;
    a. the station that receives your call will either handle your problem or immediately put you in touch with the station that can do the most for you;
    b. be prepared to announce your position and problem so that they can assist you in finding the best landing site and so that Search and Rescue (SAR) will get to you quickly.

SECTION 43—FORCED LANDINGS

6. Almost simultaneously with the selection of a landing spot, setting up your glide and getting on the radio, you should be taking every possible step to restore power, including the following:
    a. apply full carburetor heat. There may be carburetor icing;
    b. be sure your fuel shutoff valve is ON;
    c. check your magnetos as follows:
        (1) turn the ignition switch to the right mag and then to the left mag;
        (2) if one mag has shorted out, both mags are shorted out while the ignition switch is in the BOTH position;
        (3) however, if this is the case, the engine will start again when you turn the ignition switch to the good magneto position;
        (4) be sure that the mixture is FULL RICH. It is easy to pull out the fuel mixture thinking you are pulling on carburetor heat;
        (5) be sure that the primer is securely locked.
7. Assuming that your altitude has been sufficient to set up an orderly landing, there are additional precautions that you should take;
    a. check your chart to see the altitude of the area so that you can determine your own pattern altitude;
        (1) while this would normally be 800 feet AGL, using 1,000 feet will enable you to stretch a final approach;
    b. if your altitude or remaining power is enough, drag the field;
        (1) that is, fly over it and check the condition of the terrain, obstacles, etc.;
        (2) make a final check of wind direction from smoke, cloud shadows, dust, etc.;
    c. if your power and/or altitude permits, use the regular landing pattern, since this is the way you are most experienced in getting the plane onto the ground;
    d. if you still have power, apply power to 1,500 rpm every 20 seconds to clear the engine;
    e. keep your airspeed up (65 KIAS with flaps up and 60 KIAS with flaps down) throughout the landing and while on final approach to avoid the danger of a stall;
    f. don't apply flaps until you are absolutely sure of reaching the selected spot and then use up to 30 degrees of flaps;
    g. use the usual short field landing procedures (See Sec. 27);
    h. if the field appears to be soft, use the usual soft field landing procedures (See Sec. 27);
    i. be sure that all seat belts and shoulder harnesses are firmly secured;
    j. unlatch the doors just before touchdown;
    k. have all passengers remove eyeglasses and cover their faces with coats, etc.;
    l. land with the tail slightly low;
    m. apply heavy braking action, but with the wheel all the way back.
8. When your forced landing is simulated, during flight instruction, follow this procedure when you are advised to go around:

a. apply full power;
   b. remove carburetor heat;
   c. when you have reached a safe airspeed, lift your flaps slowly;
   d. from this point you will follow your regular departure procedures.
9. If your forced landing will be into water:
   a. follow usual emergency procedures outlined above;
   b. secure or jettison all baggage, etc.;
   c. determine the wind direction, remembering that the white caps appear to move *into* the wind;
   d. if the swells are heavy, land parallel to them;
   e. if the swells are not heavy, land the way the white caps are moving;
   f. apply 30 degrees of flaps;
   g. set up a 300 feet-per-minute descent at 55 KIAS;
   h. before flareout, open your cabin doors and prop them open with anything available, since you won't be able to open them after you hit the water;
   i. start your flareout when you are about 10 feet above the water;
   j. try to touch the water while in a level attitude, descending at 300 feet per minute;
   k. when you are just about to touch down on the water, stall your airplane out completely, to stop all forward travel;
   l. get out quickly and inflate your life vests and raft.

Section 44
INSTRUMENT FLYING

1. One of the most important parts of your training will be the time you spend flying by instruments;
    a. of course, as a student, you will *only* do this with your instructor present and in simulated instrument flight, rather than flight under IFR conditions;
    b. while there are several different ways to do this, you will probably do your instrument flying under a hood which permits you to see the instrument panel, but keeps you from seeing outside.
2. The time spent under the hood has a number of practical advantages to you:
    a. the experience gives you a much better feel for the operation of the airplane;
    b. it prepares you to meet emergencies that you could not handle if you had never had anything comparable;
        (1) but time spent under the hood should never make you overconfident or careless about entering situations that might be dangerous;
    c. it makes you more familiar with the instruments, how they operate, and how they can be most useful for you;
    d. it helps to prepare you for more advanced certificates, such as the instrument and commercial.
3. Time spent under the hood must be entered separately in your logbook.
4. Simulated instrument flying attempts to duplicate the conditions that will be encountered if there is sudden loss of visibility;
    a. without a horizon, or anything on the ground to refer to, we quickly lose our sense of balance;
    b. instrument flying is done the same as any other flying, except that, rather than determining the attitude of the airplane by reference to the ground and the horizon, we must do so through the eyes of the instruments which tell us the airplane's attitude;
    c. the artificial horizon becomes the principal source of information about the airplane's attitude;
        (1) it usually responds instantly to changes in attitude and is, therefore, more reliable than the vertical speed indicator, which is always somewhat delayed behind the actual change in attitude;

- d. the turn and bank indicator becomes more important than usual because it is used to avoid and correct slips and skids;
    - (1) *remember:* if the ball is out of center to the right, use the right rudder to get it back to the center;
- e. during instrument flight, it is highly essential that your eyes keep moving over *all* the instruments, never permitting your eyes to become glued on any particular one;
    - (1) you should learn to get the meaning of each instrument in as brief a period of time as possible;
    - (2) train yourself not to rest your eye on one instrument for more than a second or two at a time.
5. The 180-degree turn becomes very important if you should accidently fly into poor visibility;
    - a. it is important because often poor visibility can be left behind by a 180-degree turn and a few minutes of straight flight away from the place you encountered it;
    - b. note your heading and prepare to turn to its reciprocal;
    - c. make a smoothly coordinated turn to the left or right;
    - d. establish a two minute turn on your turn and bank coordinator;
    - e. continue the turn for 60 seconds;
    - f. avoid climbs and descents by constantly referring to the artificial horizon and the VSI, as well as the altimeter and ASI
    - g. use your elevator to maintain your altitude and airspeed.
6. A shallow descending turn is a descent at the rate of 500 feet per minute, with a bank of about 15 degrees;
    - a. the rate of descent is controlled by the reduction of the power to about 2,000 rpm;
    - b. the airspeed of a 152 will normally be 87 KIAS;
        - (1) trim the airplane to maintain desired airspeed without use of your elevator;
    - c. start to level off about 50 feet above the desired altitude;
    - d. return power to 2,450 rpm upon reaching 50 feet above the desired altitude.
7. A shallow climbing turn to a predetermined altitude is a climb at about 400 feet per minute, at a 15-degree bank;
    - a. use your turn and bank indicator to establish a standard rate turn;
        - (1) this is a turn that takes two minutes to make a 360-degree change in direction if the needle is kept on the "doghouse";
    - b. the power is increased to full power;
    - c. the turn should be well coordinated;
    - d. start to level off about 20 feet before arriving at the desired altitude;
    - e. after leveling off, let the airspeed build up to 87 KIAS and then throttle back to 2,450 rpm.
8. In your flight test, you may be required to make normal turns of at least 180 degrees to within ± 20 degrees of a preselected heading;
    - a. this is sometimes known as a 180-degree timed turn;

SECTION 44—INSTRUMENT FLYING

    b. accuracy is achieved with the least effort if you use your turn and bank indicator to establish a standard rate turn;
       (1) if the air is turbulent, don't try to keep the needle exactly in the right position. Instead, try to keep the bank so that the *average* position of the needle is correct;
    c. continue to check the other instruments regularly;
    d. climbs and descents must be made to within ± 100 feet of a preselected altitude;
    e. rely upon the gyro compass rather than the magnetic compass because of the vagaries of the magnetic compass (See Sec. 18);
    f. constantly bear in mind the desired heading so that you do not become too engrossed in reading the instruments and forget to straighten the airplane to attain the desired heading.

9. You may be required to recover from the approach to a climbing stall;
    a. this maneuver, together with the recovery from the start of a power-on spiral, is sometimes known as the "recovery from critical flight attitudes";
    b. you may be asked to close your eyes and lower your head until you cannot see the instruments until asked to look up at them;
    c. after an assortment of climbs, descents and turns, the instructor (and later your flight examiner) will put the airplane into an attitude that will lead to a climbing stall;
       (1) he will turn the controls over to you with some comment such as "It's all yours";
    d. check the instruments as quickly as possible if you are approaching a stall, especially by checking your airspeed;
       (1) make the normal correcting action to recover from a stall (Sec. 23);
       (2) if the airspeed is decreasing, lower the nose smoothly to gain airspeed;
    e. if power has been reduced, return to full power;
    f. constantly check the altimeter in leveling off;
    g. when the airplane is leveled off, resume cruise speed and then reduce rpm to 2,450.

10. Recovery from the start of a power-on spiral is handled in much the same way as the recovery from the approach to a climbing stall;
    a. check the instruments immediately. These will indicate:
       (1) the airspeed will be high;
       (2) the rate of climb indicator will show a rapid loss of altitude;
       (3) the artificial horizon will show the bank and a steep angle of descent;
    b. take the following corrective action, and in this order:
       (1) cut the power;
       (2) level the wings by referring to the artificial horizon;
       (3) bring the nose up slowly and smoothly, being sure not to do so too quickly because of the great increase of load factor placed upon the airplane;
    c. after you have the airplane under control, establish your desired direction, altitude and airspeed.

Section 45
NIGHT FLYING

1. You are not required to perform night flying to get your Private Pilot Certificate, but if you don't, you won't be able to fly at night as a private pilot;
    a. while night flying can be about as safe as daytime flying, there are special hazards at night that require special training, care and precautions;
    b. the greatest danger to the non-instrument pilot is that of flying into clouds at night, particularly when visibility is poor and/or there is no moon;
        (1) never fly VFR at night when the weather conditions are bad or deteriorating;
    c. some nations consider night flying so dangerous that they forbid VFR flights at night;
    d. never fly at night without adequate instruction.
2. Even as a private pilot, you must never carry passengers at night without having met the recency of experience requirements;
    a. in order to carry passengers from one hour after sunset to one hour before sunrise you must have made at least 3 takeoffs and 3 landings to a *full stop* at night within the preceding 90 days in the category and class of aircraft to be used.
3. In addition to the instruments and equipment required for VFR daytime flights (see Sec. 9.7) you must have the following for nighttime flight:
    a. approved position lights;
    b. an approved aviation red or aviation white anticollision light;
    c. an adequate source of electrical energy for all installed electrical and radio equipment;
    d. one spare set of fuses, or three spare fuses of each kind required.
4. You are not *required* to have a landing light unless you are operating for hire, but you *should* have a landing light, anyway.
5. In addition, you should have one flashlight in good operarting condition and preferably have a second for a backup.
6. Your preflight planning should include everything you normally do, but with additional precautions:
    a. check the weather very carefully and don't go unless it will be good;
    b. check the lighting aids at your own and destination airports, and along the way;
    c. study the lighting equipment in your airplane so that you can operate it in the dark;

SECTION 45—NIGHT FLYING

     d. prepare your flight plan with great care so that you will know exactly where you are throughout your flight;
     e. without fail, file a flight plan;
     f. check the temperature and dewpoint, as a narrow spread indicates the likelihood of fog at night.

7. Your preflight check should include all the usual steps, plus the following:
     a. be sure that your position lights, anticollision light and strobe lights (if any) are working properly;
     b. be very sure that your electrical systems are functioning properly;
     c. be sure your flashlights are handy and in good condition.

8. You will take off the same way you do in the daytime, but with certain special precautions:
     a. check your flight instruments carefully as you take off, at least until you see the horizon and are fully oriented;
     b. avoid bright lights before you take off;
     c. avoid violent or abrupt maneuvers;
     d. be alert for the disappearance of ground lights or for a red or green glow around your position lights, as that may indicate you are flying into clouds.

9. There are other special precautions to observe during night flight;
     a. you and all passengers should avoid smoking as that impairs night vision;
     b. fly as high as practical;
     c. avoid excessive lighting in the cockpit.

10. Your landing at night will be about the same as in the daytime, but with some differences:
     a. take special pains to check the conditions at your destination airport, including runway directions, winds, field elevation and altimeter setting;
     b. check for any obstructions around the field, their elevation and how you will avoid them;
     c. since altitude and speed are deceptive at night, maintain a continuous and careful scan of your instruments;
     d. a normal approach at night can seem steeper than normal so that there is a danger that you will *undershoot* the runway;
     e. be sure to remember to turn on your landing light about 5 miles from the airport;
     f. landing lights can almost hypnotize you so be sure that you don't keep staring straight ahead;
     g. keep some power right up to point of touchdown.

11. While flying at night, constantly look in all directions for the lights of other airplanes; determine their position in relation to you by their position lights;
     a. if you see the green light on the left and the red light on the right, the plane is coming right at you, demanding immediate action to evade it;
     b. if you see the red and white light, it is going from your right to your left;
     c. if you see the green and white light, it is going from your left to your right.

12. When you are flying at night, always be aware that:
    a. if there are not visible lights on the ground, it is very easy to become disoriented;
    b. you can quickly fly into a cloud that you are unable to see, forcing you to fly entirely by instruments until you can get back out of the clouds;
    c. it is easy to confuse the lights that you see, such as a star for a light on the ground or an airplane, and vice versa.

Section 46
YOUR FIRST SOLO FLIGHT

1. Before you can solo, you must have:
    a. your Student Pilot Certificate, which must be signed on the reverse side by your instructor certifying you for solo flight;
    b. your Third Class Medical Certificate;
    c. your Radiotelephone Permit.
2. Before you can solo, you must demonstrate to your authorized flight instructor that you know the rules of Part 91 of the FARs;
    a. these rules are discussed throughout this Guide under appropriate headings;
    b. solo flight includes flight both when you are the sole occupant and when you are pilot in command of the airplane;
    c. you do *not* have to pass a written examination before you solo;
    d. a sample test on the general and visual flight rules is shown in Fig. 46.1.
3. You must have received ground and flight instruction from an authorized flight instructor in at least the following procedures and operations:
    a. flight preparation and procedures (Sec. 8 & 9), including preflight inspection (Sec. 10) and powerplant operation (Sec. 7);
    b. ground maneuvering (Sec. 12) and runups (Sec. 13);
    c. flight at minimum controllable airspeeds (Sec. 23) and stall recognition and recovery (Sec. 23);
    d. straight and level flight, climbs, turns, descents (Sec 15);
    e. normal takeoffs (Sec. 14) and landings (Sec. 27);
    f. airport traffic patterns, including collision avoidance precautions (Sec. 25 & 51) and wake turbulence (Sec. 22);
    g. emergencies (Sec. 42), including elementary emergency landings (Sec. 43).
4. Your instructor must certify on your Student Pilot Certificate that you are able to make solo flights:
    a. this endorsement must be made *before* your first solo flight;
    b. the endorsement to solo does not permit you to fly solo cross-country (Sec. 47).
5. You must carry your Student Pilot Certificate and Medical Certificate with you when you fly solo.
6. Some apprehension is only natural when you first solo an airplane;

a. your instructor will not let you solo the airplane until he is confident that you will be *absolutely* safe in so doing;
b. if your performance is satisfactory, you will normally be asked to make three solo flights during your first solo period;
c. no further solo flights will be authorized until after a rest period and further dual review of basic maneuvers.
7. Do not make the common mistake of assuming that you are now a thoroughly qualified pilot;
   a. there is much instruction ahead, and much to learn after your first solo flight and before you will be qualified to receive your Private Pilot Certificate.
8. Even though you have soloed, you cannot continue to fly solo unless your logbook has been endorsed within the preceding 90 days by an authorized flight instructor that:
   a. he has given you instruction in the make and model of aircraft in which your solo flight is made;
   b. he finds that you have met the requirements listed above for solo flight;
   c. he finds that you are competent to make a solo flight in that aircraft.
9. For the limitations on solo cross-country flight by a student pilot, see Sec. 47.
10. Here is a sample test on General and Visual Flight Rules that you should know before you solo:
    1. Do the Federal Aviation Regulations specifically prohibit the operation of an aircraft in a careless or reckless manner? See Sec. 20.4.
    2. Are deviations from control tower instructions allowed in the case of an emergency? See Sec. 20.3.
    3. Which aircraft has the right-of-way when two or more aircraft at different altitudes, but not on final approach, are approaching an airport for the purpose of landing? See Sec. 20.6.
    4. What are the restrictions on the proximity of one aircraft to another in flight? See Sec. 20.5.
    5. When aircraft are approaching each other head-on, in which direction should each pilot alter course? See Sec. 20.6.
    6. Is any preflight action required of a student pilot prior to solo flight in a local area? See Sec. 9 & 46.
    7. Is an intentional maneuver that exceeds a bank of 60-degrees considered an acrobatic maneuver? See Sec. 20.11.
    8. If an airplane is converging with a glider at approximately the same altitude, which has the right-of-way? See Sec. 20.6.
    9. May an aircraft be operated after sunset without displaying position lights? See Sec. 45.3.
    10. What are the standard light signals for the control of airport traffic and what is the meaning of each signal—on the ground? In the air? See Sec. 31.7.

SECTION 46—YOUR FIRST SOLO FLIGHT

11. What is the minimum safe altitude over congested areas as established by regulations? See Sec. 16.7.
12. Are there any restrictions to operating within an airport traffic area except for the purpose of landing or taking off? See Sec. 31.1.
13. Is a pilot required to comply with the instructions of a control tower when operating at an airport with a control tower? See Sec. 31.
14. What is the standard direction for all turns for an airplane approaching to land at an airport without a control tower? See Sec. 25.4.
15. Do instructions received from an airport ground controller have the same authority as those received from the in-flight controller? See Sec. 31.2.
16. Is buzzing or intentionally flying in close proximity to the ground, other than for takeoff or landing, considered to be careless or reckless operation? See Sec. 20.3.
17. Assume there is no altimeter setting available at your airport, what setting would you use for a local flight? See Sec. 16.6.
18. Except when necessary for takeoff or landing, which is considered to be a minimum safe altitude for all flight situations? See Sec. 16.7.
19. When operating an aircraft equipped with a two-way radio at an airport with a control tower, is the pilot required to maintain communications with the control tower? See Sec. 31.1.
20. Is a visual display appropriate to indicate non-standard traffic directions for an airport without a control tower? See Sec. 25.6.
21. In what direction should the pilot circle the airport when approaching to land at an airport with a control tower? See Sec. 31.5.
22. What are the basic VFR weather minimums in a control areas? See Sec. 9.2.
23. What communications action is required of the pilot when operating an aircraft with a radio receiver only at an airport with a control tower? See Sec. 31.7.
24. What are the dimensions of the standard airport traffic areas? See Sec. 25.11.
25. May a pilot at an airport with a control tower taxi an aircraft on a runway before receiving clearance from the appropriate controlling agency? See Sec. 31.2.
26. What are the basic VFR weather minimums outside controlled airspace at or below 1,200 feet above the ground? See Sec. 9.5.
27. What are appropriate altitudes when operating an aircraft under VFR in level cruising flight of an altitude of more than 3,000 feet above the surface on a magnetic course of 0 through 179 degrees? 180 through 359 degrees? See Sec. 16.8.
28. Is it mandatory that pilots keep seatbelts fastened while at the controls of an aircraft? See Sec. 20.8.
29. If overtaking another aircraft, in which direction should the course be altered to pass well clear of the other aircraft? See Sec. 20.6.
30. What are the basic VFR weather minimums in a control zone? See Sec. 25.9.

31. Which aircraft has the right-of-way when one aircraft is being overtaken by another? See Sec. 20.6.
32. How can control areas and control zones and their limits be identified on sectional aeronautical charts? See Sec. 47.
33. In the case of lost radio contact with a control tower, what is the prescribed action for the traffic pattern entry, approach, and landing? See Sec. 25.7.
34. What does the operation of a rotating beacon at an airport located within a control zone, during daylight hours mean? See Sec. 26.2.
35. What information is provided to a pilot by the Automatic Terminal Information Service (ATIS)? See Sec. 35.
36. What visual display is used to indicate that an airport runway or taxiway is closed to traffic? See Sec. 25.5.
37. If the wind is calm, where should you look for traffic, if the following radar traffic advisory is received? TRAFFIC 2 O'CLOCK, 1 MILE, WEST BOUND. . . . ? See Sec. 33.11.
38. What do the letters "VHF/DF" that appear in the *AIM Airport/Facility Directory* for a certain airport mean? See Sec. 41.
39. What information should a pilot provide when telephoning a weather briefing facility for preflight weather information? See Sec. 39.15.
40. Assume you are crossing the flightpath of a large jet airplane that is ahead of you at the same altitude, to avoid wake turbulence what should you do? See Sec. 22.4.

Section 47
PLANNING THE CROSS-COUNTRY FLIGHT

1. As a student pilot, your right to make cross-country flights is strictly regulated:
    a. except in an emergency you may not make a solo cross-country flight or make a solo flight landing at any point other than the airport of takeoff until you meet the requirements listed below.
2. An authorized flight instructor may allow you to practice solo landings and takeoffs at another airport within 25 nautical miles from your home airport if he finds that you are competent to do them.
3. Before your solo cross-country flight, you must receive instruction from an authorized instructor in at least the following pilot operations pertinent to the aircraft you will be flying:
    a. the use of aeronautical charts, pilotage and elementary dead reckoning using the magnetic compass;
    b. the use of radio for VFR navigation and for two-way communication;
    c. control of an airplane by reference to flight instruments;
    d. short field and soft field procedures and crosswind takeoffs and landings;
    e. recognition of critical weather conditions, estimating visibility while in flight, and the procurement and use of aeronautical weather reports and forecasts;
    f. cross-country emergency procedures.
4. Before you can make any cross-country flight, you must have:
    a. an endorsement from an authorized flight instructor on your Student Pilot Certificate which states that you have received instruction in solo cross-country flying and the applicable training requirements set forth above, and are competent to make cross-country solo flights in the category of aircraft involved;
    b. an endorsement by your instructor in your pilot logbook that he has reviewed the preflight planning and preparation for *each* solo cross-country flight and that you are prepared to make the flight safely under the known circumstances and the conditions listed by the instructor in the logbook;
    c. the instructor may also endorse your logbook for repeated solo cross-country flights under stipulated conditions over a course not more than 50 nautical miles from the point of departure if he has given you instruction in both directions over the route, including takeoffs and landings at the airports to be used.

5. A principal tool in planning and flying a cross-country flight is your aeronautical chart. The principal kinds of charts used by the student and by the non-instrument rated private pilot are published by the government (the National Ocean Survey, or NOS) and are:
    a. the Sectional Aeronautical Chart. Students use this kind of chart almost exclusively. See Sec. 47.7;
    b. Local Aeronautical Charts have a scale of about 4 statute miles per inch, and are used primarily for use on VFR flights in highly congested areas;
        (1) they show more topographical detail than any other charts;
        (2) they are identified by the names of cities, such as Atlanta Local;
    c. Aeronautical Planning Charts have a scale of about 80 statute miles per inch, and are designed for planning long flights;
    d. World Aeronautical Charts are better known as WACs and have a scale of about 16 statute miles per inch. They supply on a smaller scale much of the information given on Sectional Charts. They are used primarily by experienced private and commercial pilots who frequently fly cross-country.
6. Pilots other than jet airline pilots, flying on IFR flight plans, use Low Altitude Enroute Charts which give very little topographical information and are published by the NOS and by Jeppesen;

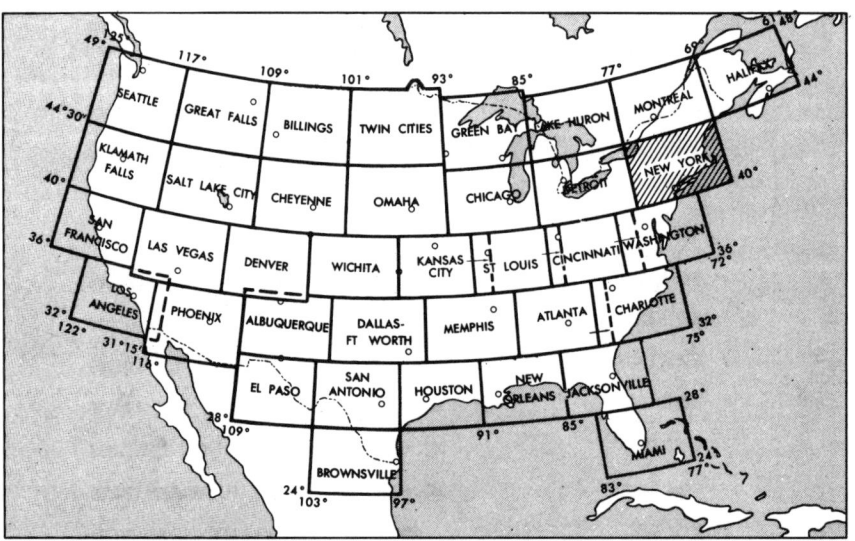

FIG. 47.1—INDEX OF SECTIONAL CHARTS

a. another very useful tool for both the instrument and non-instrument rated pilot is *Sky Prints* published by Sky Prints Corp., 6617 Clayton Rd., St. Louis, Missouri 63117.
7. The 48 states are depicted on 37 Sectional Charts, which are printed on both sides:
   a. each sectional chart has a name or title;
   b. each chart is marked with an effective date and indicates the date on which it will become obsolete for use in navigation;
   c. you should supply yourself not only with the sectional chart that covers your area but also with adjoining charts since bad weather and other conditions may compel you to land at an airport outside your chart area.
8. You should study the aeronautical symbols and the information concerning terrain and contour elevations until you know what they all mean;
   a. by referring to these symbols, you may identify aeronautical, topographical and obstruction symbols;
   b. many landmarks that are easily recognizable from the air are identified by brief descriptions beside the small black squares.
9. Relief, that is, the elevations of the land surface, is shown on the chart by brown contour lines drawn at 250-foot intervals.
10. All airports that have permanent hard-surfaced runways are shown by runway patterns for more positive identification and to help provide you with landmarks;
    a. recognizable runways are shown to aid in visual identification;
    b. information that relates to an airport with an airport traffic area is given in blue figures in a blue box adjacent to the airport symbol;
    c. information relating to other airports is given in magenta.
11. Draw the course of your flight on the sectional chart or charts;
    a. your route may be (1) direct from one point to another, (2) along Victor airways shown on the chart, or (3) a combination of both;
    b. the course line should begin at the center of the airport of departure and end at the center of the destination airport;
    c. if the route is direct, it will consist of a single straight line.
12. For safety and convenience, you will probably use the VOR system for a trip of any substantial length;
    a. the Victor system consists of airways established from 7,001 feet AGL to, but not including, 18,000 feet MSL;
    b. the VOR airways are based solely on VOR/VORTAC navigation aids;
       (1) they are shown on your aeronautical charts by a "V" ("Victor"), followed by the airway number, e.g., V12;
       (2) these Victor airways are numbered similarly to U.S. highways;
       (3) as in the highway numbering system, a segment of an airway which is common to two or more routes carries the numbers of all the airways which coincide in that segment;

(4) when such is the case, you will indicate only that airway number of the route which you are using, when you file a flight plan;

c. when you intend to make an airway flight using VOR facilities, you specify the appropriate Victor airway(s) in your flight plan.

13. Select appropriate checkpoints along your route;
    a. these may be VORs, or easy-to-locate points such as large towns, large lakes and rivers, towns with a network of highways and railways entering and departing;
    b. large rivers are especially good checkpoints when they have prominent loops or bends, or in combination with other prominent checkpoints;
    c. note these checkpoints on your flight log.
14. Check along and to either side of your route for caution, restricted and prohibited areas, military climb corridors, Air Defense Identifying Zones (ADIZ), etc. (see Sec. 19).
15. Study the terrain along your route;
    a. check the highest and lowest elevations along your route so you can choose an appropriate altitude;
    b. check for *rugged terrain,* mountains, forests, swamps, and large bodies of water, so you can avoid them;
    c. check for tall obstructions.
16. Make a list of the navigation aids and their frequencies that you will use along your route;
    a. indicate those aids that have voice facilities so you will know on which stations you can receive weather broadcasts.
17. Make a list of flight service stations along your route and the frequencies which you can use for transmitting and receiving;
    a. the frequencies can be found in the Sectional Chart, *Sky Prints,* and the *AIM:*
    b. check NOTAMS for any frequency changes or VOR shutdowns.
18. Study available information about each airport at which you intend to land. This study of the *AIM* will include:
    a. *The Airport Directory,* if the airport has no control tower;
    b. *The Airport/Facility Directory,* if the airport has a control tower;
    c. NOTAMS (issued every 14 days) will show additional information on hazardous conditions or changes that have been made since the issuance of the *Airport Directory* and the *Airport/Facility Directory* sections.
19. Your computer is an important tool in your preflight planning. The use of the computer is treated in detail in your ground school course. However, as a refresher, we here set forth the steps in using your E6-B computer to determine your ground speed and wind correction angle:
    a. rotate the azimuth so that the *wind direction* appears directly under the True Index mark;
    b. slide the grid in the computer until the grommet (small black circle in the center) is on any of the heavy left to right lines, such as 120 or 160;

SECTION 47—PLANNING THE CROSS-COUNTRY FLIGHT

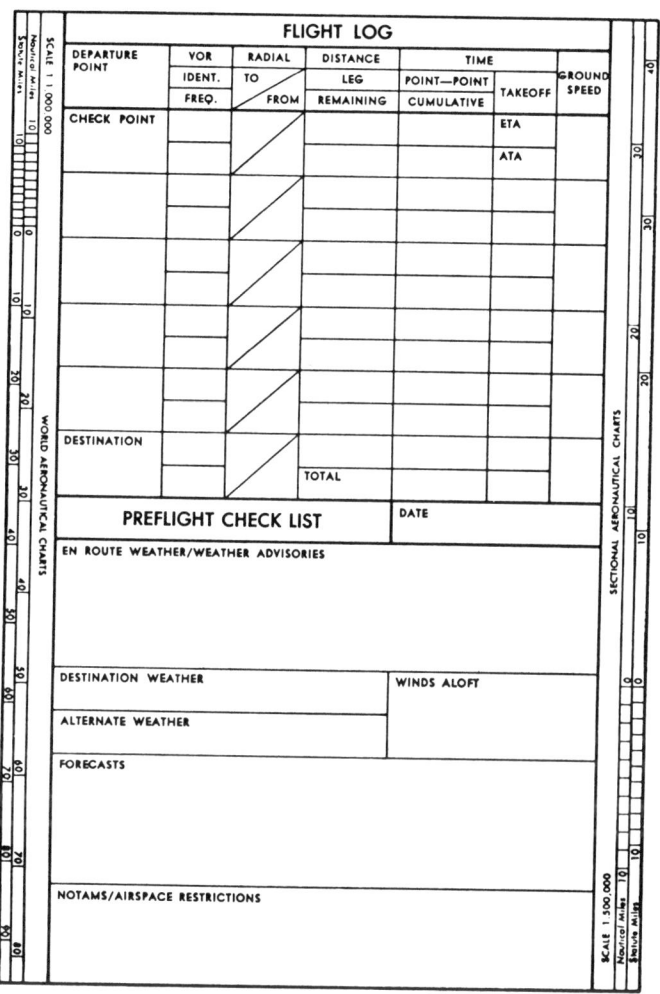

FIG. 47.2—FLIGHT LOG

c. place a pencil mark on the clear plastic to indicate the velocity of the wind in miles per hour;
   (1) this is measured up from the heavy line the grommet is on;
   (2) each faint line represents two miles per hour and each heavy line represents ten miles per hour;
   (3) for instance, if the grommet is on 120 and the wind velocity is 20 mph, the pencil mark is placed on 140;
d. rotate the azimuth until the *true course* is immediately under the True Index mark; place pencil dot on your true airspeed;
e. the Wind Correction Angle is then read by:
   (1) reading the number of degrees to the left or right of center you find the pencil mark;
   (2) if the pencil mark is to the left of the center line, *subtract* that number of of degrees from the *true course* to obtain the *true heading;*
   (3) if it is to the right, *add* the Wind Correction Angle to the *true course* to obtain the *true heading;*
f. the headwind or tailwind factor is under the grommet.

20. Review the problems of direction in Sec. 18. Determine your compass heading (CH) as follows:
    a. using the straight line drawn on your chart, use the plotter to determine your true course (TC);
    b. determine the wind direction and velocity;
       (1) using your computer, determine the *wind correction angle;*
       (2) this is *added* to your true course if the wind is from the *right* and *subtracted* if the wind is from the *left;*
       (3) the *true course* (TC) corrected for the wind, gives the *true heading* (TH);
    c. your true heading (TH) plus or minus the magnetic variation equals the magnetic heading (MH);
    d. refer to the chart to find the closest isogonic line;
       (1) it will indicate the magnetic variation which is expressed in number of degrees east or west, thus: 5°E or 4°W;
       (2) when the variation is east, it is *subtracted.* When it is west, it is *added.* "East is least and West is best;"
    e. the magnetic heading (MH) must be corrected for compass deviation to arrive at your compass heading (CH);
       (1) deviation is caused by magnetic influences within the plane itself;
       (2) the amount of this deviation is shown in your airplane on the compass correction card, mounted near the compass.

21. Briefly summarized:
    a. *true course* (TC) is the direction toward destination, as measured on the chart;
    b. *true heading* (TH) is the *true course* (TC) corrected for the wind;

c. *magnetic heading* (MH) is the *true heading* (TH) corrected for variation;
d. *compass heading* (CH) is the *magnetic heading* (MH) corrected for deviation as shown on the deviation card;
e. *magnetic course* is the true course corrected for magnetic variation;
f. *magnetic course* is used in determining your altitude (odd or even thousand feet plus 500) when flying above 3,000 feet AGL;
g. the compass heading is the direction in which the nose of the airplane should point to make good the desired course.

22. Some pilots find it convenient to remember these relationships by learning the statement: "*T*rue *V*irgins *M*ake *D*ull *C*ompany;"
    a. T—True Heading
    b. V—Variation
    c. M—Magnetic Heading
    d. D—Deviation
    e. C—Compass Heading
    f. TH plus or minus V = MH
    g. MH plus or minus D = CH.

23. Determine your ground speed, as follows:
    a. correct your indicated airspeed (IAS) to reflect density altitude;
        (1) the airspeed indicator registers true airspeed under *standard sea level conditions;* that is, when the pressure is 29.92 and the temperature is 15°C (59°F) and you are flying at sea level;
        (2) the true airspeed increases over indicated airspeed as the altitude increases (air pressure decreases) and as the temperature increases;
        (3) true airspeed may be determined by the use of your computer, or by the rule of thumb that true airspeed increases by 2 percent of the indicated airspeed for each 1,000 feet of altitude;
    b. use true airspeed on the wind side of your computer to figure ground speed.

24. Using the performance chart, determine the time required to reach each checkpoint and your destination;
    a. if you expect a headwind or tailwind, you should check your time for the *return* flight, as it will be different.

25. Determine the amount of fuel you will consume by referring to the performance chart in the *Pilot's Operating Handbook;*
    a. if the fuel aboard will be insufficient to reach your destination, with a *large margin of safety,* plan intermediate stops for refueling.

Section 48
FILING YOUR VFR FLIGHT PLAN

1. One of the greatest of all services to the student and private pilot is the VFR flight plan;
    a. you are not required to file a flight plan for your cross-country flights, but it could save your life if you encounter trouble;
        (1) a flight plan *is* required for operations in or penetrating a Coastal or Domestic ADIZ or DEWIZ;
    b. the VFR flight plan differs considerably from the IFR flight plan;
        (1) the IFR flight plan is filed only by instrument rated pilots who fly under the constant control of Air Traffic Control (ATC);
    c. unlike IFR flight plans, your VFR flight plan does not reserve a block of airspace for you and you are not in constant contact with ATC.
2. To obtain the maximum benefits from your flight plan, you should file it directly with your nearest FSS;
    a. you may use your radio to file if no other means are available;
    b. you are encouraged to give your departure time directly to the FSS where you filed the plan;
        (1) this will insure more efficient flight plan service and will allow the FSS to advise you of significant changes in aeronautical facilities or weather conditions.
3. A VFR flight plan will be held until one hour after the proposed departure time unless:
    a. the actual departure time is received;
    b. a revised proposed departure time is received;
    c. at the time of filing, the FSS is informed that the proposed departure time will be met, but actual time cannot be given because of inadequate communications;
    d. on your request, at a location having an active tower, your aircraft identification will be forwarded to the tower for reporting the actual departure time;
        (1) this procedure should be avoided at busy airports.
4. The FSS works on the 24 hour clock and adjusts it to Greenwich Mean Time (GMT), sometimes known as Zulu (Z) time;
    a. this is the time observed at the Prime Meridian, which passes near London;
    b. the uniform use of this time removes ambiguities as you move from one time zone to another and from daylight to standard time;
    c. the United States is divided into time zones;

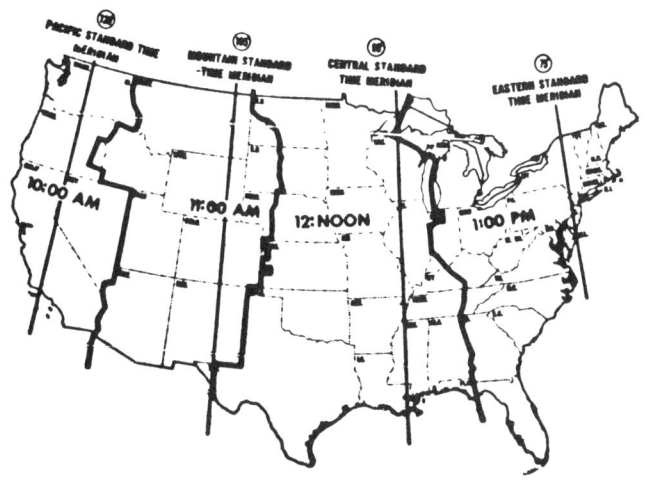

FIG. 48.1—UNITED STATES TIME ZONES

d. To convert your own local time and that along your route and at your destination, refer to Fig. 48.2.

To Convert From:	To Greenwich Mean Time:
Eastern Standard Time	Add 5 hours
Eastern Daylight Time	Add 4 hours
Central Standard Time	Add 6 hours
Central Daylight Time	Add 5 hours
Mountain Standard Time	Add 7 hours
Mountain Daylight Time	Add 6 hours
Pacific Standard Time	Add 8 hours
Pacific Daylight Time	Add 7 hours

FIG. 48.2—CONVERSIONS TO GREENWICH MEAN TIME (GMT)

5. The flight plan has a standard format which you fill out and file with the FSS but you can read it off in the same order if you are filing by telephone or radio;
   a. use these suggestions to enable you to fill out the flight plan accurately:
      (1) *Type*—As a student, you will always check VFR;
      (2) *Aircraft identification*—Enter your N number, such as N2151S;
      (3) *Aircraft type/special equipment*—Enter your type of airplane, such as Cessna 152, followed by a slash and the equipment code identifier;

SECTION 48—FILING YOUR VFR FLIGHT PLAN

DEPARTMENT OF TRANSPORTATION— FEDERAL AVIATION ADMINISTRATION **FLIGHT PLAN**						Form Approved OMB No. 04-R0072	
1. TYPE ☐ VFR ☐ IFR ☐ DVFR	2. AIRCRAFT IDENTIFICATION	3. AIRCRAFT TYPE/ SPECIAL EQUIPMENT	4. TRUE AIRSPEED KTS	5. DEPARTURE POINT		6. DEPARTURE TIME PROPOSED (Z) | ACTUAL (Z)	7. CRUISING ALTITUDE
8. ROUTE OF FLIGHT							
9. DESTINATION (Name of airport and city)	10. EST. TIME ENROUTE HOURS | MINUTES		11. REMARKS				
12. FUEL ON BOARD HOURS | MINUTES	13. ALTERNATE AIRPORT (S)		14. PILOT'S NAME, ADDRESS & TELEPHONE NUMBER & AIRCRAFT HOME BASE				15. NUMBER ABOARD
16. COLOR OF AIRCRAFT	CLOSE VFR FLIGHT PLAN WITH_____FSS ON ARRIVAL						

FAA Form 7233-1 (5-72)   ☆ U.S. GOVERNMENT PRINTING OFFICE: 1975 - 671-921/561/7

FIG. 48.3—FLIGHT PLAN

/X   No transponder
/T   Transponder with no altitude encoding capability
/U   Transponder with altitude encoding capability
/D   DME, no transponder
/B   DME, transponder with no altitude encoding capability
/A   DME, transponder with altitude encoding capability

(Other suffixes for RNAV—Area Navigation)

FIG. 48.4—SPECIAL EQUIPMENT SUFFIXES

SECTION 48—FILING YOUR VFR FLIGHT PLAN

  (4) *True airspeed*—Enter your expected airspeed in KNOTS, as 87;
  (5) *Departure point*—Use the identifier code, such as UIN for Quincy, Illinois;
  (6) *Departure time*—Enter your departure time in Greenwich Mean Time (GMT) or (Z). If you are airborne when filing, give the actual or proposed departure time, as appropriate;
  (7) *Cruising altitude*—Enter the appropriate VFR altitude, to assist the FSS specialist in giving you wind and weather information;
  (8) *Route of flight*—Define your route of flight by using the navaid/identifier codes, or the names if you don't have the codes, as well as the airways. If any segment will be direct, use navaids to define your route, and use radials/bearings to define other unpublished routes;
  (9) enter the airport identifier code or the name of the airport, if you don't have the identifier. Include the name of the city (and state if there is any chance of confusion);
  (10) enter your estimated time en route (ETE), based on latest forecast winds;
  (11) these are normally comments relating to IFR flight plans;
  (12) insert the amount of fuel on board from your point of departure. Check the endurance profile for this computation.
  (13) the alternate airport is normally used for IFR flight plans but you can name one if you wish on a VFR flight plan;
  (14) enter your complete name, address and telephone number, and enough information to identify your home base, airport or FBO, all of which will be helpful if they have to look for you;
  (15) enter the *total* number of people on board;
  (16) enter the predominant colors of your plane.
6. You should give position reports from time to time as you progress on your flight;
  a. this is not required but is a good practice that could facilitate finding you if you are forced to land;
  b. such contacts permit the FSS to pass on significant information to you and also serve to check the progress of your flight in case it should become necessary to find you.
7. If you are making a "stopover" flight which you anticipate will cover an extended period of time, you should file separate flight plans for each leg when you expect the stop to be more than one hour's duration.
8. Notify the nearest FSS if at any time you change your destination, your ETA, or otherwise alter your flight plan.
9. Be sure to close your flight plan upon arrival;
  a. if there is a FSS on or close to the field, you can close your flight plan on the ground just after landing;
  b. if there is no FSS nearby but there is a VOR which is remoted to a FSS, you can close

it through the VOR by transmitting on 122.1 and receiving on the VOR frequency (be sure that *both* volumes are turned up);

   c. if there is no other way, you must find a telephone to the nearest FSS to close your flight plan;

      (1) be sure that you have the telephone number of the FSS;

      (2) many FBOs have a direct line to the FSS;

      (3) in a place like Cross City, Florida, you may have to pay a bundle to phone the FSS;

   d. a tower will not close your VFR flight plan automatically, so you should either close your flight plan with the FSS while you are in the air, contact the FSS through a VOR on or near the field, or telephone them immediately upon landing.

10. If you have failed to close your flight plan within 30 minutes of your ETA, a check of all local airports will be made to determine if your airplane has arrived there;

   a. this action will not happen if they have established communication with you, or if you have reported;

   b. if your airplane has not been located within one and one-half hours after your ETA, an extensive communications inquiry will be made throughout the flight range of your airplane;

   c. if the results of this inquiry are negative or your airplane has not been located within one hour after those inquiries were begun, the facilities of Search and Rescue (SAR) will be activated;

   d. your failure to close a flight plan will start an unnecessary search for you, with the consequent hazards to search pilots, and needless waste of thousands of dollars.

Section 49
MAKING YOUR CROSS-COUNTRY FLIGHT

1. Before taking off, have all your equipment and supplies well organized including the following:
    a. all necessary charts;
    b. your plotter and computer (or calculator);
    c. your flight plan;
    d. your flight log;
    e. your logbook, for signature at the destination airport;
    f. your Student Pilot Certificate and Medical Certificate;
    g. your FCC Radio Operator's License.
    h. a flashlight
2. Be sure you have taken all preflight procedures listed in Sec. 9 and 10.
3. After taking off, fly the normal departure pattern;
    a. you will probably be off course to begin with, due to the departure pattern for the runway in use;
    b. you may either take up a heading that will intercept your course, or, climb to at least 2,000 feet AGL and fly directly over the airport and then turn directly on course;
    c. go to your intended altitude and trim your airplane for level flight;
    d. hold the chart on your lap for easy access.
4. Even though you are busy, constantly:
    a. check your location;
    b. check for other airplanes;
    c. check your heading and altitude;
    d. check your engine instruments;
    e. listen to the radio for traffic in the area, and weather reports, etc.;
    f. reset your altimeter to conform to the report from the nearest FSS;
    g. reset your directional gyro every 15 minutes, or as needed, to conform to your magnetic compass.
5. In addition to the use of the radio and VOR, you should constantly check your course by *pilotage* (navigation of an airplane by reference to visible landmarks);
    a. the Sectional Charts identify the aeronautical and topographical symbols;
    b. as a student pilot, you should be familiar with these symbols, since cross-country

flying can be a very "busy" activity allowing little or no time to check the meaning of symbols.
6. In addition to your use of the radio, VOR and pilotage, you will also use *dead reckoning;*
    a. dead reckoning is the form of navigating an airplane wherein direction and distance are computed by reference to a known position;
    b. determine the actual ground speed from time to time;
       (1) place the distance flown over the elapsed time, on the computer;
       (2) read the ground speed above the speed index;
    c. if you know the direction and ground speed, it is relatively easy to know your approximate location at any time.
7. Well before you arrive at your destination:
    a. recheck the information about the airport, such as altitude, radio frequencies, etc.;
    b. if you have *Sky Prints,* The Jeppesen Directory of Airports, or similar maps, glance again at the layout of the runways and taxiways;
    c. begin your descent in sufficient time so that you are down to traffic pattern altitude prior to entering the traffic pattern;
    d. if there are radio facilities at the airport, call in well in advance;
    e. follow your usual pre-landing checklist, being particularly careful to return your mixture control to "full rich" in case you have leaned out your mixture at higher altitudes.
8. Take your logbook to the fixed base operator or other available personnel, and have them note therein a verification of your arrival at their airport, together with their signature.

Section 50
REQUIRED MANEUVERS AND HOW TO PERFORM THEM

1. During the check ride, you will be required to perform certain maneuvers, by reference to ground objects;
    a. these maneuvers are usually performed at traffic pattern altitude over a predetermined groundpath while you are required to divide your attention inside and outside your airplane;
    b. these maneuvers will be flown at 800 feet AGL and at regular cruise power.
2. One ground reference maneuver is known as *S-turns along a road;*

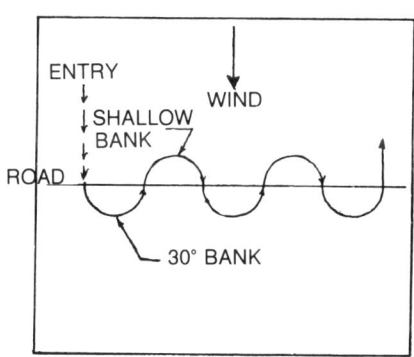

FIG. 50.1—S-TURNS ALONG A ROAD

   a. select a road that runs at right angles to the wind direction;
   b. enter the pattern on the upwind side of the road flying downwind;
      (1) after crossing the road, start a smooth, well coordinated turn;
   c. the steepest bank will be while on the downwind side of the road;
      (1) the *steepest* bank should be at least 30 degrees;
   d. the shallowest bank will occur on the upwind side of the road;
      (1) the amount of wind will determine the difference between the steepest and shallowest bank;

(2) the less wind, of course, the less difference there will be in the upwind bank and the downwind bank;
  e. vary your bank so that your track over the ground will be a series of perfect half circles;
  f. check your turn and bank indicator frequently to be sure that your turns are well coordinated;
  g. maintain your altitude to within 100 feet of the selected altitude;
  h. keep your distances from the road equal on both sides of the turn.
3. Another maneuver that you will practice is known as *eights along a road;*

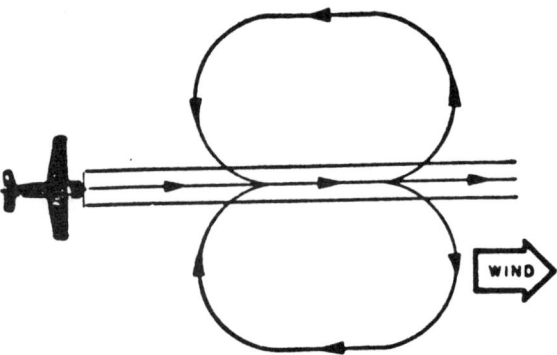

FIG. 50.2—EIGHTS ALONG A ROAD

  a. select a road parallel to the wind and go to 800 feet AGL;
  b. fly with the wind (downwind) above the road;
  c. execute a medium-banked 360-degree turn;
   (1) note that this brings you back over the road at a point downwind of the place where you entered the turn;
  d. in order to enter at the same point where you began the turn, you will have to fly straight, while flying parallel to the road and into the wind;
  e. make these turns in both directions.
4. A variation of the Eights Along a Road is the maneuver known as *eights across a road;*
  a. select the intersection of two roads;
  b. select a track over the ground so that the 8 crosses at the intersection of the roads;
  c. enter the pattern parallel to the road and downwind from the road;
   (1) the road used for the base of your maneuver will be that which is crosswind or perpendicular to the wind direction;
  d. maintain your altitude to within 100 feet of the selected altitude;
  e. be sure that all turns are smooth and coordinated;
  f. as in all turns, do not attempt to lean away from the turn;
   (1) instead, keep your body perpendicular to the wings of the airplane.
5. One of the maneuvers that you will be required to perform is the *rectangular course;*

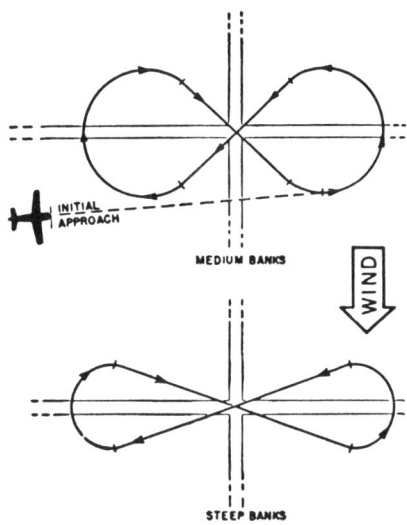

FIG. 50.3—EIGHT ACROSS A ROAD

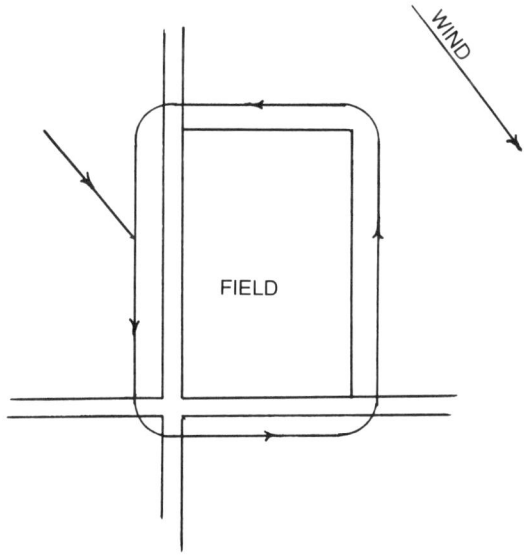

FIG. 50.4—RECTANGULAR COURSE

a. this simulates the traffic pattern and is primarily designed to teach you to correct for wind drift while in the pattern;
b. check the wind so you will be prepared in advance to correct for it;
c. select a rectangular pattern such as a field, preferably with a wind that is not blowing parallel to any of its sides;
d. you will be expected to fly around and outside the selected area;
e. enter at one corner of the field at a 45-degree angle to what will simulate a downwind leg in the traffic pattern;
f. on each leg of the rectangle, crab sufficiently into the wind so that you will remain parallel to each side of the rectangle;
   (1) avoid excessive maneuvering to correct for wind drift;
g. maintain the selected altitude to within ± 100 feet.

6. One of the maneuvers that you are required to demonstrate is *turns about a point;*

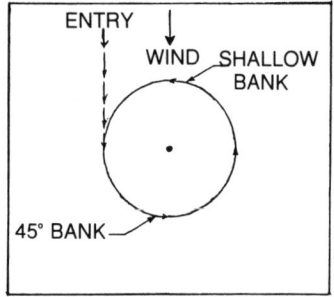

FIG. 50.5—TURNS ABOUT A POINT

a. select a prominent landmark, such as an intersection of a road, as your point;
b. enter the maneuver while flying downwind;
   (1) enter with a smoothly coordinated turn;
c. fix the radius of your turn so that your maximum angle of bank during the turn will be 45 degrees;
   (1) your maximum angle of bank will be while you are on the downwind side, because the wind is blowing you away from the point;
   (2) the minimum angle of bank will be while the airplane is on the upwind side;
d. constantly maintain your altitude to within ± 100 feet of your selected altitude;
e. keep your distance from the point constant at all times;
f. constantly refer to your needle and ball indicator to be sure that your turn is well coordinated;
   (1) if the ball is out of the center, correct the slip or skid by pushing on the rudder on the same side the ball is.

7. An advanced figure 8 maneuver is that which is known as *eights around pylons;*

SECTION 50—REQUIRED MANEUVERS AND HOW TO PERFORM THEM

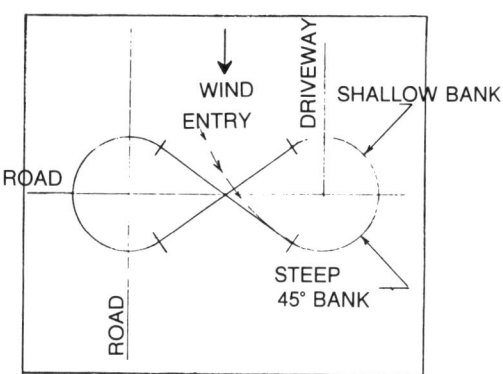

FIG. 50.6—EIGHTS AROUND PYLONS

a. select a road which is perpendicular to the wind and with suitable pylons along the road;
   (1) the pylons selected are prominent landmarks such as two road intersections;
   (2) the pylons should be about a half mile apart;
b. enter downwind, crossing the road at the point midway between the pylons;
c. be sure that all turns are well coordinated;
d. check the turn and bank indicator to assist in avoiding slips and skids;
e. the steepest angle of bank will be 45 degrees.
   (1) this will occur when you are on the downwind side;
f. while turning around the pylon, keep the distance from the pylon constant;
g. after turning three-fourths of a turn about a pylon, forget that one and find the other pylon;
   (1) fly the pattern so that you will cross the line between the pylons at a point equal distant between them, flying straight and level;
h. your flight should be straight and level at the place where the 8 crosses between the pylons;
   (1) crab into the wind to compensate for wind drift;
i. maintain your altitude to within ± 100 feet of your selected altitude.

Section 51
ACCIDENTS AND HOW TO AVOID THEM

1. Accidents can be avoided. But avoiding accidents requires a lot of thought and planning, and extreme caution *at all times.*
2. Your airplane is well designed and constructed. It will *never* be the cause of an accident if you maintain it properly;
    a. if you lease the airplane, check the aircraft and engine logbooks to be sure that it is being maintained properly;
    b. if you own the airplane that you are using, it is your responsibility to see that it has received its annual inspection and oil changes.
3. Comply strictly with the FARs.
4. Fly defensively;
    a. it is never safe to presume that all other pilots will observe all the rules, even assuming that *all* pilots *know* all the rules. Instead, *always* operate your airplane on the assumption that others around you will fly in violation of the rules;
    b. *never* relax your vigil while in flight;
        (1) keep a constant lookout for other aircraft;
        (2) check all the instruments frequently;
        (3) keep constantly alert for any changes in the weather, as well as any indications that there may be a change in the weather.
5. Never fly when you are fatigued;
    a. fatigue slows your reaction time and impairs your judgment;
    b. to avoid fatigue during flight:
        (1) get adequate rest prior to the flight;
        (2) avoid too long a flight in one day;
        (3) carry along candy or other quick-energy food;
        (4) keep active and mentally alert making ground checks, plotting your position with the aid of radio, VOR, etc.;
        (5) stop at an airport along the way to freshen up, walk around, etc.
6. No person may act as a crewmember of a civil aircraft within 8 hours after consumption of any alcoholic beverage or while under the influence of alcohol;
    a. nor may you act as a crewmember while using any drug that affects your faculties in any way contrary to safety;

SECTION 51—ACCIDENTS AND HOW TO AVOID THEM

   b. you may not allow anyone who is obviously under the influence of liquor or drugs to be carried in your plane, except in an emergency, and in the case of a medical patient under proper care.
7. Do not fly if you are not in good health;
   a. your possession of a medical certificate is some assurance of your good health but is far from conclusive;
   b. even though you have a valid medical certificate, you may not act as pilot in command while you have a known medical deficiency, or increase of a known medical deficiency that would make you unable to meet the requirements for your current medical certificate.
8. The use of drugs, even mild medications, can seriously impair your judgment and the coordination needed for flying;
   a. prior to and during a flight you should strictly refrain from using aspirin, antihistamines, cold tablets, cough mixtures, laxatives, tranquilizers and appetite suppressors.
9. Do not fly after SCUBA diving;
   a. while under water, the body absorbs excess nitrogen which can cause the bends at high altitudes if you have not let sufficient time elapse before takeoff.
10. Never run out of gas;
    a. this should never happen, if you will check your tanks—including the security of the caps—before leaving, and then stop for refueling at reasonable intervals during flight;
    b. running out of fuel is almost always the sign of flagrant negligence.
11. Avoid mid-air collisions by taking the following precautions *before* beginning your flight:
    a. obtain from the proper charts all the information pertinent to your route, such as headings, distances, checkpoints, altitudes, etc., and note them on your flight log;
    b. have all necessary charts folded in proper sequence and conveniently located in the cockpit;
    c. check all pertinent information in your *AIM,* with particular attention to NOTAMS and *Airport/Facility Directory* sections;
       (1) *all* radio frequencies to be used on your flight should be written on your flight log, for quick reference during your flight;
    d. note on your flight log all airport data and VFR procedures for approaches to busy air terminals, from the *AIM Airport Directory* and the *Airport/Facility Directory* sections;
    e. check your *Sectional Charts* carefully to be sure that your route will not cross any Prohibited, Restricted, Caution or Warning Areas. (See Sec. 19);
    f. check the Special Notices-Area section of your *AIM* before leaving for such notices as "Terminal Radar Service Areas" and "Terminal Area Notices."
12. Avoid mid-air collisions by taking the following precautions *during* flight:
    a. comply strictly with all the requirements discussed in this guide and related to taking off and landing your airplane;

b. constantly look around, *very* carefully, for other aircraft and particularly when in the traffic pattern;
   (1) this is especially true during landing, when it is very easy for another airplane to get into your blind spot, or you into his;
   (2) a special problem of blind spots occurs when a faster low-winged airplane approaches the airport from behind and above you, so he cannot see you;
   (3) strict adherence to a practice of making fairly sharp 90-degree turns onto base leg and onto final approach will reduce these dangers;
c. when leaving or approaching an airport, use your radio to advise others of your position and intentions;
d. while you are climbing or descending on Victor airways, fly to the right side of the center line of the radial forming the airway;
   (1) you will thus better avoid IFR and VFR cruising traffic operating along the center line of the airway;
e. be *extremely* careful in flying over and in the vicinity of a VOR facility;
   (1) a large proportion of the aircraft in cross-country flight converges over the VOR;
   (2) during a test period, 89 percent of the near mid-air collisions occurred over a VOR facility;
f. adhere strictly to the hemispherical rule, requiring you to maintain the proper altitude when more than 3,000 feet (see Sec. 16.7);
   (1) but don't place too much confidence in this protection since other aircraft may be traveling faster or slower, may be ascending or descending, or may have ignored the rule.

13. You should constantly study the rules of safe flying until they become part of your instinctive thinking. In addition to those in this section and throughout the book are the following:
   a. always maintain sufficient flying speed to avoid stalls, with a margin to spare;
   b. never let your haste to get there cause you to break any of the rules of safe flying;
   c. never take a chance on the weather. If in doubt, don't go, unless you have your instrument rating;
   d. never (absolutely never) do anything cute or brazen to show off or to prove something about yourself. These things only prove that you are stupid;
   e. never let your pride force you to do something that could increase your chances of having an accident. Pride can be fatal if it keeps you from making a 180-degree turn when you encounter bad weather;
   f. always avoid flying over large cities unless absolutely necessary, and then at sufficient altitude to permit a safe landing;
   g. never let yourself get caught in any situation where there isn't a way to get out safely;
   h. always fly enough to keep your proficiency. This is a lot more than most people think. Your ability to fly well deteriorates quickly when you are not flying.

Section 52
REPORTING ACCIDENTS AND NEAR COLLISIONS

1. The FAA is vitally interested in all near mid-air collision incidents;
    a. each reported incident is thoroughly investigated as soon as received.
2. You are urged to report accidents and near collisions as follows:
    a. contact the nearest FAA Air Traffic Control facility or FSS by radio;
    b. telephone report at your next point of landing, to the nearest FAA Air Traffic Control facility or FSS:
    c. write to the nearest Air Carrier District Office or General Aviation District Office.
3. Give them the following information, if available:
    a. date, time (GMT), location and altitude of incident;
    b. identification and type of reporting aircraft; aircrew destination; name and home base of pilot;
    c. identification and type of other aircraft; aircrew destination; name and home base of pilot;
    d. type of flight plans; station altimeter setting used;
    e. detailed weather conditions at flight altitude/level;
    f. approximate courses of both aircraft; indicate if one or both aircraft were climbing/descending;
    g. reported separation in distance at first sighting; proximity at closest point horizontally and vertically; length of time in sight prior to evasive action;
    h. degree of evasive action taken, if any (from both aircraft, if possible); injuries, if any.
4. If you are the *operator* of the airplane, you are required to notify the National Transportation Safety Board, Bureau of Aviation Safety Field Office when you have any of the following:
    a. an aircraft accident;
    b. flight control system malfunction or failure;
    c. inability of any required flight crewmember to perform his normal flight duties as a result of injury or illness;
    d. in-flight fire;
    e. aircraft collide in flight;
    f. an aircraft is overdue and is believed to have been involved in an accident.

5. The required notification shall include:
    a. type, nationality, and registration marks of the aircraft;
    b. name of owner, and operator of the aircraft;
    c. name of the pilot-in-command;
    d. date and time of the accident;
    e. last point of departure and point of intended landing of the aircraft;
    f. position of the aircraft with reference to some easily defined geographical point;
    g. number of persons aboard, number killed, and number seriously injured;
    h. nature of the accident including weather factors and the extent of damage to the aircraft so far as is known;
    i. a description of any explosives, radioactive materials, or other dangerous articles carried.

Section 53
KEEPING YOUR LOGBOOK

1. All pilots are required to keep a logbook, recording all aeronautical training and experience required to meet the requirements for (1) any certificate or rating, and (2) the recent flight experience requirements;
   a. while you are not required to log other flight time, it is a good idea to do so since your experience is also important for other purposes such as your insurance and additional ratings.
2. Your logbook should be a bound book, carefully maintained so that you meet the requirement that it be a reliable record of your flight time and should contain the following information for each flight:
   a. date and total time of the flight;
   b. place, or points of departure and arrival;
   c. type and identification of airplane;
   d. whether you flew as pilot-in-command, second-in-command or solo;
   e. the flight instruction received from an authorized flight instructor;
   f. any pilot ground trainer instruction received and other flight time;
   g. the conditions of flight, such as day or night, actual instrument and simulated instrument conditions.
3. As a student, you may log as solo flight only that flight time when you are the *sole occupant* of the airplane.
4. As a private pilot, you will be able to log as pilot-in-command only that flight time during which you are the sole manipulator of the controls of an aircraft for which you are rated or when you are the sole occupant of the aircraft or when you act as pilot-in-command of an aircraft on which more than one pilot is required under the type certification of the aircraft, or the regulations under which the flight is conducted.
5. There are special rules for logging flight time as second-in-command and instrument flight but they do not apply to the student pilot.
6. All time logged as flight instruction, instrument flight instruction, pilot ground trainer instruction, or ground instruction time must be certified by the appropriately rated and certificated instructor from whom it was received.

7. You are required to present your logbook for inspection upon reasonable request by the administrator, an authorized representative of the National Transportation Safety Board, or any State or local law enforcement officer.
8. As a student, you must carry your logbook with you on all solo cross-country flights, as evidence of the required instructor clearances and endorsements.

Section 54
GETTING READY FOR YOUR FLIGHT TEST

1. Before you can take your flight test for the Private Pilot Certificate, you must:
    a. have passed the written test since the beginning of the 24th before the month in which you take the flight test;
        (1) if you have lost your grade slip, you can send a telegram to Federal Aviation Agency, Oklahoma City, Oklahoma for a substitute;
    b. have the applicable instruction and aeronautical experience described in Sec. 1.7;
    c. hold a third class or better medical certificate issued since the beginning of the 24th month before the month in which you take the flight test;
    d. be at least 17 years of age;
    e. have a written statement from an appropriately certificated flight instructor on Application Form FAA 355, certifying that he has given you flight instruction in preparation for the flight test within 60 days preceding the date of application, and finds you are competent to pass the test and that you have satisfactory knowledge of the subject areas in which you are shown to be deficient by your FAA written test report;
    f. have your radio operator's license, Form 753 B issued by the FCC;
    g. if you failed an earlier flight test, you must have with you the Notice of Disapproval which you received.
2. You can take your flight test by any General Aviation District Office (GADO) or from an appropriately designated pilot examiner;
    a. your flight instructor will advise you the most readily available examiners;
    b. there is no charge for the flight test if it is given by an FAA inspector;
    c. any other flight examiner will make a reasonable charge for the test, which charge is payable whether you pass the test or not.
3. You are required to furnish the airplane used for the test;
    a. it must be of U.S. registry and have a current standard or limited airworthiness certificate.
4. The airplane you use must have:
    a. the equipment for each pilot operation required for the flight test (see Sec. 9.10 and 45.3);
    b. no prescribed operating limitations that prohibit its use in any pilot operation required on the test;

c. pilot seats with adequate visibility for each pilot to operate the airplane safely, except when you are flying under the hood;

d. engine power controls and flight controls that are easily reached and operable in a normal manner by both pilots.

5. You are required to furnish a hood for use during flight on instruments.
6. The examiner conducts the flight test in order to observe your ability to perform the procedures and maneuvers in a satisfactory manner;

    a. he is not the pilot-in-command during the flight test unless he acts in that capacity for the flight, or a portion of the flight, by prior arrangement with you.

7. If you fail the flight test, you may not apply for retesting for 30 days;

    a. however, you can apply for retesting within that period upon presenting a written statement from an authorized instructor certifying that he has given you flight or ground instruction as appropriate and finds that you are competent to pass the test.

8. When your flight instructor has certified that you are ready for your flight test, make an appointment with the examiner to take the test;

    a. be prepared to have the appointment cancelled one or more times because of bad weather or conflicts on the part of the examiner;

    b. be sure that the airplane you will use for the test will be available for a sufficient period the day of your test;

    c. be sure that the plane will have the required equipment for the test.

9. If the flight test will be taken at an airport other than that where you have received your instruction:

    a. make one or more cross-country flights to *that* airport *before* the day of the appointment;

        (1) if you have planned well in advance, these may have been cross-country flights taken earlier, in logging your needed cross-country time;

    b. make a number of takeoffs and landings of various kinds to familiarize yourself with the airport;

    c. study the runways and the taxiways, so that you feel comfortable in taxiing to and from the runways and are oriented to the traffic patterns for each runway;

    d. fly around the airport, studying the terrain, the roads, possible emergency landing areas, and the other information that you may need very quickly during a flight test.

10. Check with your instructor before the flight test to be sure that he has certified you for your cross-country flight.
11. Allow yourself plenty of time to check carefully to be sure that all necessary documents are in place in your airplane. They include:

    a. the *Pilot's Operating Handbook;*

    b. check lists;

    c. a registration certificate showing the present owner's name;

    d. an airworthiness certificate;

e. the aircraft logbook;
    (1) it must contain a certificate of a mechanic dated within the past 12 months that he has inspected the aircraft in accordance with the annual inspection and found it airworthy;
    (2) if the airplane is used commercially, it must have the same type of certificate entered within the last 100 hours of operation of that airplane;
f. an Aircraft Radio Station License;
g. weight and balance data;
h. your own Sectional Chart (and possibly those for nearby areas);

12. On the day of your appointment, go to the airport well in advance of your appointment, allowing enough time to get ready, make final checks and still arrive well in advance of the time of your appointment.

13. It is possible that, with you and your instructor, your airplane will exceed the maximum weight, if your gas tanks are full;
    a. check the weight and balance data and see if you and a large adult male passenger can ride in the plane if its tanks are full. If not, arrange to have them at the required levels before the flight test begins.

14. Arrive early for your appointment, make your presence known and make the best use of the remaining time;
    a. make a check of the wind direction and velocity and its effect on the selection of the preferred runway, the runway(s) to be used for crosswind takeoffs and landings, as well as your selection of a field, etc. for forced landings;
    b. check the forecast winds aloft so that you are mentally ready for the wind when you perform your flight maneuvers.

15. There are a few points that give many students difficulty. Some of them are:
    a. be sure to make clearing turns before maneuvers; be sure that you are at sufficient altitude;
    b. *always* keep in mind the direction of the wind, and be oriented as to your direction, so that you are prepared, without notice, to pick a field and proceed to make an emergency landing;
    c. pay special attention to your coordination of aileron and rudder on all your turns;
    d. before taking off on the flight test, check to be sure that the gyro compass is properly set;
        (1) from time to time while in straight and level flight, check to be sure during your flight test, that the gyro compass is correct.

16. One of the more important things is to develop a proper frame of mind;
    a. your instructor would not have certified you for the flight test unless he was completely confident that you could pass it;
    b. the best frame of mind is positive thinking. It tells you that you *can*. The only thing that can defeat you is a negative approach.

SECTION 55—YOUR FLIGHT TEST

Section 55
YOUR FLIGHT TEST

1. You will not merely be required to duplicate on your flight test the maneuvers you learned in training:
    a. you will be required to demonstrate competency in all *pilot operations* listed in Sec. 1.7;
    b. your instructor is permitted to select procedures and maneuvers from FAA approved training publications pertinent to the Private Pilot Certificate;
    c. your instructor must endorse in your logbook that you have demonstrated competency in all the required pilot operations and that he considers you to be qualified to pass the flight test.
2. On the flight test, the examiner will select the procedures and maneuvers that you are to perform to show competency in each *pilot operation;*
    a. you do not have to be tested on *every* procedure or maneuver within each pilot operation, but only those that your examiner considers necessary to determine your competency in each pilot operation;
    b. if, in the judgment of your examiner, certain demonstrations are impractical (such as night flying or equipment malfunction) he may determine your competency in those areas by oral testing;
    c. emphasis will be placed on procedures, knowledge and maneuvers which are most critical to a safe performance as a pilot;
    d. the demonstration of prompt stall recognition, adequate control, and recovery techniques will receive special attention;
    e. other areas of importance include spatial disorientation, collision avoidance and wake turbulence hazards.
3. You will be expected to know the meaning and significance of the airplane performance speeds important to the pilot, and be able readily to determine those speeds for the airplane you are using (see Sec. 17).
4. Your ability to perform the required pilot operations is based on the following:
    a. executing procedures and maneuvers within the aircraft's performance capabilities and limitations, including the use of the aircraft's systems;
    b. executing emergency procedures and maneuvers appropriate to the aircraft;

c. piloting the aircraft with smoothness and accuracy;
d. exercising judgment;
e. applying aeronautical knowledge;
f. showing mastery of the aircraft, with the successful outcome of a procedure never seriously in doubt.

5. If you fail any of the required pilot operations, you have failed the flight test;
   a. either you or the examiner can discontinue the test at any time when the failure of a required pilot operation makes you ineligible for your Private Pilot Certificate;
   b. if the test is discontinued, you are entitled to credit for only those entire pilot operations that you have successfully performed;
   c. therefore, even if you fail to pass one portion, seek to complete as much of the test as possible since that will mean that much less to prepare for and complete on re-examination.

6. You will be asked to present appropriate pilot and medical certificates and to locate and explain the airplane's registration certificate, airworthiness certificate, operating manual, airplane equipment list, and required weight and balance data;
   a. you must be able to explain the airplane and engine logbooks or other maintenance records;
   b. you must be knowledgeable regarding the location, purpose and significance of each required item.

7. You may be orally quizzed on the performance capabilities, approved operating procedures and limitations of your airplane;
   a. this includes normal power settings, critical and recommended speeds, and fuel and oil requirements (Sec. 7);
   b. you should use the manufacturer's recommendations to determine the effects of temperature, pressure altitude, wind, and gross weight on the airplane's performance. (Sec. 17.3);
   c. you will be evaluated on your ability to obtain, explain and apply the information that is essential in determining the performance capabilities and limitations of the plane you are using.

8. You may be asked to demonstrate the application of the approved weight and balance data for your airplane to determine that the gross weight and center of gravity location are within allowable limits (Sec. 8);
   a. you may use the charts and graphs provided by the manufacturer;
   b. your performance will be evaluated on your ability to determine the empty weight, CG, maximum allowable gross weight, useful load (fuel, passengers, baggage) by reference to appropriate publications, and your ability to apply this information to determine that the gross weight and CG are within approved limits.

9. You may be asked to demonstrate knowledge of how to select weather information that is pertinent and how best to obtain this information (Sec. 39);

a. you must show ability to interpret and understand its significance with respect to the proposed flight.
10. You may be asked to demonstrate a visual inspection to determine the airplane's airworthiness and readiness for flight (Sec. 10);
    a. this includes all required equipment and documents;
    b. you should use the manufacturer's checklist;
    c. you must use an orderly procedure in conducting the preflight check of the airplane and must know the significance of each item checked and recognize any unsafe condition.
11. You may be asked to demonstrate a visual inspection to determine that the fuel is of the proper grade and type and the supply of fuel, oil and other required fluids is adequate for the proposed flight (Sec. 7);
    a. you should take appropriate action to eliminate possible fuel contamination in the airplane (Sec. 7.3);
    b. you must know the grade and type of oil and fuel specified for your airplane and be able to determine the amount of fuel required to complete the flight (Sec. 7);
    c. you must know where to find all the fuel and oil filters, the capacity of each tank, and the location of the battery, hydraulic fluid reservoirs, anti-icing fluid tanks, etc., and must know the proper steps for avoiding fuel contamination during and following the servicing (Sec. 4 & 7).
12. You may be asked to demonstrate a check to determine that the engine is operating within acceptable limits and that all systems, equipment and controls are functioning properly and are adjusted for takeoff (Sec. 13);
    a. for this purpose, you should use the manufacturer's checklist;
    b. you must use proper procedures in engine starting and runup and in checking the airplane's systems, equipment and controls to determine that the airplane is ready for flight (Sec. 13);
    c. careless operation in close proximity to obstructions, ground personnel, or other aircraft will be disqualifying.
13. You may be asked to demonstrate the use of designated frequencies and recommended voice procedures to report your position and state your intentions as well as to obtain information and clearances (Sec. 29 & 30);
    a. where applicable, you are expected to use Airport Terminal Information Service (ATIS) (Sec. 35), Airport Advisory Service, (Sec. 29), Control Tower (Sec. 31), Approach and Departure Control, (Sec. 31), UNICOM, (Sec. 29.7), and ATC signal lights (Sec. 31.8);
    b. you must determine the type of communication facilities available, and use the appropriate necessary information;
    c. if you fail to comply with airport traffic procedures or instructions without permission to do so you will be disqualified.

14. Where available, you may be asked to demonstrate the proper use of wind and traffic direction indicators, and markings indicating closed runways, displaced thresholds, taxiways, holding lines, and basic runways (Sec. 25);
    a. you are also expected to be familiar with taxiway and runway lighting (Sec. 26.5), rotating beacons (Sec. 26.2), obstruction lights (Sec. 26.4), and VASI (Visual Approach Slope Indicator) (Sec. 26.7);
    b. you must know the meaning of standard wind and traffic indicators, markings and lighting (Sec. 25), and how they relate to airplane operation;
    c. failure to use these aids properly, creating an unsafe situation, will disqualify you.
15. You may be asked to demonstrate safe operating practices while in close proximity to other aircraft, persons or obstructions;
    a. emphasis should be placed on the use of brakes and power to control taxi speeds, proper positioning of the flight controls for existing wind conditions, awareness of possible ground hazards, and compliance with taxi procedures and instructions (Sec. 12);
    b. you must maneuver your airplane on the surface without endangering persons or property or conflicting with the smooth and orderly flow of traffic.
16. You may be asked to demonstrate prescribed arrival and departure procedures (Sec. 14 & 27);
    a. you are expected to maintain appropriate altitudes, airspeeds and ground track consistent with instructions received or the established traffic pattern;
    b. your performance will be evaluated on your ability to maneuver the airplane relative to the runway in use;
    c. you must give consideration to the application of wind drift correction, adequate spacing in relation to other aircraft, and maintaining and controlling altitude and airspeed;
    d. any deviation of $\pm$ 100 feet from the prescribed traffic altitudes of of $\pm$ 10 knots from the recommended airspeeds will be considered disqualifying unless corrected promptly.
17. You are expected to exercise continuous surveillance of the airspace in which you are operating, to guard against potential mid-air collisions (Sec. 51);
    a. you must use adequate clearing procedures before executing maneuvers which involve rapid altitude and heading changes;
    b. you must perform whatever clearing is necessary to ascertain that the area is clear before you perform maneuvers such as stalls, flight at critically slow airspeeds, etc.;
    c. you must not delay in entering a maneuver after completing the clearing turns;
    d. you can accomplish this by performing the necessary conditions of flight (such as reducing airspeed, adding carburetor heat, etc.) while you are in the clearing turns;
    e. in addition to "see and avoid" practices, you are expected to use VFR Advisory

Service at nonradar facilities, Airport Advisory Service at nontower airports or FSS locations, and Radar Traffic Information Service, where available;
  f. you must maintain continuous vigilance for other aircraft and take immediate actions to avoid any situation which would result in a mid-air collision;
  g. you must take extra precautions, particularly in areas of congested traffic, to ensure that your view of other aircraft is not obstructed by your airplane's structure;
  h. when you are using the traffic advisory service, you must understand the terminology used by the radar controller in reporting the positions of other aircraft (Sec. 33.8);
  i. Your failure to maintain proper surveillance will disqualify you.
18. You may be asked to explain how, where, and when wingtip vortices are generated and what are their characteristics and associated hazards (Sec. 22);
  a. you must follow recommended courses of action to remain clear of these hazards;
  b. you must identify the conditions and locations in which wingtip vortices may be encountered and adjust your flight path to avoid these areas.
  c. Failure to follow recommended procedures for avoiding the hazards of wingtip vortices can disqualify you.

Section 56
FLYING YOUR CHECK RIDE

1. *"S" TURNS ACROSS A ROAD.* (Sec. 50.2). You may be asked to demonstrate a series of "S" turns across a straight ground reference line approximately perpendicular to the wind;
    a. you should plan your bank variations to compensate for the wind so that each half circle is equal on opposite sides of the line;
    b. at each reversal of direction, you should cross the selected line at a 90 degree angle with the wings level;
    c. you should maintain a constant altitude throughout the maneuver;
    d. you must readily select ground references and maneuver the airplane in relation to these references;
    e. you are required to demonstrate coordinated turns, smooth control usage and division of attention;
    f. any deviation of $\pm$ 100 feet from the selected attitude shall be considered disqualifying unless you correct it promptly;
    g. excessively steep banks, flight below minimum safe altitude prescribed by the FARs, or inadequate clearance of other aircraft shall be disqualifying.
2. *EIGHTS ALONG OR ACROSS A ROAD.* (Sec. 50.3). You may be asked to maneuver along a ground track starting above and parallel to a road, then perform 360° turns left and right:
    a. This is known as "eights along a road" or "eights across a road";
    b. you are expected to vary the bank to correct for wind to arrive back over the road at a starting point upon completion of each 360 degree turn;
    c. the ground track should be in the form of a figure 8;
    d. you may be asked to perform a similar ground track maneuver starting over the intersection of two roads or some point on a road;
    e. the turns should be made so the intersection or point, which forms the center of the "8" is crossed in straight-and-level flight;
    f. you should maintain a constant altitude throughout the maneuver;
    g. you must maneuver the airplane so the loops of the "8" are symmetrical;
    h. your performance will be evaluated on proper wind drift correction, airspeed control coordination, altitude control and vigilance for other aircraft;

i. excessively steep banks, flight below minimum safe altitude prescribed by the FARs, or inadequate clearance of other aircraft shall be disqualifying.
3. *RECTANGULAR COURSE.* (Sec. 50.5). You may be asked to follow a rectangular or square course around and outside a selected area;
    a. you are expected to correct for wind drift so the ground track is parallel to the sides of the selected area and equidistant from each side;
    b. you should maintain a constant altitude throughout the maneuver;
    c. this pattern should be performed to the right and to the left;
    d. you must readily select the ground reference and maintain the desired tract in relation to that reference;
    e. you are required to demonstrate properly coordinated turns, smooth control usage and division of attention;
    f. deviation of ±100 feet from the selected altitude shall be considered disqualifying unless corrected promptly;
    g. excessive maneuvering to correct for wind drift, flight below minimum safe altitude prescribed by the FARs, or inadequate clearance from other aircraft shall be disqualifying.
4. *TURNS ABOUT A POINT.* (Sec. 50.6). You may be asked to perform a ground track maneuver in which a constant radius of turn is maintained by varying the bank to compensate for wind drift, so as to circle and maintain a uniform distance from a prominent reference point on the ground;
    a. you should maintain a constant altitude throughout the maneuver;
    b. this maneuver should be performed to the right and to the left;
    c. you must maneuver your airplane so that the ground track is a constant distance from the reference point;
    d. your performance will be evaluated on proper wind drift correction, airspeed control, coordination, altitude control, and vigilance for other aircraft;
    e. deviation of more than ±100 feet from the selected altitude shall be considered disqualifying unless corrected promptly;
    f. excessively steep banks, flight below minimum safe altitude prescribed by the FARs, or inadequate clearance from other aircraft shall be disqualifying.
5. *EIGHTS AROUND PYLONS.* (Sec. 50.7). You may be requested to perform right and left turns around two ground reference points or pylons;
    a. a turn should be made in each direction, varying bank to correct for wind drift, resulting in a constant distance from each point;
    b. the ground track should be in the form of a figure "8";
    c. you must maneuver your airplane so that both loops of the "8" are of equal size;
    d. your performance will be evaluated on proper wind drift correction, airspeed control, coordination, altitude control and vigilance for other aircraft;

e. deviation of ±100 feet from the selected altitude shall be considered disqualifying unless corrected promptly;

f. excessively steep banks, flight below minimum safe altitude prescribed by the FARs, or inadequate clearance from other aircraft shall be disqualifying.

6. *FLIGHT AT CRITICALLY SLOW AIRSPEEDS (SLOW FLIGHT).* (Sec. 23). You may be asked to maneuver in various configurations and at such airspeeds that controllability is minimized to the point that if the angle of attack is increased by an increase in load factor or a decrease in airspeed, an immediate stall would result;

   a. you will be evaluated on your ability to establish the minimum controllable airspeed, to positively control the airplane, to use proper torque corrections, and to recognize incipient stalls;

   b. primary emphasis will be placed on airspeed control;

   c. during straight-and-level flight at this speed, you must maintain altitude within ±100 feet and heading within ±10 degrees of that assigned by the examiner;

   d. inadequate surveillance of the area prior to and during the maneuver or an unintentional stall induced by your own actions shall be disqualifying.

7. *IMMINENT STALLS.* (Sec. 23). You may be asked to demonstrate recoveries from imminent stalls entered from straight flight and from turning flight with power-on or power-off;

   a. you are expected to place the airplane in the attitude and configuration appropriate for flight situations such as takeoffs, departures, landing approaches, and accelerated maneuvers, as directed by the examiner;

   b. you should apply control pressures which result in an increase in angle of attack until the first buffeting or decay of control effectiveness is noted;

   c. your recovery should be accomplished immediately be reducing the angle of attack with coordinated use of flight and power controls;

   d. you must recognize the indication of an imminent stall and take prompt, positive control action to prevent a full stall;

   e. you will be disqualified if a full stall occurs or if it becomes necessary for the examiner to take control of the airplane to avoid excessive airspeed, excessive loss of altitude, or a spin.

8. *FULL STALLS.* (Sec. 23). You may be asked to demonstrate recoveries from full stalls entered from straight flight and from turning flight with power-on or power-off;

   a. you are expected to establish the altitude and configuration for flight situations such as takeoffs and departures, landing approaches, and accelerated maneuvers;

   b. then, you will increase your angle of attack smoothly until a stall occurs, as indicated by a sudden loss of control effectiveness or uncontrollable pitching;

   c. you should accomplish recovery by reducing the angle of attack immediately, and positively regaining normal flight attitude with coordinated use of flight and power controls;

d. you are expected to be aware of the loss of altitude necessary to recover from a stabilized high rate of descent with the elevator control fully back, if this condition is encountered before a stall develops;

e. you must recognize when the stall has occurred and take prompt action to prevent a prolonged stalled condition;

f. you will be disqualified if a secondary stall occurs or if it becomes necessary for the examiner to take control of the airplane to avoid excessive airspeed, excessive loss of altitude, or a spin.

9. *NORMAL AND CROSSWIND TAKEOFFS.* (Sec. 14). You may be asked to demonstrate normal and crosswind takeoffs by aligning the airplane with the runway or takeoff surface and applying takeoff power smoothly and positively while maintaining directional control;

   a. you should establish pitch attitude to permit normal acceleration to the manufacturer's recommended lift-off speed and then smoothly increased to establish a straight climb at the desired climb speed;

   b. you may be asked to make at least one crosswind takeoff with sufficient crosswind to require the use of crosswind techniques, but not in excess of the crosswind limitations of your airplane;

   c. in the crosswind takeoff, you are expected to hold aileron into the wind and maintain a straight path by use of your rudder;

   d. these crosswind corrections should be maintained until after lift-off and the airplane is then crabbed into the wind to prevent drift;

   e. your performance of normal and crosswind takeoffs will be evaluated on application of power and flight controls, directional control, coordination and smoothness in establishing lift-off and climb;

   f. you must maintain a track aligned with the runway and a climb speed within ± 5 knots of the desired climb speed after lift-off.

10. *NORMAL AND CROSSWIND LANDINGS.* (Sec. 27). You may be asked to demonstrate normal and crosswind landings;

    a. normal landings should be made using a final approach speed which is 60–70 KIAS with flaps up, or 55–65 KIAS with flaps down;

    b. you should take action to reduce power progressively so that the throttle is closed when the desired touchdown point is assured or while rounding out for touchdown;

    c. you may be asked to make landings with full flaps, partial flaps or no flaps;

    d. forward slips and slips-to-a-landing may be performed with or without flaps unless prohibited by the airplane's operation limitations;

    e. your touchdown should be on the main wheels with little or no weight on the nosewheel;

    f. you must maintain adequate corrections and positive directional control during the after-landing roll;

    g. you may be asked to make at least one crosswind landing with sufficient crosswind

to require the use of crosswind techniques but not to exceed the crosswind limitations of your airplane;
- h. in crosswind conditions, wind drift corrections should be made throughout the final approach and touchdown;
- i. you may be asked to discontinue a landing approach at any point and execute a go-around;
- j. your performance of normal and crosswind landings will be evaluated on the basis of your landing technique, judgment, wind drift correction, coordination, power techniques and smoothness;
- k. you must maintain proper approach speed within ± 5 knots and touchdown in the proper landing attitude within the portion of the runway or landing area specified by the examiner;
- l. touching down with an excessive side load on the landing gear or poor directional control shall be disqualifying;
- m. on go-arounds, you must maintain positive airplane control and appropriate airspeeds.

11. *BASIC MANEUVERS ON INSTRUMENTS.* (Sec. 44). You may be asked to demonstrate your ability to control and maneuver your airplane solely by reference to flight instruments while performing straight-and-level flight, turns, climbs and descents, and while recovering from critical flight attitudes;
    - a. your performance will be evaluated on coordination, smoothness and accuracy;
    - b. you must perform turns at least 180 degrees to within ±20 degrees of the preselected heading, and climbs and descents to within ±100 feet of a preselected altitude;
    - c. you will be disqualified if the examiner finds it necessary to take over to avoid a stall or to avoid exceeding the operating limitations of the airplane.

12. *USE OF RADIO AIDS.* Under simulated conditions, you will be asked to follow a VOR radial (Sec. 36), or "home" to a radio station, (Sec. 37), using ADF (Automatic Direction Finder) as appropriate to the radio equipment in your airplane;
    - a. no prescribed orientation procedure will be required;
    - b. you must follow a radial or "home" to a station while effectively controlling altitude, heading and airspeed.

13. *USE OF RADAR OR DF HEADING INSTRUCTIONS.* You may be asked to demonstrate the proper procedures for contacting Approach Control or Flight Service Stations to request emergency assistance;
    - a. you should be able to follow radar (Sec. 33), or DF (Sec. 41), heading instructions while in simulated instrument conditions. (Sec. 44);
    - b. your performance will be evaluated on your ability to obtain and follow radar or DF heading instructions and emergency approach assistance received by radio, while effectively controlling altitude, heading and airspeed.

14. *PLANNING THE CROSS-COUNTRY FLIGHT.* (Sec. 47). You may be asked to plan a cross-country flight to a point at least 2 hours away at the cruising speed of your airplane;
    a. you must include at least one intermediate stop;
    b. your planning should include the obtaining of pertinent and available weather information, plotting the course on an aeronautical chart, selecting checkpoints, measuring distances, and computing flight time, headings and fuel requirements;
    c. you should use the *Airman's Information Manual (AIM)* as a reference for airport information, NOTAMS, and other appropriate guidance as may be extracted from its contents;
    d. all flight planning operations shall be meaningful, accurate and applicable to the trip proposed;
    e. you must explain the plan for the flight, verify the calculations and present the sources of your information and data.
15. *CONDUCT OF PLANNED FLIGHT.* (Sec. 49). You may be asked to perform the planned flight using pilotage, dead reckoning, and VOR and ADF radio aids as appropriate to the equipment in the airplane;
    a. you should make good the desired track, determine your position by reference to landmarks, and calculate estimated times of arrival (ETA) over checkpoints;
    b. you may also be asked to "home" to a radio station using ADF, recognize station passage, and determine your position by means of cross-bearings;
    c. you should set out on the cross-country flight that you planned before takeoff;
    d. you should follow the planned course at least until you have established the compass heading necessary to stay on course and can give a reasonable estimate of ground speed and time of arrival at the first point of intended landing;
    e. you must (1) establish and maintain headings required to stay on course, (2) correctly identify your position, (3) provide reasonable estimates of times of arrival over checkpoints and destination with an apparent error of not more than 10 minutes, and (4) maintain altitude within ±200 feet of the planned altitude;
    f. when requested by the examiner to divert to an alternate airport, as might be necessary to avoid adverse weather, you are expected to turn to the new course promptly;
    g. this may be accomplished by means of pilotage, dead reckoning or radio navigation aids;
    h. you must establish an appropriate heading for the course to the alternate airport and within a reasonable time to give an acceptable estimate of the flying time and required fuel.
16. *MAXIMUM PERFORMANCE TAKEOFFS, SHORT FIELD TAKEOFF AND MAXIMUM CLIMB.* (Sec. 14). You may be asked to demonstrate a takeoff from a short takeoff area and over simulated obstacles:
    a. power should be applied promptly and smoothly, and the airplane rotated to liftoff just as the best angle-of-climb airspeed is attained;

b. you are expected to maintain that speed until the assumed obstacles have been cleared;

c. you are expected to know and understand the effectiveness of the best angle-of-climb airspeed and the best rate-of-climb airspeed of your airplane to obtain maximum climb performance;

d. your performance will be evaluated on the basis of planning, smoothness and directional control and accuracy;

e. the liftoff and climb must be performed within ±5 knots of the best angle-of-climb speed and assumed obstacle cleared by a safe margin.

17. *SHORT FIELD LANDING.* (Sec. 27). You may be asked to demonstrate a landing from over an assumed 50-foot obstacle;

   a. the final approach speed should result in little or no floating after the throttle is closed during the flare for touchdown;

   b. the airplane should clear the obstacle by a safe margin and touchdown within the area designated by the examiner, at minimum controllable airspeed;

   c. upon touchdown, you are expected to properly apply brakes to minimize the after-landing roll;

   d. power, flaps, or moderate slips may be used as necessary on the last segment of the final approach;

   e. your performance will be evaluated on planning, coordination, smoothness and accuracy;

   f. you must control the angle of descent and airspeed on final approach so that the assumed obstacle is safely cleared and floating is minimized during the flare;

   g. after touchdown, you must bring your airplane smoothly to a stop within the shortest possible distance consistent with safety.

18. *SOFT FIELD TAKEOFF.* (Sec. 14). You may be asked to demonstrate a takeoff from a simulated soft field;

   a. you should accomplish this with the wing at a relatively high angle-of-attack so as to transfer the weight from the wheels to the wing as soon as possible;

   b. as soon as the elevators become effective a positive angle-of-attack should be established to lighten the load on the nosewheel;

   c. after becoming airborne, you should adjust the pitch attitude with the wheels just clear of the surface to allow the airplane to accelerate;

   d. be sure to exercise care to prevent settling back to the ground;

   e. as your airplane reaches the best angle-of-climb or best rate-of-climb airspeed, whichever is appropriate for the field conditions, adjust the pitch attitude to maintain the desired climb speed;

   f. the flap setting used should be in accordance with the manufacturer's recommendations;

g. your performance will be evaluated on planning, directional control, smoothness and accuracy;

h. you must lift off at a speed not higher than the power-off stalling speed and maintain the proper climb speed within ± 5 knots.

19. *SOFT FIELD LANDING.* (Sec. 27). You may be asked to demonstrate a simulated soft field landing from a normal approach with touchdown at the lowest possible airspeed to permit the softest possible touchdown and a short landing roll;

   a. you should maintain a nose-high attitude during the after-landing roll and retract the flaps promptly, to prevent damage from mud or slush thrown by the wheels;

   b. your performance will be evaluated on planning, smoothness and accuracy;

   c. you must maintain the final approach airspeed within ± 5 knots of that prescribed;

   d. you must exercise extreme caution and maintain positive control during flap retraction.

20. *NIGHT FLYING.* (Sec. 45). You may be asked to demonstrate how to prepare for a local or cross-country night flight;

   a. this requires familiarity with (1) airport lighting, (2) the airplane's lighting system and its operation, (3) the need for a personal flashlight, and (4) the weather conditions pertinent to night flight;

   b. you should give particular attention to the temperature/dewpoint spread due to the possibility of ground fog forming during night flights;

   c. you must explain the significance of the items peculiar to the preparation for night flights;

   d. you may be required to give an actual demonstration of takeoffs and landings at night;

   e. if required, you are expected to explain and/or demonstrate (1) proper use of power during the approach and landing phase, (2) efficient use of landing lights, (3) safe climb and approach paths, (4) safe taxi speeds, (5) recognition of position relative to other aircraft by the location and color of their lights, and (6) the dangers of spatial disorientation;

   f. if an actual demonstration is not required, the foregoing requirement may be satisfied by oral quizzing;

   g. your performance will be evaluated on your ability to explain or demonstrate, as required by the examiner, the various techniques and aspects of night takeoffs and landings;

   h. you will be required to demonstrate an understanding of the importance of constant vigilance for other aircraft on the ground and in the air and the precautions necessary to avoid wake turbulence and spatial disorientation;

   i. you may be required to give an actual demonstration of night navigation. If so required, you are expected to follow procedures similar to those described above under cross-country flying. If an actual night demonstration is not required, the foregoing may be satisfied by a daylight demonstration or oral quizzing;

j. your performance will be evaluated on the same principles outlined above under cross-country flying, with special emphasis on night flying.
21. *PARTIAL OR COMPLETE POWER MALFUNCTION.* You may be asked to demonstrate a knowledge of corrective actions for: (1) partial loss of power (Sec. 42.1), (2) complete engine failure (Sec. 42.2), (3) rough engine (Sec. 42.1), (4) carburetor or induction system ice (Sec. 21.1), (5) fuel starvation (Sec. 42.3), and (6) fire in the engine compartment. (Sec. 42.4);
    a. the examiner may, with no advance warning, reduce power to simulate engine malfunction;
    b. your performance will be evaluated on the basis of your prompt analysis of the situation and the remedial course of action;
    c. the emergency procedures shall be performed in compliance with the manufacturer's recommendations;
    d. any action which creates unnecessary additional hazards shall be disqualifying.
22. *SYSTEMS OR EQUIPMENT MALFUNCTIONS.* You may be asked to demonstrate a knowledge of corrective actions for: (1) inoperative electrical system (generator, alternator, battery or circuit breaker) (Sec. 42.5), (2) electrical fire or smoke in cockpit, (Sec. 42.6), (3) flap malfunction (Sec. 42.8), (4) door opening in flight, (Sec. 42.9), and (5) inoperative elevator trim tab. (Sec. 42.10;
    a. When practicable, the examiner may, with no advance warning, simulate flap malfunctions, or an inoperative electrical system;
    b. you are expected actually to perform the recommended emergency procedures for the simulated malfunction;
    c. your performance will be evaluated on your prompt analysis of the situation and your remedial course of action;
    d. the emergency procedure shall be in compliance with the manufacturer's recommendations;
    e. any action which creates unnecessary additional hazards shall be disqualifying.
23. *LOST PROCEDURES.* You may be asked to explain the proper course of action to be taken if you become lost (Sec. 40), are trapped on top of an overcast (Sec. 39.18), have lost radio communications (Sec. 40.8), or encounter unanticipated adverse weather. (Sec. 29.22);
    a. your performance will be evaluated on your ability promptly and correctly to analyze the situation and describe the appropriate remedial action.
24. *WHEN YOU PASS THE CHECK RIDE.* When your flight examiner determines that you have passed the check ride, he will issue a temporary Private Pilot Certificate;
    a. this is good for 90 days;
    b. your permanent Private Pilot Certificate will be mailed to you in about 3 weeks;
    c. there is no charge for the Private Pilot Certificate.

Section 57
AFTER YOU GET YOUR PRIVATE PILOT CERTIFICATE

1. Whenever you act as pilot-in-command, be sure that you have your Private Pilot Certificate and your Third Class Medical Certificate in your possession;
    a. your Third Class Medical Certificate expires at the end of the 24th month after it is issued;
    b. you may not act as pilot-in-command or in any other capacity as a required pilot flight crewmember while you have a known medical deficiency that makes you unable to meet the requirements for your current medical certificate;
    c. your Private Pilot Certificate will not expire but can be suspended or revoked for violation of the FARs;
    d. you can obtain a replacement for a lost or destroyed airman certificate by sending a letter to the DOT, FAA, Airman Certification Branch, P.O. Box 25082, Oklahoma City, Oklahoma 73125, informing them of your name, permanent mailing address with Zip Number, your Social Security number, date and place of birth, and all available information about the grade, number and date of issue of the certificate and ratings on it, together with your check or money order for $2.00;
    e. you can obtain a replacement of a lost or destroyed medical certificate by sending your check or money order for $2.00 to DOT, FAA, Aeronautical Certification Branch, P.O. Box 25082, Oklahoma City, Oklahoma 73125;
    f. you can obtain a telegram from the FAA confirming the issuance of a lost or destroyed airman certificate or medical certificate, good for 60 days.
        (1) you obtain this by a request or prepaid telegram. See FAR 61.29(c);
    g. if you move your permanent address, your pilot certificate expires in 30 days unless you notify the Airman Certification Branch in writing. (See Paragraph d. above).
2. Your certificate permits you to fly a single engine aircraft, land;
    a. you may not be permitted to act as pilot-in-command of any of the following unless you hold a type rating for that aircraft: A large aircraft (except lighter-than-air), a helicopter, for operations requiring an airline transport pilot certificate, a turbo-jet powered airplane, or other aircraft specified by the administrator through aircraft type certificate procedures;
    b. you may not act as pilot-in-command of an airplane that has more than 200 horse-

power, or that has a retractable gear, flaps and a controllable propeller, unless you have received instruction from an authorized flight instructor who has certified in your logbook that you are competent to pilot an airplane that has more than 200 horsepower, or that has a retractable landing gear, flaps, and a controllable propeller, as the case may be;
- (1) this requirement does not apply if you logged flight time as pilot-in-command in high performance airplanes before Nov. 1, 1973.

3. As a private pilot you may not carry passengers or property for hire or, for compensation or for hire, act as pilot-in-command, except that you may:
   a. for compensation or hire, act as pilot-in-command of an aircraft in connection with any business or employment if the flight is only incidental to that business or employment and the aircraft does not carry passengers or property for compensation or hire;
   b. share the operating expenses of a flight with your passengers;
   c. demonstrate an aircraft in flight to a prospective buyer if you are a salesman and have at least 200 hours of logged flight time;
   d. act as pilot-in-command of an aircraft used in a passenger carrying airlift sponsored by a charitable organization under certain conditions listed in Sec. 61.118 of the FARs.

4. You may not carry passengers unless you meet the recency of experience requirements;
   a. you must have made at least 3 takeoffs and 3 landings as the sole manipulator of the flight controls in the same category and class of aircraft within the preceding 90 days;
      (1) these do not have to be to a full stop unless you are flying a tailwheel airplane;
      (2) these must be shown in your logbook;
   b. to fly at night (from one hour after sunset to one hour before sunrise) with passengers you must have logged at least 3 takeoffs and 3 landings to a full stop at night within the preceding 90 days.

6. Whether you own the airplane you fly or not, it is your duty to be sure that the aircraft has had its annual inspection;
   a. a 100-hour inspection is required for aircraft being flown for hire;
   b. an approved aircraft inspection program may be used rather than the annual inspection.

7. In order to act as pilot-in-command, you must, within the preceding 24 months have accomplished a biennial flight review given to you in an aircraft for which you are rated;
   a. this is given by an appropriately certificated instructor or other person designated by the administrator;
   b. your logbook must be endorsed by the person who gave you the review certifying that you have satisfactorily accomplished the flight review;

- c. you do not have to have the flight review if, within 24 months, you have satisfactorily completed a pilot proficiency check, such as your private pilot, instrument or commercial;
- d. a flight review consists of a review of the current general operating flight rules of Part 91 of the FAR and a review of those maneuvers and procedures which in the discretion of the person giving the review are necessary for the pilot to demonstrate that he can safely exercise the privileges of his pilot certificate.

8. You may not fly at night if your certificate is endorsed "Night flying prohibited";
   - a. this limitation can be removed when you show you have 3 hours of night flying, including 10 takeoffs and landings.

9. You should never fly over mountains unless:
   - a. you have received mountain flying instruction from a qualified mountain flying instructor;
   - b. you have made very careful plans for the entire flight;
   - c. you have good weather assured for the entire flight;
   - d. you have filed a flight plan;
   - e. you have provided yourself with suitable clothing in case of a forced landing;
   - f. you have checked your ADF for proper operation;
   - g. you have provided an adequate survival kit for your aircraft;
   - h. you have oxygen for those portions of your flight over 10,000 feet.

10. You should make similar precautions for any flight over water, deserts, swamps and forests.

SECTION 58
THE WONDERFUL WORLD OF FLIGHT

Your continued enjoyment of flying demands that you *always* be a safe pilot. You must constantly study your airplane, techniques of flying, the information that is available to you to make your flights safe, as well as the constant changes and improvements that persistently alter your problems and opportunities as a pilot.

Build a good flying library. The experts have given us the advantage of their lifetimes of experience. Buy their books. Read them carefully. Reread them from time to time. You will be surprised how much you will learn (or remember something forgotten) each time you read them. The FARs and *AIM* are very poorly written and difficult (almost impossible) to read. But read them over and over. Note the changes frequently. Many important changes are made that receive little or no fanfare.

Keep up on the advancements in aviation. The best way to do so is to read magazines such as *Flying.* Save your copies and go over the back issues. It makes a pleasant way to spend a rainy Saturday afternoon.

Your Pilot's Operating Handbook is a motherlode of important, lifesaving information. You have studied it carefully for your private pilot flight test. Get it out and reread it, very carefully, at least once a year. When you change to a different airplane, take the new Manual home and study it thoroughly. It will save you from making costly, even disastrous, mistakes.

The government is doing a good job of providing essential information to pilots. Get a list of their publications and add as many of them to your flying library as possible. These should include the VFR and IFR Exam-O-Grams, Advisory Circulars and many other publications available free or at low cost.

The aphorism that there are old pilots and there are bold pilots but there are no old, bold pilots has become a cliché. But it is loaded with truth that can save your life. As a pilot you have assumed heavy new responsibilities. You must exercise extreme care at all times, not just to save your own life. You owe it to your husband or wife and even more to children who will need you until they are grown. You owe it to your business associates, your employees and the stockholders of your company.

Getting your Private Pilot Certificate has been a long, arduous struggle. The alcoholics, drug addicts, criminals and other irresponsible people have no business piloting a plane. Most such people have been weeded out in the process. You are the right sort of person or you would not have made it this far. But you can't let your professionalism lapse. In fact, your constant goal should be to think and conduct yourself like an airline pilot. You will do everything in your power to protect yourself, your airplane, your passengers, others in the sky around you and those on the ground.

Under no circumstances will you do such stupid things as aerobatics (other than legally, under carefully controlled conditions). You will never fly low over people or buildings. You will never try to be cute or show off. You know that such juvenile antics are dangerous, that they turn the public against general aviation and mark you in the eyes of other pilots as immature.

As a pilot, you are a special goodwill ambassador for general aviation. The public has little understanding (and often less love) for the "little planes" that they think delay commercial planes, crash into homes and otherwise make a nuisance of themselves. It is up to you to help to change this image. If you and all other pilots don't help in this effort, we will continue to lose the friends we need so desperately.

Help spread the good word about flying. Be a true ambassador of goodwill for general aviation. Use your plane to help others. Volunteer to help in worthy projects, whether it be to take a city official to the state capital, pick up medicine for a critically ill baby, search for a lost child, or whatever you can do to help others. In so doing, your community will realize the importance of the light airplane to their well being.

A few words of caution about taking up passengers—the mere fact that you can do so legally does not mean that you can do so safely. In the first place, you should have somewhat more experience than that required for a private pilot's certificate before you start carrying your family and friends. Coping with emergencies can be very difficult for the inexperienced pilot. It can become overwhelming when you have a planeful of people.

Be particularly careful if your passengers have never flown in a "little airplane." Pick a nice day when there is no turbulence. Talk to your passengers. Explain everything you do as you do it. Tell them that you are required to use checklists, and that all pilots, including those on airlines, use them. You don't want them to think you have to get out a book to read up on how to fly the airplane.

Tell your inexperienced passengers what you are looking for as you preflight the plane. Tell them you will circle the field and will return immediately if they feel too uncomfortable. On takeoff, use a low angle of climb. All turns should be done slowly and smoothly. Quick descents should be avoided. Also, avoid quick power changes, or cutting off the power. They tend to alarm the novice. Above all, do nothing to frighten your passenger. If there is anything that marks the pilot who should not be flying, it is the sadist who wants to scare his passenger. Such antics instantly destroy good will that responsible pilots have spent lifetimes in building.

Of course, you will never fly unless you are adequately insured. Whether you rent or own, your own policy should contain adequate coverage against all damages to the person and property of others, as well as to the airplane you are flying. Don't rely on the owner of the plane to have insurance that covers you. Never let anyone fly your airplane who is not listed in your policy. Also, it is up to you to see that he is qualified to fly the plane, has a proper medical certificate, has passed a Biennial Flight Review within the preceding two years and meets all the recency of experience requirements for that flight.

Now that you have your Private Pilot Certificate, a whole new world is open to you. It is an interesting and exciting world. It can be profitable. No longer are you handcuffed to the 55 mile per hour snail's pace on the roads below. Now you can move quickly and easily to any place in this hemisphere.

Flying opens entire new vistas in your life. It gives you time and opportunity to see and do things that could not possibly be accomplished without an airplane. You can visit family and friends, while less fortunate earthlings have to be content with an occasional telephone call or letter.

Up until now you probably had to be content for your vacation to use your car to drive, slowly, laboriously and tiringly to one or two destinations. Now, your airplane can turn a weekend into a full vacation. A week of flight can bring you to dozens of fascinating places scattered over hundreds, even thousands, of miles.

The United States, Canada and Mexico are teeming with places of enormous beauty. The Atlantic and Pacific Oceans, the Rockies and Appalachians, the Great Lakes and Gulf of Mexico are worth seeing but would take a lifetime if you were not a pilot. They are even more beautiful from the air. Unlike the jet passenger, you can fly low enough to drink in the dazzling grandeur of America.

Ours is a glorious history. Whether it be the homes of colonists in Williamsburg or the inspired courage of the defenders of the Alamo, the shrines of the Revolution in Concord and Lexington, the battlefields of Gettysburg and Bull Run, or where history is now being made in Washington or the United Nations, your plane can whisk you and your family there in a small fraction of the time it takes to drive.

Whether you want to hunt, fish or just explore with your camera, delightful rivers, streams and lakes can be quickly reached in your plane, even though they are in distant and seemingly inaccessible spots.

Your airplane will soon become an essential tool in your business. It will enable you to enlarge your business world. There is scarcely a city that does not have an airport where you can meet your customers and suppliers as quickly and as often as you want. Your plane can probably bring you home in time for dinner with your family.

As a pilot, new hobbies and pleasures will be opened up to you, such as aerobatics, gliding and parachute jumping. Thousands have found delight in collecting and restoring antique planes. Others get immense pleasure from building and flying their own homebuilts and experimental planes.

Of course, for many new pilots, there is much more ahead in aviation. The job opportunities are almost unlimited, if you will continue to develop as a pilot.

You may want to go on to be a pilot in the Air Force or other branch of the armed forces. Or, you may set your sights on the glamor, prestige and high salary of the airline pilot. And there are many other rewarding jobs in flying, such as the flight Instructor, charter pilot, corporate pilot, crop duster, or any one of dozens of others that demand the abilities of the capable pilot.

But never lose sight of the most important fact about flying. It's fun!!! It adds new flavor and excitement to your life. It is a constant challenge. It demands the best of the best of us. It is constantly changing. Flying is a recreation that lifts you above the dreary world. Just to get in your plane and fly for an hour erases your tensions. It reminds you that you have reached a level of achievement that is shared only by a few fortunate fellow pilots.

Regardless what your reason or reasons for flying may be, having a good time is a very legitimate objective of all your flights. So take advantage of it. Enjoy the pleasures of flying to the very fullest, *every* time you fly.

GLOSSARY OF AERONAUTICAL TERMS

absolute altitude—the actual altitude of an aircraft above the surface or terrain over which it is flying

absolute ceiling—the greatest altitude at which an airplane can continue horizontal flight in a standard atmosphere

acceleration—an increase in velocity; also, the rate of such change

acceleration error—the error of the magnetic compass that occurs during and because of the airspeed changes

accuracy landing—landing an airplane as close as possible to a designated mark on the ground

acrobatic—used to describe stunt flying such as acrobatic flight or the pilot of such flight

acrobatic flight—an intentional maneuver involving an abrupt change in the aircraft's attitude, an abnormal acceleration, not necessary for normal flight

adjustable—the capability of an airfoil or other aircraft component of being fixed or set in two or more positions

adjustable-pitched propeller—a propeller the angle of whose block can be adjusted while the airplane is on the ground

administrator—the Federal Aviation Administrator or any person to whom he has delegated his authority in the matter concerned

advection fog—a fog that results when warm, moist air moves over a cold surface

aerodrome—all areas normally used for the takeoff and landing of both seaplanes and land planes

aerodynamic—the field of dynamics that deals with the forces (resistance, pressure, etc.) exerted by air or other gases in motion

aerodynamic force—a force that acts on a body, such as an airplane, in motion through the air or in relative motion with respect to the air

aileron—a hinged control surface on the trailing edge of the wing. It is used to cause a bank about the longitudinal axis.

aileron tab—a trim tab on an aileron. There is none on the Cessna 152

airborne—to describe an airplane in the air

air carrier—a person who undertakes directly by lease, or other arrangement, to engage in interstate, overseas, or foreign air transportation or the transportation of mail by aircraft

aircraft—a device that is used or intended to be used for flight in the air

aircraft call sign—the sign given by the pilot to a radio station and consisting of the make of the airplane, followed by the complete certification number, thus: "Cessna N8424 Juliet"

aircraft engine—an engine that is used or intended to be used in propelling aircraft. It includes engine appurtenances and accessories necessary for its functioning but does not include propellers

aircraft instrument—see instrument

aircraft position charts—aeronautical charts used for flights of the North Atlantic and Pacific, Mediterranean and Caribbean areas

air current—a stream of air that moves vertically or in any other direction, other than horizontally

Air Defense Identification Zone—the area of airspace over land or water within which the ready identification, the location and the control of aircraft are required in the interest of national security

airfield—an area used for takeoff and landing of aircraft but having limited facilities

airfoil—any airplane surface or member, such as a wing, propeller blade or rudder; its principal purpose is to deflect the airflow

airframe—the fuselage, booms, nacelles, cowlings, facings, airfoil surfaces and landing gear of an aircraft, and their accessories and controls

Airman's Information Manual—a publication prepared by the Department of Transportation of the Federal Aviation Administration, giving much information of value to airmen

airmanship—degree of skill in flying aircraft

airmarker—a sign visible from the air, showing the name of the town and an arrow showing the direction and distance to the nearest airport

air mass—a large body of air that has approximately uniform temperature and moisture characteristics in a horizontal cross section

air meet—an event where pilots gather for racing, stunting and similar events

AIRMET—an advisory from the FSS concerning weather that is potentially hazardous to inexperienced pilots, or to pilots using an aircraft with limited equipment

air navigation radio aids—radio aids used by a pilot in navigating, such as VOR and VORTAC. For instrument flying, there are also radar and instrument landing systems (ILS)

airplane—an engine driven fixed-wing aircraft heavier than air, that is supported in flight by the dynamic reaction of air against its wings

air plot—the position of an airplane that would be plotted, when based upon true heading and airspeed, but assuming no wind

air pocket—an air space marked by strong current flow which, when entered or encountered by an aircraft, causes the craft suddenly to rise or drop (especially to drop) as if into a pocket. However, most non-flyers who witness a crash caused by a stall attribute it, erroneously, to an "airpocket"

airport—an area on land or water used for the takeoff and landing of aircraft, including its buildings and facilities, if any. More strictly, it is a facility with complete servicing facilities

airport advisory area—the area within five statute miles of an uncontrolled airport on which is located a Flight Service Station so depicted on the appropriate Sectional Aeronautical Chart

airport advisory service—a service provided by a Flight Service Station where there is no control. It includes information on wind and weather, as well as about traffic known to be in the area

Airport Surface Detection Equipment (ASDE)—radar used to determine positions of aircraft and vehicles on the ground at an airport

airport surveillance radar (ASR)—a radar center system used in a ground controlled approach system to detect aircraft within a 30 mile radius of an airport and to present continuously to the radar operator information as to position, in distance and azimuth, of these aircraft

airport traffic area—the airspace within a horizontal radius of 5 statute miles from the geographical center of any airport at which a control tower is operating, extending from the surface up to, but not including 3,000 feet above the surface

airport traffic control—service provided by an airport traffic control tower for aircraft on and in the vicinity of an airport

Air Route Surveillance Radar (ARSR)—a long range (approximately 150 mile radius) used by Air Route Traffic Control Centers to control air traffic between terminals

Air Route Traffic Control Center (ARTCC)—commonly called a Center. This operating facility provides air traffic control service to airplanes operating on IFR within controlled airspace, principally during the en route phase of flight

airship—an engine-driven lighter-than-air aircraft that can be steered

airspeed—the aircraft's speed in relation to the air through whch it is passing

airspeed indicator—an instrument in an airplane that indicates the speed of an airplane in relation to the air through which it is flying

air stream—a body of air in motion relative to a solid body

airstrip—an unimproved strip of land that is used for the takeoff and landing of airplanes

air traffic—aircraft operating in the air or an airport surface exclusive of loading ramps and parking areas

air traffic clearance—an authorization by air traffic control for the purpose of preventing collision between known aircraft, for an aircraft to proceed under specified traffic conditions within controlled airspace

Air Traffic Control (ATC)—a service provided to keep aircraft flying under IFR safely separated while operating in controlled airspace—taking off and climbing, en route and when approaching and landing at air terminals

air traffic controller—a specialist responsible for providing air traffic control service

Air Traffic Rules—those parts of the Federal Aviation Regulations (FAR) that regulate airplanes in flight, as distinguished from Field Rules

air transportation—interstate, overseas or foreign air transportation or the transportation of mail by aircraft

airways—designated paths through the airspace at three levels—low, intermediate and high. The low altitude airways are 10 miles wide and extend upwards to 14,500 feet above MSL. The intermediate altitude airways are 16 miles, or more, wide and extend from 14,500 to 24,000 feet above MSL. The high altitude routes extend upward from 24,000 feet and are designed solely for jets.

airworthy—the status of being in a suitable condition for safe flight

alternate airport—an airport specified in a flight plan at which an aircraft may land, if a landing at the intended airport becomes inadvisable

alternator—an alternating current generator used in aircraft to supply needed electric current

altimeter—an instrument used in an airplane to register its altitude by measuring barometric pressure

altimeter setting—the setting of the altimeter to adjust for known barometric pressure so that the altimeter will correspond with the actual elevation of the airport

altitude—the elevation of an airplane. It may be specified as above sea level (MSL) or above ground level (AGL)

ambiguity meter—the TO-FROM indicator of a VOR receiver

anemometer—an instrument used to measure wind velocity

angle of attack—an acute angle formed by the chord of an airfoil and the relative wind

angle of glide—the angle that is formed by the flight path of a descending airplane and the horizon

angle of incidence—the angle of wing fixed between a wing and the axis of the fuselage

angle of pitch—the acute angle between the longitudinal axis of an airplane and the direction of the wind relative to the airplane

angle of roll—the acute angle between the lateral axis of an airplane and the horizontal

angle of yaw—the acute angle between the longitudinal axis of an airplane and its line of travel, looked at from above

appliance—any instrument, mechanism, equipment, part, apparatus, appurtenance, or accessory, including communications equipment, that is used or intended to be used in operating or controlling an aircraft in flight, is installed in or attached to the aircraft and is not part of an airframe, engine or propeller

approach—the direction from which an aircraft comes for a landing or from which it approaches a traffic pattern

approach and landing chart—a chart used for instrument approach and landing at a properly equipped airport

approach control—a service by terminal facilities for arriving and departing IFR traffic and, under certain circumstances, for VFR traffic

approach control tower—a control tower that directs airplanes approaching for a landing. It transmits on voice channel or associated ranges and ILS in addition to listed frequencies

approach fix—the geographic point over which an aircraft flying by IFR begins its final approach to the airport before landing. This point is usually identified by a navigation aid

Approach Lighting System (ALS)—a lighting system that aids a pilot in landing, after a breakthrough on an instrument approach

approach sequence—the order in which tower controllers position aircraft approaching a terminal for landing

apron—see ramp

arresting barriers—yellow lines painted on the front end of a runway to indicate any portion of the runway not be used in landing

arrival—the action or event of an aircraft arriving at a place; an instance of such action, as in "four arrivals, four departures"

artificial horizon—the instrument with a miniature aircraft and horizon bar that gives a picture of the attitude of the real aircraft

atmosphere—the air that surrounds the earth

attitude—the position of an aircraft considering the inclination of its three axes in relation to the horizon attitude indicator—artificial horizon

Automatic Direction Finder (ADF)—a radio compass that seeks out signals from commercial broadcast stations and non-directional homing beacons permitting the pilot to determine his bearing to that station

automatic pilot—a gyroscopic device used in some airplanes to operate the flight controls without the pilot's supervision

Automatic Terminal Information Service (ATIS)—a transcribed broadcast, continuously repeated and frequently changed, which gives airport advisory on wind, altimeter, visibility, ceiling, runway in use, etc.

avionics—aircraft equipment used for radio communication, navigation and certain functions of control over the aircraft

axis—the theoretical line extending through the center of gravity of an airplane in each major plane—fore and aft, crosswise, and up and down. These are longitudinal, lateral and vertical axes, respectively

azimuth—bearing in the horizontal plane, usually expressed as the angle, and in air navigation measured clockwise from true north, or magnetic north, from 1 degree to 360 degrees

back—the top part of any airplane's fuselage, usually used in connection with the action of flying on an airplane's back

bail out—to jump from an airplane in flight

balance—the conditions of an aircraft that is capable of steady flight without pitch, roll or yaw

balloon—a lighter-than-air aircraft that is not engine-driven

bank—to use the ailerons to cause the airplane to tip or roll about the longitudinal axis of the airplane

barometer—an instrument for measuring the pressure of the atmosphere. The principal types are the mercurial and the aneroid

barrel roll—a stunt in which an airplane executes a complete roll by revolving once around an axis but parallel to its longitudinal axis

base-leg—a flight path at right angles to the landing runway off its approach end and extending from the downwind leg to the intersection of the extended runway center line

bearing—the position of an object or point with reference to the position of some other object or point, or point on the compass

belly-land—to land an airplane on its belly, without benefit of landing gear. This cannot happen in your 152 because its landing gear cannot retract

bent—(of an aircraft) damaged or destroyed in any kind of accident

best angle of climb airspeed—the airspeed which results in the greatest increase in altitude in a given distance

best climb speed—the airspeed that enables the pilot to achieve the best compromise in his effort to obtain maximum climb, airspeed, passenger comfort, visibility engine cooling and efficiency. This is subjective and is normally somewhat less than the best rate of climb airspeed

best rate of climb airspeed—that airspeed which permits the pilot to achieve the greatest increase in altitude in a specified period of time

biplane—an airplane having two main wings, with one above the other

blade—the part of the propeller that bites the air

blade angle—the angle of a propeller blade

blade tract—the path preversed by the propeller while the propeller is rotating; the blade is said to be in or out of tract

blade twist—the twist built into a propeller

blip—the echo from an aircraft or other object reflected visually on the radarscope. It usually appears as an elliptical object about the size and shape of a large grain of rice

boost—to increase the manifold pressure or throttle setting

bracket—a distinct feature of the terrain which bounds the course on one side and serves as a guide line. Brackets include large rivers, prominent highways, railroads, and mountain ranges

brake horsepower (BHP)—the power delivered at the propeller shaft of an aircraft engine

buffeting—the beating effect of the disturbed airstream on an airplane's structure during flight

buffeting limit—the extreme amount of buffeting that an airplane can sustain without material failure

bunt—the first half of an outside loop

burble—a condition that exists around an airplane wing when there is a breakdown of smooth airflow around the wing, resulting from a high angle of attack and leading to a stall burble point—the point at which burble begins as the angle of attack is increased

buzz—to fly low over some point on the ground in a reckless, illegal manner

cabin—the portion of an airplane occupied by the pilot, passenger(s) and, in some aircraft, the baggage

cage—to lock an instrument, as the artificial horizon, to prevent damage to the instrument during acrobatics

calculator side—the side of a pilot's computer that is used to work problems that involve true airspeed, conversions from statute to nautical miles, time, distance and fuel

calibrated airspeed (CAS)—the indicated airspeed corrected for position and instrument error. It is equal to true airspeed in standard atmosphere at sea level

calibrated altitude—the indicated altitude corrected for instrument errors

camber—the curve of an airfoil section from the leading edge to the trailing edge

carburetor—that part of the fuel system that mixes vaporized fuel with air to produce a combustible or explosive mixture

carburetor heat—a system that permits engine heat to be diverted through the carburetor to melt any ice

carburetor heat control—the device in an airplane that is pulled out to cause hot air to pass through the carburetor and melt any ice

carburetor ice—ice formed in the carburetor throat caused by the rapid reduction in temperature that results because of the vaporizing of fuel and the increase in the velocity of the air, passing through the carburetor venturi. This ice reduces or stops the flow of fuel

category—as used with respect to the certification, ratings, privileges and limitations of airmen, means a broad classification of aircraft, such as airplanes, gliders, rotorcraft and lighter-than-air. When used with respect to the certification of aircraft, category means a grouping of aircraft based upon the intended use or operating limitations, including transport, normal, utility, acrobatic, limited, restricted and provisional

caution area—an area in which flight is permitted but where special caution must be exercised due to the existence of visible hazard to flight, such as flight testing, flight training, military maneuvers, parachute drops, etc.

CAVU—clear or scattered clouds and visibility greater than 10 miles

ceiling—the height above the earth's surface of the lowest layer of clouds or obscuring phenomena that are reported as "broken," "overcast," or "obscuration," and not classified as "thin" or "partial;" also, the maximum altitude attainable by a particular airplane under standard conditions

Celsius (C)—a temperature scale identical to the Centigrade scale, with 0° as the melting point of ice and 100° as the boiling point of water

center line—a line which may be real or imaginary, and which runs longitudinally through the center of anything, such as a runway

center line thrust—twin engine airplanes with both engines in line, one pulling and other pushing, thus eliminating asymetrical thrust, or outboard torque

center of gravity—the point in an airplane when it will balance

center of gravity range—the allowable range where the center of gravity may fall. The exact location of the range, usually near the wing root, is specified for each type of aircraft

center of pressure—the point in the airfoil section where the force of lift is deemed to act for purposes of computations concerning the airplane

center section—the central panel or section of an airplane wing

centrifugal—moving or directed away from the center of location, as in "centrifugal acceleration"

centigrade—a temperature scale upon which the difference between freezing water (0°) and boiling water (100°) is divided into 100 degrees

chart—a map used in navigation, at sea or in the air, with certain features omitted and other exaggerated to accentuate their value as landmarks

chandelle—an abrupt climbing turn in which the airplane almost stalls while its momentum provides additional acceleration for the climb

changeover point—the point approximately midway between omnis where the pilot changes from the station behind to the station he is approaching

checklist—a list of items or procedures. The Operating Checklist is one such list and is used to avoid forgetting any essential flight procedure

checkout—the procedure wherein a qualified person

instructs another in the proper procedures to follow in flying a particular airplane

check pilot—a pilot designated by the FAA to administer check rides for other pilots

checkpoint—a prominent landmark on the ground, either visual or radio, used in air navigation, used to help establish the airplane's position in flight

chronometer—an accurate timepiece, especially used in navigation

circuit breaker—a device used in place of a fuse to break an electrical circuit if there is an overload

civil aircraft—aircraft other than public aircraft

clearance—authorization by an air traffic control facility for an aircraft to proceed within controlled airspace, taking into account the location of other known aircraft

clearance limit—the point to which an aircraft is cleared

clear ice—ice formed on an airplane's wings by the constant, slow freezing of water upon the airplane's surface; distinguished from rime ice

climb—the act of an airplane in ascending under power

climb corridor—an area indicated on aeronautical charts, having a ceiling and a floor. It is restricted airspace adjoining a military airport and is reserved for the landing and takeoff of military jets

climb indicator—the instrument that indicates the rate-of-climb

cockpit—the space occupied by the pilot and passengers

code—a series of impulses transmitted by a transponder in an airplane in response to interrogation from the ground

Combined Station/Tower (CS/T)—a Flight Service Station (FSS) which is located and combined with a control tower, indicated on the chart

compass—a device used in the airplane to point to the North Pole. It may be magnetic or gyroscopic

compass correction card—a card mounted in the airplane to show the compass heading when the magnetic heading is known. The difference is due to magnetic interference by various parts of the airplane

compass heading—the heading on the compass which must be followed to make good the desired course, being true course corrected for wind, variation and deviation

compass rose—a circle divided into 32 points or 360 degrees numbered clockwise from true or magnetic north, printed on a chart and used for navigation

compressibility error—an erroneous indicated airspeed experienced in highspeed airplanes which results from the compression of air at the pitot-static tube

computer—a device used by pilots to assist in and simplify computations involving speed, distance, time and wind correction

consolan—navigation used for transocean flying

constant power operation—the operation of aircraft at the same engine power throughout a given flight, regardless of change in the gross weight of the aircraft

constant speed propeller—a propeller that tends to maintain the revolutions of an engine at a constant rate by automatically increasing or decreasing pitch

contact conditions—weather conditions permitting contact flying at a given altitude

contact flying—a method of flying in which a pilot determines the altitude and position of his plane by visual reference to the horizon, to landmarks or to clouds

conterminous U.S.—forty-eight states and the District of Columbia

continental control area—the area which includes the airspace within the conterminous U.S. at and above 14,500 feet MSL, excluding airspace less than 1,500 feet above the terrain, and prohibited and restricted areas (except certain specified restricted areas)

continental U.S.—the original 48 states and Alaska

contour—an imaginary line on the ground. Every point on the same line is the same height above sea level

control area—controlled airspace extending upward from specified height above the surface of the earth. Unless other provided in appropriate cases, control areas extend upward from 700 feet above the surface until designated from 1,200 feet above the surface or from at least 500 feet below the MEA, whichever is higher, to the base of the continental control area

controllability—the quality of an aircraft that makes for effectiveness and ease of control

controllable-pitch propeller—a variable-pitch propeller so constructed that its blade angle may be changed to either one or two angles by the pilot in the cockpit while the propeller is rotating

controlled airspace—airspace designated as continental control area, control area, control zone or transition area, within which some or all airplanes may be subject to air traffic control

controlled spin—a normal spin

controlled visual flight regulations (CVFR)—the regulations in effect in a control zone where VFR minimums do not exist but a pilot can keep clear of clouds. Departures and landings may be permitted under the control of the tower

control lock—a wire appliance that is inserted through a hole in the control column to lock the control wheel so that the ailerons and elevator cannot be moved

controls—the devices used by a pilot in operating an airplane

control surface—any hinged airfoil exposed to the airflow used to guide or control an aircraft in the air, including the rudder, elevator, ailerons, flaps and trim tabs

control tower—a facility for controlling traffic in the vicinity of and on an airport

control wheel—the wheel held by the pilot with which he controls the ailerons and elevator

control zone—controlled airspace extending upwards from the surface of the earth. Control zones may include one or more airports and are normally circular areas 5 statute miles in radius with extension where necessary to include instrument approach and departure paths

convection currents—also known as thermals

conventional—that which conforms or adheres to accepted standards. The term is used in describing airplanes, tools, methods, etc.

coordinated turn—a turn of the airplane without any skid or slip, resulting when the amount of aileron and rudder are smoothly coordinated. In a coordinated turn, the ball in the turn-and-bank indicator stays at the bottom, instead of moving to either side

coordination—the movement or use of two or more controls in their proper relationship to obtain the results desired

course—in air navigation, a planned route or direction of flight by reference to a line on the earth

course deviation indicator (CDI)—the part of omni equipment that includes a needle which swings to the left or right, indicating whether the airplane is to the left or right or on course. It is also known as the "Left-Right needle"

course selector—the Omni Bearing Selector of omni equipment

cowl flaps—small doors that open out of the cowling and which are controlled from the cockpit

cowling—the covering around the engine

crab—the act of turning an aircraft into the wind to compensate for drift

crewmember—a person assigned to perform duty in an aircraft during flight time

critical angle of attack—the angle of attack equal to or greater than the angle of attack for maximum lift, at which the flow of the air about an airfoil changes abruptly with the result that the lift is sharply reduced and drag is sharply increased

crosswind—a wind blowing from one side or the other, as distinguished from a headwind or a tailwind

crosswind leg—a flight at right angles to the landing runway off its upwind leg

cruise—to fly at cruising speed, which is normally 75% of full power for a light airplane; also, to fly at a constant altitude

cruise control—the operating of an airplane to obtain the maximum efficiency, particularly on extended flights

cruising altitude—an altitude maintained during a flight or a portion of a flight

cruising ceiling—the altitude above which the rate of climb for a particular airplane is less than 300 feet per minute

cruising speed—the speed which results from a power setting recommended by the manufacturer for cruising the airplane

culture—man constructed features on the ground such as highways, railroads, cities and bridges, which are shown on charts and used to assist in navigation

cut—to turn off an aircraft engine

danger area—former name for restricted area

dead reckoning—the form of navigation of an airplane wherein direction and distance are computed by reference to a known position

dead stick landing—a landing without any engine power

deceleration—the act of decreasing velocity

Defense Visual Flight Rules (DVFR)—the rules that apply to a VFR flight over an ADIZ, and which require the filing of a DVFR flight plan unless the airplane is being flown at a true airspeed under 180 knots

density altitude—the pressure altitude that has been corrected for existing temperature

departure control—the function of an air traffic control center in controlling the departure of aircraft

deplane—to disembark from an airplane

deviation—the error induced in a magnetic compass by steel structure, electrical equipment and similar disturbing factors in the airplane

deviation card—a card installed in the airplane's cockpit to permit the pilot to correct the magnetic compass for errors caused in the reading by metals and electrical accessories

deviation indicator—the needle of a VOR receiver that indicates whether the airplane is on course, or to the left or right of course

dew point—the temperature at which moisture will begin to condense. If the dew point is within several degrees of the temperature, some form of fog or precipitation results

dihedral—the angle either downward or upward, from a wing's root to wingtip

directional antenna—an antenna used in the aircraft in conjunction with the automatic direction finder (ADF) to determine the bearing to the transmitting station

direction finder—a radio instrument used to determine the direction of arrival of a radio signal

directional gyroscope (gyro) (DG)—also known as the gyro compass or heading indicator. It is a compass that operates upon gyroscopic principles and therefore is much easier to read than a magnetic compass

Distance Measuring Equipment (DME)—equipment on some airplanes used to supply the distance of the airplane from a navigation aid

ditching—the process of landing a land plane in water

dive—a rapid descent by an aircraft, nose downward, with or without power

down-aileron—an aileron that is in the down position. It creates lift and is distinguished from the up-aileron

down-draft—a draft of atmospheric air which moves toward the ground, the opposite of updraft

downwash—the downward thrust imparted on the air to provide lift for the airplane

downwind—the direction in which the wind is blowing

downwind landing—a landing made with a downwind heading

downwind leg—a flight path parallel to the landing runway in the direction opposite to landing

downwind turn—a turn that causes an airplane to turn downwind

drag—force opposing the motion of the airplane through the air

drift—deflection of an airplane from its intended course by action of the wind

drift angle—the angle formed by the true heading of an airplane and its track over the ground

drift meter—a navigation instrument for determining visually the amount of drift, in degrees

drift sight—an instrument found on transport and military aircraft which is gyro-stabilized and detects drift and ground speed

dual control—two sets of cockpit controls in an airplane which permit either the pilot or co-pilot to fly the aircraft. The system is used for training and is found in the 152

dual ignition—a system of fuel ignition consisting of two magnetos (right and left) and two spark plugs for each cylinder. This provides greater safety and more efficient combustion

dual instruction—instruction given by instructor to student in an airplane equipped with dual flight controls

east variation—the angle that is shown on a sectional chart, by its isogonic line, when magnetic north is to the west of true north

echelon—a flying formation in which groups are disposed in parallel lines, each to the right or left of the one in front, giving the appearance of steps

eddies—gusts of wind with sudden changes in velocity and direction

elevation—the vertical height above sea level of some geographic point such as an airport

elevator—a hinged, horizontal control surface used to raise or lower the tail in flight

emergency landing—a forced landing or one that is made for precautionary reasons

emergency locator transmitter (ELT)—a small compact, radio transmitter used by downed aircraft to signal their location to search and rescue parties. It may be activated manually or by an impact (crash) force of a certain number of G's or both. It transmits on the emergency frequencies of 121.5 MHz or 243 MHz, or both

empennage—the entire tail group of the airplane including the fixed and movable tail surfaces

en route charts—a series of charts providing only the information required for IFR flights, and formerly known as RF or radio facility charts

en route control—the control exercised by an air traffic control center over flights under Instrument Flight Rules

equitime point—the point on a chosen route where the time needed to reach a destination equals the time needed to return to the original point of departure

equivalent airspeed—the calibrated airspeed of an aircraft corrected for adiabatic flow for the particular altitude. Equivalent airspeed is equal to calibrated airspeed in standard atmosphere at sea level

exhaust gas temperature gage (EGT)—gage that measures the temperature of an airplane's exhaust gas

factor of safety—the ratio of maximum stress that an airplane or a structural part thereof can withstand to the maximum stress that it is estimated that it receive in the use for which it is designed

fahrenheit—a temperature scale upon which the temperature of freezing water is 32° and that of boiling water is 212°

fairing—a member or structure, the primary function of which is to produce a smooth outline and reduce drag

falling leaf—a stunt in which the airplane is caused to simulate the movements of a falling leaf

fan marker—a radio aid that is part of ILS which is located along the localizer beam and provides information as to distance to go and a position fix

feedback—pressures felt by a pilot, resulting from aerodynamic forces on the control surfaces

field elevation—the altitude of an airport above sea level

Field Rules—the portion of the Federal Aviation Regulations (FAR) that govern activities on and about an airport, as distinguished from Air Traffic Rules

fin—a fixed airfoil to increase the stability of an airplane; usually applied to the vertical surface to which the rudder is hinged

final approach—a flight path in the direction of landing along the extended runway center line from the base leg to the runway

firewall—the wall that separates the engine from the remainder of the aircraft

fix—a geographical position determined visually, by reference to one or more navigational aids, by celestial plotting, or by another navigational device

fixed base operator—one who leases the pilots' lounge, hangars and other space from the owner of the airport and, in turn, provides such facilities as fuel, hangar rental, flight instruction, plane rental and charter flights

flag—a signal strength indicator of the VOR receiver

flap—an appendage to an airfoil, usually the wing, for changing its lift characteristics, and to permit slower landings

flap speed—the highest speed permissible with wing flaps extended

flare—to raise the nose of the airplane in a smooth curve just before the stall and touching down

flareout—to round out a landing by decreasing the rate of descent and airspeed by slowly raising the nose

flares—magnesium lights of high intensity usually electrically operated, which can be dropped suspended from small parachutes for night emergency landings

flat dive—a dive at slight angle from the horizontal

flat glide—a glide at small angle to the horizontal

flat-out—at full speed

flat spin—a spin in which the airplane's nose is at a slight angle below the horizontal

fledgling—a novice pilot

flight advisory service—advice and information provided by air traffic control facilities and FSS to assist pilots in the safe conduct of flight

flight check—the checking of a pilot's proficiency in actual flight. Also, any check of an aircraft to determine the quality of operation of some piece of equipment

flight clearance—an authorization for a departure from an airfield or for a flight under designated conditions

flight following service—a service provided to pilots on some VFR flight plans. The pilot reports to FSS at specified times and transferred from one station to another until the flight is completed

flight formation—two or more aircraft flying in a fixed relation to each other

flight indicator—artificial horizon

flight instrument—an aircraft instrument that indicates direction, altitude, airspeed or attitude of an aircraft

flight level—a level of constant atmospheric pressure related to a reference datum of 29.92 inches of mercury. Each is stated in three digits that represent hundreds of feet. For example, flight level 250 represents a barometric altimeter indication of 25,000 feet; flight level 255, an indication of 25,500 feet

flight line—the portion of an airport that includes hangars, ramps and surrounding grounds where airplanes are serviced and parked. It does not include taxiways or runways

flight log—see log

flight maneuver—any performance or maneuver of an aircraft in the air

flight path—the path of an airplane as it flies through the air

flight-path deviation indicator (FPDI)—the deviation indicator of the VOR

flight plan—specified information, relating to the intended flight of an aircraft, that is filed orally or in writing with FSS or air traffic control

flight profile—a graphic outline of an airplane's altitude of flight

flight rating—an aeronautical rating

flight service specialist—a FSS representative who gives information on weather, field conditions and other flight information

Flight Service Station (FSS)—a facility operated by the FAA to provide flight assistance service

flight simulator—a training device that simulates the conditions of actual flight

flight strip—a runway but usually the term denotes a strip of cleared land to be used as an emergency runway

flight test—a performance test of an airplane, equipment or a person in flight

flight time—the time from the moment the aircraft first moves under its own power for the purpose of flight until the moment it comes to rest at the next point of landing; also, time a flight is to begin;

flight track—the path of an airplane over the ground

flight visibility—the average forward horizontal distance, from the cockpit of an aircraft in flight, at which prominent objects may be seen and identified by day and prominent lighted objects may be seen and identified by night

flipper—any movable control surface

float—a bouyant water-tight structure which is a part of the landing gear of a seaplane

flutter—a vibrating and oscillating movement of a wing, control surface, or the like, caused by aerodynamic forces acting upon an airfoil or surface

fly—to cause an aircraft to move through air, or ride as an occupant of an aircraft

flying—the movement of an airplane and its passenger(s) through the air; also, the act of piloting an airplane

flying hour—an hour of airplane flight, including takeoff and landing

flying stress—the stress on a person in flight, resulting from fatigue, airsickness, etc.

foehn—a dry wind with strong downward component, warm for the season, characteristic of any mountainous regions. It is called a chinook in the Rocky Mountains

fog—a cloud at or near the earth's surface. Fog consists of numerous droplets of water, which individually are so small that they cannot readily be distinguished by the naked eye

forced landing—an unintended landing, made because of difficulty or impossibility of keeping the airplane flying, usually made at a place other than an airport

fore—the front portion of an airplane

fore-and-aft axis—the longitudinal axis

former—false rib, bulkhead or other structural piece used at right angles in a wing, fuselage, etc.

frequency selector—a component of the VOR receiver used to select any of the frequencies between 108.0 and 118.1 MHz

front—the line of demarcation between two different types of air mass

fuel strainer—a strainer placed at the lowest point in the fuel system and used to drain accumulated moisture and foreign matter from the system

full-flap—the condition of an airplane with flaps fully extended

full-flap takeoff or landing—made with full flaps

full rich—the condition is which the mixture control is pushed all the way in so that the greatest amount of fuel can be supplied to the engine

full throttle—full power

fuselage—the body of an airplane to which the wings, landing gear and tail are attached

G—the gravitational force or pull of the earth

gascolator—a type of fuel strainer that incorporates a sediment bulb

general aviation—the aircraft, airmen and flight operations of every kind and description other than those which are classified as civil air carrier or military

generator—a source of direct current for aircraft

glaze ice—clear ice

glide—sustained forward flight in which speed is maintained only by the loss of altitude

glide angle—the acute angle formed by the horizontal and the airplane's glide path

glide path—the path traversed by an airplane as it glides downward

glide ratio—the ratio of distance traveled over the ground to the vertical distance descended in a glide during the same period of time

glide slope—an element of ILS which provides an inclined surface for the airplane to follow to the landing surface

glider—a heavier-than-air aircraft that is supported in flight by the dynamic reaction of the air against its lifting surfaces and whose free flight does not depend principally on an engine

glide ratio—the ratio of distance traveled over the ground to the vertical distance descended in a glide during the same period of time

Global Navigation Chart—chart used for world-wide flight planning with a scale of 1:5,000,000 or about 80 statute miles to the inch

go-around—the procedure of going around in a traffic pattern, rather than touching down

gosport—a speaking tube system, attached to the student's helmet, or to the earphones, to use in conversation in the air

gradient tints—the colors on an aeronautical chart that indicate elevation above sea level. These range from green at sea level to dark brown at highest elevations

gravity—the force that makes a body fall toward the center of the earth

Greenwich Mean Time (GMT)—the time in Greenwich, England, and the time used by the FAA for all operational purposes; sometimes indicated by the letter "Z", for "Zulu" Time

grommet—a small circle in the center of the wind side of a pilot's computer

gross weight—the total weight of an airplane, including its empty weight, oil, pilot and passengers (if any), fuel and baggage

ground control—a function performed at an airport where there is a control tower; it controls airplanes on the ground from parking space to the runway, and back

ground controlled approach (GCA)—a ground radar system. It provides verbal instructions which enable a pilot to land by complying with such instructions

ground effect—a cushion effect of the air compressed against the ground as an airplane flies close to the ground

ground-loop—an uncontrollable violent turn on the ground

ground plot—the position of an airplane that is plotted, taking into consideration the airspeed, true heading, and wind

ground roll—the roll of an airplane from touching down until it begins to taxi

ground run—the run of an airplane up to the point of taking off

ground speed (GS)—the rate of the airplane's progress over the ground

ground vector—in air navigation, a vector representing the track and ground speed of an aircraft and forming a part of the wind triangle

ground visibility—the prevailing horizontal visibility near the earth's surface as reported by the United States Weather Bureau or an accredited observer

guard—to guard a frequency is to have the airplane's radio tuned to that frequency with the volume up

gust—a sudden, brief increase in the speed of the wind

gust lock—a lock used to avoid wind damage to ailerons, elevators and rudders

gyro compass—directional gyroscope or heading indicator

gyro-horizon—artificial horizon, directional gyroscope, heading indicator

gyroscope—(or gyro)—a rotating wheel or disc designed to utilize Newton's laws of motion. Gyroscopes are used in the gyroscopic instruments, including the attitude indicator, the turn indicator and the heading indicator

hail—precipitation consisting of balls of irregular lumps of ice often of considerable size; a single unit of hail is called a hailstone. Large hailstones usually have a center surrounded by alternating layers of clear and cloudy ice. Hail falls almost exclusively in connection with thunderstorms, and has been found up to 17 inches in circumference and weighing a pound and a half

hangar—a building designed and used to house aircraft

heading—the horizontal direction in which an aircraft is pointed

heading indicator—the directional gyroscope

head-on wind (head wind)—a wind that blows directly from the front of an airplane

hedge-hopping—flying an airplane low, close to the ground, tree tops, buildings, etc.

helicopter—a rotorcraft that, for its horizontal motion, depends principally on its engine-driven rotors

heliport—an area of land, water or structure used or intended to be used for the landing and takeoff of helicopters

hemispheric rule—the requirement imposed by the FAA that the altitude of flight is determined by the direction of flight for aircraft flying at an altitude of 3,000 feet or more above ground level

hertz (Hz)—a unit of frequency equal to one cycle per second

high-speed stall—a stall occurring when the speed becomes great enough to induce the wing or other airfoil into a critical angle of attack and resulting in a turbulent separation

high-wing—a monoplane wing attached at or near the top of the fuselage

hinge axis—an axis about which a control surface swings

hold—to maintain the position of an airplane at the same altitude and about the geographic point while awaiting instructions to proceed

holding—a standard maneuver, executed at the direction of a traffic controller, which keeps an aircraft circling within a specified block of airspace while awaiting further clearance

holding fix—a specified location at which holding is accomplished

homing—to fly with the airplane's heading directly toward a station at the destination by use of ADF or VOR

hood—an extended visor cap worn by the student while flying on instruments; it permits him to see the instruments without seeing outside the airplane

horizon—the line formed by the apparent meeting of the earth and sky as observed from any point, a line that indicates a plane on a flight instrument, as in the artificial horizon

horizontal axis—either the lateral or the longitudinal axis of an airplane

horizontal flight—a flight in which the aircraft maintains a uniform altitude above sea level

horizontal stabilizer—the horizontal portion of the empennage which is fixed and which provides horizontal stability for the airplane

horsepower—a unit for measurement of power output of an engine; it is the power required to raise 550 lbs. one foot in one second

hypoxia—oxygen deficiency in the blood cells or tissues

identifier—the abbreviation used to identify a Flight Service Station (FSS) and Combined Station/Tower (CS/T); e.g. MHK is the identifier for Manhattan, Kansas; these may be found in Part 3 of the *AIM*

idle—to run an aircraft engine slowly, without sufficient power being developed for movement of the aircraft;

IFR conditions—weather conditions below the minimum prescribed for flights under VFR

IFR over-the-top—the operation of an aircraft over-the-top of an IFR flight plan when cleared by air traffic control to maintain "VFR conditions" or "VFR conditions on top"

Immelmann turn—a maneuver in which an airplane makes a half-loop and then resumes its normal, level position by making a half roll

incidence, angle of—the angle between the mean chord of the wing and the longitudinal axis of the airplane

indicated airspeed (IAS)—the direct instrument reading the pilot obtains from the airspeed indicator, uncorrected for variations in atmospheric density, installation error and instrument error

indicated altitude—the altitude indicated by an altimeter than is set for the atmospheric pressure existing at the time and place of such reading

indicator—an airplane instrument used to show a position, angle attitude, or the like; short for "airspeed indicator," "bank and turn indicator," etc.

indraft—the inflow of air through a revolving propeller

induced drag—the drag produced by the low pressure of the rapidly-flowing air over the top of a wing

induced lift—that lift caused by the low pressure on the rapidly-flowing air over the top of a wing

instrument—a device using an internal mechanism to show visually or aurally the attitude, altitude or operation of an aircraft or aircraft part; it includes electronic devices for automatically controlling an aircraft in flight

instrument approach—the approach of an airplane to an airport under IFR conditions, through reference to instruments followed by a landing using visual contact after it has become possible to see the airport

instrument flight—the act of flying an airplane by reference to its instruments and radio guidance rather than visual reference to the ground

Instrument Flight Rules (IFR)—the rules that govern flight when weather conditions fall below the minimum ceiling and visibility required for VFR. To fly IFR, a pilot must pass an instrument flight test and receive a special instrument rating from the FAA

instrument landing system (ILS)—consists of four ground transmitting stations, at and in the vicinity of an airport, which radiate direction and position signals to approaching aircraft. The signals are received on an instrument in the aircraft and alert the pilot to any deviation from the safe approach path to the correct touchdown point on the runway

intensive student jet training area—airspace which contains the intensive training activities of military student jet pilots and in which restrictions are imposed on IFR flight

interphone—an electrically operated inter-communication system

interrogator—the ground surveillance radar beacon transmitter receiver which scans in synchronism with a primary radar, transmitting discrete radio signals which repetitiously request all transponders on the mode being used, to reply. The replies received are then mixed with the primary radar video to be displayed on the same plan position indicators

intersection—air traffic control reporting point which is a fix determined by the intersection of radials from radio aids

inversion—temperature inversion

inverted flight—flight in which the aircraft is upside down

inverted spin—a spin in which the airplane is in an inverted flight position throughout

isobar—equal barometric pressure indicated by a black line on a weather map

isogonic line—a dashed line on an aeronautical chart that indicates, for the area, the number of degrees that the magnetic North Pole is displaced to the east or west of true north

jury strut—a secondary structural member; often used to brace a main strut near its center

kilo Hertz (kHz)—a unit of frequency equal to 1000 cycles per second

kilometer—a unit of length equal to 1000 meters, 3280.8 feet or 0.621 miles

kinesthesia—a person's sense which detects and measures motion without reference to a sight or hearing

knot—a nautical mile per hour, which is equal to 1.1516 statute miles per hour

Koch Chart—a chart used to simplify the computation of takeoff distances and rate-of-climb, as they are affected by temperature and altitude

laminar flow—the flow of air in parallel layers of particles about the airplane and its airfoils

land—to bring an airplane down onto the ground according to plan, as distinguished from a crash

landing—the act of terminating flight and bringing the airplane to rest

landing area—any area suitable for the landing of an airplane

landing check—the check made by a pilot just before landing

landing clearance—permission to land

landing distance—the distance covered by an airplane during its landing roll

landing flap—a flap of an airplane used to slow its airspeed for landing

landing gear—the under structure of the airplane which supports its weight while at rest

landing run—the airplane's run after it has touched down

landmark flying—pilotage

land plane—an airplane designed to rise from and land on the ground large aircraft—an aircraft of more than 12,500 lb., maximum certificated takeoff weight

lateral axis—the imaginary line which extends crosswise, wingtip to wingtip. It is perpendicular to the longitudinal axis and the vertical axis. It is also known as the pitch axis.

lateral separation—the lateral spacing of aircraft at the same altitude by requiring operation on different routes or in different geographical areas

latitude—the angular distance from the equator of a point on the earth's surface. It is measured on the meridian of the point. One degree of latitude is equal to 60 nautical miles (about 69 statute miles)

lazy eight—a maneuver in which the airplane follows a path that is S-shaped from above and 8-shaped from the side

leading edge—the forward edge of any airfoil

lean—to reduce the fuel in the fuel-air mixture supplied to an engine

lean mixture—a mixture of fuel and air that contains a low percentage of air in comparison with a normal or rich mixture

LEFT-RIGHT indicator—the deviation indicator of the VOR receiver which shows the pilot whether he is on course, or to the left or right of course

left rudder—the cockpit control operated with the pilot's left foot, and used to turn the airplane to the left

lenticular cloud—a lens shaped cloud

lift—the supporting force induced by the dynamic reaction of air against the wing

lift component—the sum of the forces acting on a wing perpendicular to the direction of its motion through the air

lift-drag ratio—the ratio of the lift to the drag of an airfoil

lift-off—the act of listing the aircraft off the ground

light aircraft—an aircraft that weighs less than 12,500 pounds

lighter-than-air aircraft—aircraft that can rise and remain suspended by using contained gas weighing less than the air that is displaced by the gas

light gun—an intense, narrowly-focused spotlight with which a green, red or white signal may be directed at any selected airplane in the traffic on or about an airport

line—to line up an airplane so that its line of flight is in direct line with a runway or other point of reference

line inspection—preflight check

load—the forces acting on a structure. These may be static (as with gravity) or dynamic (as with centrifugal force) or a combination of static and dynamic

localizer beam—a part of the ILS used to furnish the pilot with lateral guidance to the airport runway

log—to make a record of a pilot's flight, listing flight time, area of operation and other information. The term also describes the book in which the information is recorded; logs are also kept for the operations of airplanes and engines

longitude—the angular distance of a point on the earth's surface measured from the meridian of the point to the prime meridian (Greenwich, England). One degree of longitude varies from about 60 nautical miles (69 statute miles) at the equator to zero at the poles

longitudinal axis—a longitudinal line that extends from the nose of an airplane through its center of gravity to its tail; also known as the roll axis

lubber line—the small reference line used in reading the figures from the card of an aeronautical compass

Mach number—the ratio of the true airspeed to the speed of sound

magnetic bearing—the bearing of a point in the northern hemisphere relative to that of the magnetic North Pole

magnetic compass—a device used in the airplane to determine the earth's magnetic field and which indicates the direction of the north magnetic pole

magnetic dip—the tendency of the magnetic compass to point down in certain latitudes

magnetic variation—see variation

maintenance—means inspection, overhaul, repair, preservation, and the replacement of parts, but excludes preventive maintenance

major alteration—an alteration not listed in the aircraft, aircraft engine or propeller specifications (1) that might appreciably affect weight, balance, structural strength, performance, powerplant operation, flight characteristics or other qualities affecting airworthiness; or (2) that is not done according to accepted practices or cannot be done by elementary operations

major repair—a repair (1) that, if improperly done, might appreciably affect weight, balance, structural strength, performance, powerplant operation, airworthiness; *or* (2) that is not done according to accepted practices or cannot be done by elementary operations

maneuver—any planned motion of an airplane in the air or on the ground

maneuverability—the relative ability of an airplane to have its direction or attitude changed with minimum effort

maneuverable—responsive to the movement of the controls

maneuvering speed—the maximum speed at which you can use abrupt control travel without exceeding the design load factor.

maximum climb—a climb of an airplane which is made at a maximum power setting, at an angle that gives the greatest altitude gain per minute

maximum climbing angle—the angle of climb that produces increase in altitude most rapidly

maximum cruise—the power setting on the throttle, fuel-air mixture, and rpm controls of an airplane giving maximum cruising speed at a given altitude

maximum power—the greatest amount of power that an engine is capable of producing

maximum structural cruising speed—the highest safe speed for gentle maneuvers in moderately rough air

mayday—the word used by a pilot in distress to alert ground stations

mean sea level—sea level

mean time—time based on the exact location of the sun, as distinguished from standard time

mechanical convection—the action that forces an air mass aloft as it reaches a mountain, so that it cools and the moisture in the air condenses, creating clouds

medical certificate—acceptable evidence of physical fitness on a form prescribed by the FAA Administrator

megacycle—a unit equal to one million cycles per second

meridian—a circle of the earth that passes through both poles and any particular spot on the surface of the earth

micro-second—one-millionth of a second; the unit of time common in radar use

mile (statute)—5,280 feet or 0.87 nautical miles

minimum flying speed—the lowest constant speed at which an airplane can maintain level flight without stalling

minimum gliding angle—the acute angle, as measured in still air, between the horizontal and a flight path as near as possible to the horizontal that still permits an airplane to descend steadily without benefit of thrust

minor alteration—an alteration other than a major alteration

minor repair—a repair other than a major repair

monocoque—an egglike aircraft construction in which the external skin constitutes the primary structure

monoplane—an airplane with one supporting surface

multicom—the frequency of 122.9 for use in communicating between aircraft

nacelle—enclosed shelter for a powerplant or personnel; usually secondary to the fuselage or cabin

nautical mile—6076.1 feet or 1.15 statute miles

navigable airspace—airspace at and above the minimum FAR flight altitudes, including airspace needed for safe takeoff and landing

needle and ball—turn and bank indicator

never-exceed speed—the maximum speed at which the airplane can be operated safely in smooth air

night—the time between the end of evening civil twilight and the beginning of morning civil twilight, as published in the American Air Almanac, converted to local time

non-standard departure—a departure at an airfield having a control tower, made with permission of the tower; it may authorize a) a straight out departure, b) a downwind departure, or c) a turnout in the *opposite* direction from that normally used

normal axis—the vertical axis in an aircraft

normal lapse rate—the decrease in temperature at the rate of 3½°F for every 1000 feet of increase in altitude

normal stall—the stall of an airplane caused by excessive angle of attack

nose dive—a steep dive by or in an airplane

nose-down—an aircraft with its nose pointing downward

nose-heavy—a condition of rigging in which the nose tends to sink

nose-high—the attitude of an airplane with its nose upward while in level flight

nose-low—the attitude of an airplane that has its nose inclined downward while in level flight nose-over—the turning of an airplane on its back on the ground by rolling over the nose

nose-wheel—a swivelling or steerable wheel mounted forward in tricycle-geared airplanes

NOTAM—Notice to Airmen Messages containing current and pertinent flight data such as locations of closed runways, inoperative navaids, etc.

oleostrut—a shock-absorbing strut in which the spring action is dampened by oil

omni—short for VHF omnidirectional ranges, and commonly called VOR

omnibearing selector—an azimuth in omni equipment which the pilot rotates to select a radial upon which to fly

omnirange—short for VHF omnidirectional ranges, commonly called VOR

on top—flying an aircraft above an overcast

operate—to use, cause to use or authorize to use aircraft for the purpose of air navigation, including the piloting of aircraft, with or without the right of legal control (as owner, lessee or otherwise)

Operational Navigation Chart—a chart very similar to the WAC (World Aeronautical Chart) but showing an area covered by four WACS

orientation—the act of fixing position or attitude by visual or other references

orientation flight—a flight given to familiarize a person with the airplane and the nature of flying

oscillation—any swinging back and forth by an airplane about one of its axes, as in pitching up and down

oscillation error—erratic swinging of the compass card. It is normally due to turbulence or rough pilot technique

outside loop—a loop of an airplane in flight in which the top of the airplane is on the outside of the circle

outside roll—an airplane roll that begins and ends with the airplane flying on its back

overcontrol—to move an aircraft's controls too far in one direction, then to attempt to compensate by a greater movement in the opposite direction, resulting in erratic flight

overfly—to pass over a place in an aircraft or to overshoot a place or object

overload—that part of an airplane's load which is in excess of the maximum amount prescribed for that airplane

overshoot—to fly beyond a designated area or mark

overspeed—to run an engine at a speed in excess of that recommended for cruising

over-the-top—flying an airplane over an overcast

pan—the word used by a pilot who is uncertain as to his position and wishes to alert ground stations—less urgent than "mayday"

parasite drag—drag caused by the disruption of the air flow over the airplane due to nonlifting surfaces such as landing gear, wing struts, and antennas

partial obscuration—the condition that exists when a ground observer is able to see part of the sky dome or clouds through an obscuring condition, in which case the vertical visibility does not determine the ceiling. Rather, if clouds are present, their bases and amount are reported

path—the line or route indicating the continuous positions to be occupied by an airplane moving through the air (flight path)

periodic inspection—the airframe and engine inspection of an airplane by a certificated mechanic, required at specific intervals by regulations

photogrammetry—aerial photography used to produce maps and surveys

pilot—the person who operates the controls of an airplane while it is in flight

pilotage—navigation by visual reference to landmarks, normally done with the aid of an aeronautical chart

pilot in command—the pilot responsible for the operation and safety of an aircraft during flight time

pilot weather reports (PIREPS)—reports collected by FAA stations from pilot's describing conditions aloft

pitch (propeller)—the angle of a propeller blade, measured from its plane of rotation; also, the nosing of an airplane up or down

pitch angle—the angle of pitch

pitch control—a mechanism used to control the pitch of a propeller

pitching—the movement of an airplane on its lateral axis

pitot tube—a tube exposed to the air stream for measuring impact pressure or for measuring outside undisturbed static pressure

plane—an airfoil section for deflection of air; surface or field of action in any two dimensions only; to move over the water (seaplanes) so that the weight is supported by dynamic reaction of the water rather than by displacement

plane flap—a flap affixed to the trailing edge of an airplane's wing

plotter—an instrument which combines a protractor with a straight edge, to be used by pilots in solving navigation problems

point of no return—the place beyond which an airplane cannot return to its starting point due to lack of fuel

positive control—a service provided by air traffic controllers in designated controlled airspace, whereby positive separation by radar and/or radio is provided to all aircraft regardless of weather conditions

power approach—an approach for landing with the engine under power

power dive—a dive in an airplane with its engine delivering full or considerable power

power-off—without power

power-on—with power on

power plant—the complete engine in an airplane, including its propeller, fuel tanks, etc.

Precision Approach Radar (PAR)—a radar system used by the military to guide aircraft to final approach to landing, and which furnishes range, altitude and azimuth

precision turn—a 90 or 180 degree practice turn executed with good coordination and smoothness

preflight—that which is done before a flight, usually used in reference to the preflight inspection of an airplane

preflight inspection—a careful inspection of the airplane by the pilot made before taking off

pressure—a condition that exists when force is applied to or distributed over a surface, measured as a force per unit area

pressure gradient—the decrease in atmospheric pressure per unit of horizontal distance. It is measured in the direction in which pressure decreases most rapidly

pressure altitude—the calibrated altitude that is indicated when the barometric scale is set to standard sea level pressure (29.92 in.)

prevailing visibility—the horizontal distances at which targets of known distance are visible over at least half of the horizon. It is normally determined by an observer on or close to the ground viewing buildings or other similar objects during the day and ordinary city lights at night. Under low visibility conditions the observations are usually made at the control tower. Visibility is reported in miles in the Aviation Weather Report. If a single value does not adequately describe the visibility, additional information is reported in the "Remarks" Section of the report

preventive maintenance—simple or minor preservation operations and the replacement of small standard parts not involving complex assumbly operations

primary radar—a radar system which operates by reflecting back a part of the radio pulse to the transmitting station. It is distinguished from secondary surveillance radar

prohibited area—designated airspace within which the flight of aircraft is prohibited

propeller—any device for producing thrust in any fluid

propeller thrust—the thrust developed by a rotating propeller

propeller tip—the outermost end or tip of a propeller blade

propeller wash—the backwash caused by a propeller

protractor—a device for measuring angle; usually used in navigation to determine compass courses on a chart

pusher—an airplane in which the propeller is mounted aft of the engine, and pushes the air away from it

pylon—a prominent mark or point on the ground used as a fix in precision maneuvers

R—when used in connection with a radio frequency, the 122.2R, it means that such frequency is used to *receive,* as distinguished from 122.1T, which indicates the frequency is used to *transmit*

radar—a radio device that detects the presence of bodies, such as an airplane, although they are not visible to the sight. It uses reflected radio impulses

radar advisory service—the provision of advice or information based on radar observations

radar beacon (RACON)—a fixed transponder that transmits when triggered by a properly equipped interrogator

radar contact—the term air traffic controllers use to indicate that an aircraft is identified on the radar display and that radar service can be provided until radar identification is lost or radar service is terminated

radar handoff—transferring radar identification and control (or advisory jurisdiction) over an aircraft from one controller to another without interrupting surveillance

radial—a magnetic bearing (or spoke) extending from a VOR, VORTAC, or TACAN

radiation fog—fog caused when warm air comes into contact with the surfaces that have cooled in the evening

"Radio"—the call used by a pilot contacting an omnirange or other voice facility; thus: "Quincy Radio, this is Cessna 8424 Juliet."

radio altimeter—a device that is used in an airplane to measure the height of the airplane above the ground, through the use of reflected radio waves

radio beacon—a low-frequency radio transmitter used in direction finding, for determining fixes and homing —a process of navigation whereby the pilot directs the aircraft toward the station to which he is tuned

radius of action—the distance an airplane can fly and return with its existing fuel supply, under given wind conditions along the chosen route

ramp—in common usage, the paved areas around the hangars. Strickly speaking, these are aprons since a ramp is an inclined surface used for the transportation of vehicles

range selector—a control used on a radar indicator to change the range of the display. The radar usually provides four or five different settings to cover ranges from 5 to 100 miles or more

rate of climb—the rate (expressed in hundreds of feet per minute) that an airplane climbs

rate-of-climb indicator—an instrument that indicates the rate of ascent or descent of an airplane, normally in feet per minute

rate of closure—the rate at which two airplanes come together

rate of descent—the speed at which an airplane is descending. This is indicated by the rate-of-climb indicator

rating—a statement that, as a part of a certificate, sets forth special conditions, privileges or limitations

reciprocal—the opposite direction, obtained by adding or subtracting 180 degrees to or from the given direction. 20 degrees is the reciprocal of 200; 210 is the reciprocal of 30

red line—a line that indicates a danger point, such as that on the airspeed indicator, which indicates the maximum safe speed

relative bearing—the bearing of some object, such as a radio facility, to the nose of the airplane

relative humidity—the amount of humidity in the air in comparison with the maximum amount it could contain at that temperature, expressed as a percentage

relative motion or movement—the motion that exists when one object, such as an airplane, changes its position in respect to the position of another object, such as another airplane

relative wind—the direction of the wind with respect to an airfoil

relief—the portions of a chart that show elevations through the use of contour lines, which may be emphasized by gradient or shadient tints

recover—to resume normal flight attitude after a stall, dive, spin, etc.

rendezvous—to meet at a selected location

reporting point—the intersection of radials from two omnis. A pilot flying IFR may be expected to report his time over such points

restricted area—the airspace designated under the FAR within which the flight of aircraft is restricted or prohibited, and includes prohibited areas, restricted areas, warning areas and caution areas. In its limited sense, a *restricted* area is one which cannot be entered without first obtaining permission from the controlling agency. They were formerly known as *danger* areas

rhumb line—the line drawn on a Lambert Chart between points for navigation purposes. In practice, it is the line on the map which the pilot attempts to follow

rime ice—a rough coating of granulated ice forming on the leading edges of the airplane

roll—any movement about the longitudinal axis of an airplane

roll axis—the axis of an aircraft about which it rolls; it is also known as the longitudinal axis

rollout—the roll of the airplane from the time it touches the landing strip until the airplane assumes normal taxi speed

rudder—a hinged, vertical control surface; it is attached to a vertical stabilizer, and used to guide the airplane in the horizontal

rudder pedals—controls within the airplane by means of which the rudder is operated runway—a strip of land, either paved or improved, used for takeoffs and landings of airplanes

runway-in-use—the runway that is most nearly aligned into the wind

runway visibility values (RVV)—is a measure of visibility. It is reported in miles and fractions of a mile and represents the horizontal distance a stationary observer near the approach end of the runway can see a light of 25 candlepower

runway visual range (RVR)—a measure of visibility which is similar to, and being used to replace, runway visibility value. It is reported in hundreds of feet

safety factor—any margin, factor, or element that insures a degree of safety in an operation

sailing—the use of wind and current conditions to cause a seaplane to travel the desired track while taxiing on water

scale—the proportion between a chart and the area of the earth shown on the chart; this is 1:500,000 on a sectional chart

scan—that area in space covered by the radar antenna pattern. It may be an area of 360 degrees and 50-60 miles range, as on the surveillance radar, or a smaller area such as that of the precision approach radar

scope—the face of the cathode-ray tube (Radar Indicator) on which a given area of radar coverage is displayed

scramble—the action of military aircraft in taking off pursuant to an alert, in the shortest possible time

sea level—the horizontal level that corresponds to the surface of the sea at mean (or average) level between low and high tide

seaplane—an airplane equipped with detachable floats to takeoff and land on water; it is distinguished from a flying boat

Search and Rescue (SAR)—a program of the FAA designed to locate missing pilots, including a communications search and, finally, an actual search with the cooperation of the Air Force, Civil Air Patrol, Coast Guard, state and local police, as well as civilian pilots

second in command—a pilot who is designated to be second in command of an aircraft during flight time

sectional chart (or, sometimes, simply "sectional")—an aeronautical chart of a part of the United States with a scale of 1:500,000 or about 8 statute miles to the inch

sense indicator—the TO-FROM indicator of a VOR receiver

sensitive altimeter—an altimeter that can be adjusted so that it can be set to the actual pressure at the airport where it is, or at the ground station near which it is flying

separation—spacing aircraft for safe, orderly movement while taking off, in flight and landing

separation minimums—a system of standards to insure safety in the air by specifying the spacing of airplanes in flight. For example, airplanes flying at altitudes up to and including 29,000 feet MSL are separated vertically by a minimum of 1,000 feet. Airplanes are also spaced laterally and longitudinally

sequence report—the weather report transmitted hourly to all teletype stations and available to all FAA Communication Stations

service ceiling—the altitude at which a particular aircraft becomes incapable of ascending at more than 100 feet per minute

SIGMET—an advisory concerning a significant meteorological development of such severity as to be potentially hazardous to all aircraft in flight

skid—sideward motion of an airplane in flight produced by centrifugal force

skin friction drag—the drag or resistance caused by friction caused by the moving air over the airplane

slant distance—the distance from an airplane, particularly at high altitude, to a range station or a landmark. It is distinguished from the horizontal distance, as measured along the ground

slip—the controlled flight of an airplane in a direction not in line with its longitudinal axis

slipstream—the current of air driven astern by the propeller

slow roll—slow rotation of an airplane about its longitudinal axis executed by coordinated manipulation of the controls

small aircraft—aircraft of 12,500 lbs. or less, maximum certificated takeoff weight

snaproll—an aerial maneuver in which the airplane is made to effect a quick, complete roll about its longitudinal axis

solo—a flight during which the pilot is the only occupant of the airplane

span—the distance from tip to tip. This may be the span of a wing or horizontal tail

spar—a principal longitudinal structural member in an airfoil

spatial disorientation—a confusion of the senses affecting balance impairing the ability to know what is vertical and what is horizontal

spin—a prolonged stall in which an airplane rotates about its center of gravity while it descends, usually with its nose well down

spiral—a prolonged gliding or climbing turn during which at least a 360-degree change of direction is effected

stability—the tendency of an airplane in flight to remain in straight, level, upright flight, or to return to this attitude if displaced, without effort by the pilot

stabilize—to give stability to an aircraft

stabilizer—the fixed airfoil of an airplane used to increase stability; it is usually the aft fixed horizontal surface to which the elevator is hinged

stall—the abrupt loss of lift when the airspeed decreases to the minimum which will support as airfoil at the existing loading

stall speed—the speed at which an airplane stalls

standard atmosphere—a standard of atmospheric pressure which is equivalent to 29.92 inches of mercury

standard procedure turn—standard rate turn

standard rate turn—a 360-degree turn that is completed in exactly two minutes. It is accomplished by making a turn wherein the vertical pointed of the turn and bank indicator matches a reference point

standard time—time adopted for an entire area to promote uniformity and to avoid confusion. It is distinguished from mean time

stall warning—any condition that signals the approach of a stall. Also a signal that sounds an alarm if the airplane is approaching a stall

stall warning signal—a signal sounded in an airplane with necessary equipment that indicates that the airplane is approaching a stall

straight—flying an airplane in a straight path in the air

straight-in-approach—a final approach to the airport made without entering the traffic pattern or executing turns in the established approach procedure

stress—the physical force exerted by one thing on another

strut—a compression or tension member in a truss structure; in airplanes, the term is usually applied to an external major structural member

stunt—a performance with an airplane that displays unusual skill; usually, it is an unusual and showy maneuver

sweptback wing—an airplane wing having a sweepback design in both its leading and trailing edges

swinging the compass—checking the indications of an installed compass by comparing them with an accurate compass laid out on the ground

T—when used in connection with a radio frequency, thus—122.1T—means that such frequency is used to *transmit,* as distinguished from 122.2R, which indicates the frequency is used to *receive*

tab—a small auxiliary airfoil, usually attached to a movable control surface to aid in its movement, or to effect a slight displacement of it for the purpose of trimming the airplane for varying conditions of power, load, or airspeed

tachometer—an airplane instrument that registers the speed of the engine in revolutions per minute (RPM)

tail assembly—an airplane's empennage

tail group—the airfoil members of the assembly located at the rear of the airplane

tailheavy—a condition of trim in an airplane in which the tail tends to sink

tailskid—a skid, or runner, which supports the aft end of an airplane while it is on the ground

tail slide—the rearward motion of an airplane in the air; this normally occurs only in a whip stall

tailspin—a spin of an airplane in which the tail follows a spiral action

tailwind—a wind that increases the ground speed of an airplane over its airspeed

takeoff—the action of getting an airplane from the ground into the air

takeoff clearance—authorization from an airport traffic control tower for an aircraft to take off

takeoff distance—the distance required by an airplane to take off; it is measured from beginning of the run to the point where it leaves the surface

takeoff run—the run of an airplane up to the point of leaving the ground

takeoff speed—the airspeed of an airplane at the time it leaves the ground

takeoff weight—the gross weight of an airplane at the time it takes off

tandem airplane—an airplane that has two sets of controls, one behind the other

target—the indication displayed on a radar scope resulting from a primary radar return or a radar beacon reply

target—any object that appears on the radar scope. This may be a moving object, such as an aircraft, or it may be a stationary object, such as a building

taxi—to operate an aircraft under its own power on ground or water, but not including takeoff and landing runs

temperature inversion—the condition that exists when the temperature is *higher,* rather than lower, than that at lower altitude

temperature lapse rate—the change in temperature due to change in altitude. The average temperature lapse rate is 3½°F for each 1000 feet increase in altitude

terminal forecast—a weather forecast available each six hours

terminal velocity—the hypothetical maximum speed which could be obtained in a prolonged vertical dive

terrain clearance indicator—radio altimeter

tetrahedron—a wind or runway indicator that indicated the direction from which the wind is blowing. It may operate from the pressure of the wind, or may be controlled from a tower or by land

thermal—a rising air current that results from uneven heating of the surface below

three point landing—a landing with an airplane in which the tail skid or tailwheel of the airplane and the two forward wheels come into contact with the ground at the same time

throttle—the device that is pushed in to increase down or back engine power; also, to reduce engine power

thrust—the forward force on a conventional airplane provided by the engine acting through a propeller

thrust horsepower—the horsepower delivered by the engine-propeller unit of an airplane

thrust line—the direction in which the thrust of an airplane engine acts. This is normally the axis of the propeller shaft

thrust output—the net thrust delivered by an engine

time in service—used in reference to maintenance time records and means the time from the moment an aircraft leaves the surface of the earth until it touches at the next point of landing

TO-FROM indicator—the part of the VOR receiver that indicates whether the course of the airplane is TO or FROM the station

torque—the force that produces a twisting or rotating motion as that caused by the turning of the propeller

total drag—the sum of all drag created on the airplane

touch-and-go landing—practice landings in which the airplane touches down and takes off without coming to a stop before another takeoff

touchdown—the instant in landing an airplane when the landing gear touches the ground; the point at which that happens

"tower"—the call used by a pilot in contacting an airport control tower; thus, "Springfield Tower, this is Cessna 8424 Juliet"

tower control—a facility that controls aircraft operation on and about a controlled airport

track—the path of an airplane as it flies over the ground

traffic pattern—the traffic flow that is prescribed for aircraft landing at, taxiing on, or taking off from an airport

traffic pattern altitude—the altitude above ground level that an airplane enters the traffic pattern and begins its downwind leg. Normally, this is 1,000 feet AGL for light airplanes

training device—any device or equipment used in training a pilot

transponder—equipment in an aircraft operated in conjunction with Secondary Surveillance Radar to identify the aircraft on the radar screen

trim—to adjust or balance an airplane so that it is in trim

trim tab—an adjustable-edge mounted on the trailing edge of the elevator, controlled by a trim wheel or crank. By adjusting the trim tab, the airplane can be placed in a nose-up or nose-down attitude without pressure on the elevator. Some aircraft may also have a rudder trim tab

trip forecast—a forecast of the weather that can be expected on a particular trip

true airspeed—the airspeed of an aircraft relative to undisturbed air

true altitude—the pressure altitude corrected for temperature

true course (TC)—the direction of a line drawn on a chart between the two points of departure and the destination. It is measured in degrees from true north

true heading (TH)—the direction in which the nose of the airplane should point to make good the desired course

true indicated airspeed (TIAS)—the calibrated airspeed, which is the indicated airspeed corrected for installation error and instrument error

TT—runway weight bearing capacity for aircraft with twin-tandem type landing gear

turn and bank indicator—a gyroscopic instrument that indicates the rate of turn which includes a ball that shows whether the turn is coordinated

turn and slip indicator—turn and bank indicator

turning error—northerly turning error

turtleback—the top of the fuselage aft of the cabin; in older planes, this was detachable

ultimate load—the load which will, or is computed to, cause failure in any structural member

unicom—a frequency used by pilots in communicating with certain airports to obtain advisory information. This frequency is 122.8 MHz, or, if there is a control tower, it is 123.0. New frequencies are being assigned for this purpose

upwind—into the wind

upwind leg—a flight path parallel to the landing runway in the direction of landing

useful load—in airplanes, the difference in pounds between the empty weight and the maximum authorized gross weight

variation—the angular difference between true north and the direction indicated by a magnetic compass, which is indicated on aeronautical charts, in degrees, by isogonic lines

vector—a heading issued by a radar controller for the purpose of providing navigational guidance

venturi (or venturi tube)—a tube with a restriction that is used to provide suction to operate flight instruments by allowing the slip stream to pass through it

vertical needle—the needle of a VOR receiver that shows the pilot whether he is on course, or to the left or right of course

vertical speed indicator—rate of climb indicator

vertical stabilizer—the fixed vertical portion of the empennage. To it is attached the rudder

vertigo—the loss of balance, sometimes accompanied by dizziness or nausea. It may be the result of spatial disorientation in flight

very high frequency (VHF)—a term used to describe radio equipment that transmits or receives

VFR condition on top—the maintaining of flight in VFR conditions above a cloud layer or other well defined meteorological formation

VFR traffic—aircraft operating in accordance with VFR

Victor Airway—a route on an aeronautical chart located upon VOR radials. It is represented by a blue shaded band. Each Victor Airway is given a "route" number

viscosity—the measure of the "thickness" of a fluid; it is important in determining the correct lubricating oil for any engine

visibility—the distance it is possible to see at a particular time and place. See prevailing visibility, runway visibility values and runway visibility range

Visual Approach Slope Indicator (VASI)—runway lights used during an approach which indicate, by their color, whether the airplane is on, below or above the proper glide slope

Visual Flight Rules (VFR)—those portions of the Federal Aviation Regulations (FARs) that apply when a pilot is capable of flying by referring solely to the ground and water below him, keeping certain minimum distances from clouds, and having certain minimums of ceiling and visibility

VORTAC—a navigation facility on the ground which includes a VOR, and also provides pilots of appropriately equipped aircraft with accurate distance information from the station

walk around—preflight check

warning area—an area located outside the continental United States or in off-shore waters which may not be entered without first obtaining permission from the controlling agency

wash—the disturbed air in the wake of an airplane, particularly behind its propeller

washin—a greater angle of incidence (and attack) in one wing, or part of a wing, to provide more lift; usually used to overcome torque

washout—a lesser angle of incidence to decrease lift; (see above)

weathercock—the tendency of an airplane to turn in the direction of the wind

weathervane—the tendency of an airplane while taxiing or flying to face into the wind, as a result of the pressure of the wind on the vertical surfaces of the tail group

whipstall—a type of stall in which an airplane during a vertical climb, falls forward and downward in a whip-like movement

wind correction angle (WCA)—the angle at which an airplane must be headed into the wind in comparison with true course, to make the track of the airplane coincide with the true course

wind direction—the direction from which the wind is blowing

wind drift—the amount that an airplane would drift off its intended path if a correction were not made to compensate for the effects of the wind

wind aloft—the direction and velocity of wind at a fixed altitude above ground level

wind sock—a cloth sleeve that is mounted aloft at an airport to use for estimating wind direction and velocity

wind side—the side of a pilot's computer that is used to solve true ground speed and wind correction angle problems

wind tee—a T-shaped indicator used at airports to indicate wind direction

wing—the largest airfoil of an airplane. Its major function is to provide lift to fly

wing bow—the former at the wing tip used to provide a rounded conformation. Sometimes used to denote the wing tip

wing heavy—a condition of rigging in an airplane in which one wing tends to sink

wing root—the end of a wing which joins the fuselage or the opposite wing

wingspan—the span of a wing, measured or taken between the tips of either a single-piece wing or a wing that is separated by other aircraft components

wing tip—the end of the wing farthest from the fuselage

wingtip vortices—also known as wake turbulence, the turbulence created by vortices that trail behind the wings of large aircraft

World Aeronautical Chart (WAC)—charts that show principal landmarks but omit much of the detail of a sectional chart. Their scale is 1:1,000,000 or about 16 miles to the inch

X-axis—the vertical axis in a coordinate system of axes, especially the vertical axis of an aircraft about which the aircraft yaws

yaw—to turn about the vertical axis. An airplane is said to yaw as the nose turns without the accompanying appropriate bank

Y-axis—the lateral axis in a coordinate system of axes, especially the lateral axis of an aircraft about which the aircraft pitches

zero lift angle of attack—the angle of attack of any airfoil which produces no lift

zoom—to zoom is to climb for a short time at an angle greater than the normal climbing angle, the airplane being carried upward by momentum

Zulu Time—Greenwich Mean Time

GLOSSARY OF AERONAUTICAL ABBREVIATIONS AND CONTRACTIONS

A—arctic (air mass)
A—ceiling reported from aircraft
A—also, hail (weather reports only)
A & P—airframe and powerplant (mechanic)
AAP—advise if able to proceed
AAS—Airport Advisory Service
AATM—at all times
AAWS—Automatic Aviation Weather Service
AB—continuous automatic transcribed broadcast service, air base
ABCST—automatic broadcast
ABM—abeam
ABN—aerodrome beacon
ABNML—abnormal
ABT—about
ABV—above
AC—advisory circular
AC—altocumulus
AC—severe weather outlook
ACFT—aircraft
ACK—acknowledge
ACP—altimeter check point
ACQ—All courses and quadrants
ACRBT—acrobatic
ACSL—standing lenticular altocumulus
ACRS—across
ACTG—acting
ACTV—active
AD—airworthiness directive
ADCUS—advise customs
ADF—automatic direction finder
ADIZ—Air Defense Identification Zone
ADJT—adjacent

ADMN—administration
ADVN—advance
ADVY—advisory
ADZ—advice
ADZI—advise intentions
AFCT—affect
AFDK—after dark
AFT—after
AFTN—afternoon
AGL—above ground level
AGN—again
AHD—ahead
AI—authorized inspector
AID—airport information desk
AILS—automatic instrument landing system
AIM—Airman's Information Manual
AIRAD—Airman's Advisory (local)
AIRMET—Airmen's Meterological Information
AL—approach and landing chart
ALF—aloft
ALNOT—alert notice
ALQDS—all quadrants
ALS—approach lighting system
ALSTG—altimeter setting
ALT—altitude
ALTN—alternate
AM—amplitude modulation
AMD—amend
AMDT—amendment
AME—aviation medical examiner
AMOS—Automatic Meterological Observing System
AMP—ampere
AMS—air mass
AMT—amount
ANLYS—analysis

ANRA—air navigation radio aids
ANT—antenna
AOA—at or above
AOB—at or below
AOE—airport of entry
APCH—approach
APCHG—approaching
APP CON—Approach Control
APREQ—approval request
APRXLY—approximately
APU—auxiliary power unit
ARIP—air refueling initial point
ARND—around
ARO—Airport Reservation Office
ARPT—airport
ARR—arrival/arrive
ARSR—Air Route Surveillance Radar
ARTCC—Air Route Traffic Control Center
ARTS—automated radar terminal system
AS—altostratus
AS-2—simplified surface analyses
ASDE—Airport Surface Detection Equipment
ASE—automatic stabilization equipment
ASI—airspeed indicator
ASL—above sea level
ASR—Airport Surveillance Radar (Approach)
AT—Air Traffic Service
ATC—air traffic control
ATCRBS—Air Traffic Control Beacon System
ATCT—air traffic control tower
ATD—actual time of departure
ATIS—automatic terminal information service
ATP—air transport pilot
ATZ—airport traffic zone
AUTH—authorized
AUTO—automatic
AUX—auxiliary
AVBL—available
AVG—average
AWY—airway
AWX—account weather
B—balloon measured (ceiling); also blowing; also, rotating beacon
B—rotating beacon
B—scheduled broadcasts weather at 15 min. after the hour
BCKG—backing
BCM—become
BCN—beacon
BCST—broadcast
BD—blowing dust
BDR—border
BFR—before
BGN—begin, began
BHND—behind
BHP—brake horse power
BIFR—before encounter IFR conditions
BINOVC—breaks in overcast
BKN—broken
BLD—build
BLDG—building
BLN—balloon
BLO—below
BLZD—blizzard
BMEP—brake mean effective pressure
BNDRY—boundary
BNTH—beneath
BOVC—Base of overcast
BRAF—braking action fair
BRAG—braking action good
BRAN—braking action nil
BRAP—braking action poor
BRAXP—braking action extremely poor
BRF—brief
BRG—bearing
BRK—break
BRKN—broken
BTN—between
BTR—better
BS—slowing snow
BS—broadcasting station, commercial
BYD—beyond
C—circling landing minimums
C—Control Tower, also, Celsius; also, Continental (air mass)
CAA—Civil Aeronautics Administration
CAB—Civil Aeronautics Board
CACT—civil air carrier turbojet
CAF—cleared as filed
CAP—Civil Air Patrol
CAR—Civil Air Regulation
CAS—calibrated airspeed
CAS—Collision Avoidance Systems
CAT—clear air turbulence

CAUFN—caution advised until further notice
CAVU—ceiling and visibility unlimited (clear or scattered clouds and visibility greater than 10 miles)
CB—circuit breaker
CB—citizens band (radio transceiver)
CB—crash boats
CB—cumulonimbus
CC—cirrocumulus
CC—compass course
CDI—course deviation indicator
CDT—Central Daylight Time
CFI—certified flight instructor
CFT A & I—certified flight instructor, airplane and instrument
CFN—confine
CG—center of graviey
CH—compass heading
CHG—change
CHT—cylinder-head temperature
CI—cirrus
CIFI—certified instrument flight instructor
CIG—ceiling
CIRNAV—circumnavigate
CK PT—check point
CL—coefficient of lift
CLD—cloud
CLDI—course line deviation indicator
CLR—clear
CLRNS—clearance
CLSD—closed
CN—celestial navigation
CNTR—center
CNTRL—central
CO—county
COMLO—compass locator
COMM—communication
COMM/NAV—communications/navigation (radio system)
COMSND—commissioned
COMSNG—commissioning
COND—condition
CONFIG—configuration
CONST—construction
CONSTD—constructed
CONT—continue
CONT—continuous/continuously
COP—changeover point

CORR—correction
CP—center of pressure/circular polarization
CPF—complete power failure
CPT—cockpit trainer
CSDRBL—considerable
CST—coast
CT—Control Tower
CV—cumulus
CVR—cover
D—drift angle; also dust
DA—density altitude
DABRK—daybreak
DAL—downed aircraft locator
DALGT—daylight
DAR—danger
DC—direct current
DCA—drift correction angle
DCR—decrease
DCS—double-channel-simplex
DEG—degree
DEMOL—demolition
DEMSND—decommissioned
DEP—departure
DEP CON—departure control
DER—designated engineer representative
DEV—compass deviation
DEWIZ—Distant Early Warning Identification Zone
DF—direction finder
DFVS—diffuse
DG—directional gyro
DH—decision height
DI—designated inspector
DISCNTD—discontinued
DIST—district
DL—interphone (direct line)
DLA—delay
DME—distance measuring equipment
DMSH—diminish
DMSTN—demonstration
DNS—dense
DNSLP—downslope
DO—ditto
DOD—Department of Defense
DOT—Department of Transportation
DP—deep
DPNG—deepening
DPTG—departing

DPTR—departure
DR—dead reckoning
DRFT—drift
DRZL—drizzle
DSIPT—dissipate
DSNT—distant
DSPLCD—displaced
DTRT—deteriorate
DURG—during
DURN—duration
DVFR—Defense Visual Flight Rule
DVLP—develop
E—ending of precipitation (followed in minutes past the hour on weather reports only)
E—Equatorial (airmass); also, estimated ceiling; also, sleet
EAA—Experimental Aircraft Association
EAC—expected approach clearance time
EAS—equivalent airspeed
EAT—expected approach time
EDT—Eastern Daylight Time
EFAS—enroute flight advisory service
EFC—expected further clearance time
EFCTV—effective
e.g.—for example
EGT—exhaust gas temperature
ELEV—elevation
ELSW—elsewhere
ELT—emergency locator transmitter
EMCGY—emergency
EMERG—emergency
ENDG—ending
ENG—engine
ENTR—entire
EQPMT—equipment
EQUIP—equipment
EST—Eastern Standard time
ETA—estimated time of arrival
ETC—elapsed time computer
ETD—estimated time of departure
ETE—estimated time enroute
ETOV—estimated arrival time over
EUO—emergency use only
EVE—evening
EWAS—enroute weather advisory service
EXCP—except
EXPC—expect

EXTRM—extreme
EXTSN—extension
EXTSV—extensive
F—Fahrenheit; also fog; also, fuel
FA—area forecast
F/A—fuel-air (ratio)
FAA—Federal Aviation Administration
FACIL—facility
FAR—Federal Aviation Regulations
FAS—Flight Assistance Service
FAWS—Flight Advisory Service
FBO—fixed base operator
FCC—Federal Communications Commission
FCST—forecast
FD—flight director
FD—winds aloft forecast
FFS—flight following service
FIELD—an airport
FILG—filling
FIR—flight information region
FL—flight level, given in hundreds of feet
FL—freezing level
FL—in-flight weather advisories
FLASHG—flashing
FLD—field
FLG—falling
FLIP—Flight Information Publication
FLRY—flurry
FLT—flight
FLW—follow
FLWG—following
FM—fan marker; frequency modulation
FM—from
FN—regional forecast
FN-1—regional weather prognoses
FONE—telephone
FORNN—forenoon
FPI—flight path deviation indicator
FPM—feet per minute
FPM—flashes per minute
FPS—feet per second
FQT—frequent
FRC—full route clearance necessary
FREQ—frequency
FRMN—formation
FROPA—frontal passage
FROSFC—frontal surface

FRQ—frequent
FRST—frost
FRZ—freeze
FRZN—frozen
FS-1—simplified surface prognoses
FSF—Flight Service Facility
FSS—Flight Service Station
FT—feet, foot, Fort
FT/MIN—feet per minute
FT—terminal forecast
FTS—Federal Telecommunications System
FVFR—Flight following flight plan
G—(unit of) gravity
G—ground, also gusts (wind)
GA—general aviation
GADO—General Aviation District Office
GALS—gallons
GCA—ground controlled approach
GEN—general
GFR—general flight rules
GI—government issue
GMT—Greenwich Mean Time
GND—ground
GND CON—ground control
GNDFG—ground fog
GNS—global navigation system
GP—glide path
GPH—gallons per hour
GPO—Government Printing Office
GRAD—gradient
GRDL—gradual
GS—glide slope
GS—ground speed
GWT—gross weight
H—high pressure area
H—haze
H—non-directional radio beacon (homing) power 500 watts to less than 2000 watts
HAA—height above airport
HAT—height above touchdown
HAZ—hazard
HDFRZ—hard freeze
HDTA—high density traffic airport
HDWND—head wind
HF—high frequency
HGT—height

HH—non-directional radio beacon (homing) power 2000 watts or more
HI—high
HIALS—high intensity approach lighting system
HIRL—high intensity runway lights
HLF—half
HLSTO—hailstone
HND—hundred
HP—horsepower
HR—hour, hear, here
HRZN—horizon
H-SAB—non-directional radio providing automatic weather broadcast
HURCN—hurricane
HVY—heavy
HW—hurricane advisories
HWVR—however
HWY—highway
Hz—Hertz
I—ice
IAP—(standard) instrument approach procedure
IAS—indicated airspeed
ICC—icing
ICGIC—icing in clouds
ICGICIP—icing in clouds and precipitation
ICCIP—icing in precipitation
IDENT—identification
IFF—identification friend or foe
IFI—instrument flight instructor
IFR—instrument flight rules
ILS—instrument landing system
IMDT—immediate
IMDTLY—immediately
IMPT—important
IMT—immediate
INBD—inbound
INCL—include
INCR—increase
INDC—indicate
INDEF—indefinite
INFO—information
INOP—inoperative
INREQ—information request
INS—inertial navigation systems
INST—instrument
INSTBY—instability
INT—intersection

INTL—international
INTMT—intermittent
INTR—interior
INTS—intense
INTSFY—intensity
INTSV—intensive
INVOF—in the vicinity of
IOVC—in the overcast
IP—initial point
IP/HHCL—initial point/H-hour control line
IPV—improve
IR—icy runway
ISJTA—Intensive Student Jet Training Area
ISOLD—isolated
IVFRC—in VFR conditions
IVSI—instantaneous vertical speed indicator
J-bar—jet runway barrier
JTSTR—jet stream
K—smoke; also, knots
KC—kilocycles
kHz—kiloHertz
KIAS—knots indicated airspeed
KM—kilometer
KOCTY—smoke over city
KPH—kilometers per hour
KT—knot(s)
L—low pressure; also drizzle
LAT—latitude
LBS—pounds
LC—local call
LCL—local
LCLZR—localizer
LCTD—located
LCTN—location
L/D—lift to drag (ratio)
LDA—localizer type directional air
LED—light emitting diode
LF—low frequency
LFR—Low/Medium frequency radio range
LGT—light
LGTD—lighted
LKLY—likely
LIRL—low intensity runway edge lights
L/MF—low/medium frequency
LMM—compass locator at middle marker (ILS)
LMT—limited
LND—land

LNDG—landing
LO—longitude
LOC—localizer
LONG—longitudinal
LOP—line of position
LORAN—long range navigation system
L-R—the Left-Right needle of a VOR receiver
LRR—long range radar
LST—local standard time
LTD—limited
LTGCC—lightning cloud to cloud
LTGCCCG—lightning cloud to cloud, cloud to ground
LTGCG—lightning, cloud to ground
LTGCW—lightning, cloud to water
LTGIC—lightning in clouds
LTL—little
LTLCG—little change
LTR—later
LVL—level
LWR—lower
LYR—layer
M—magnetic (after a bearing); also, Mach number, also Maritime (air mass); also, measured ceiling
MA—range (adcock, vertical radiators) power less than 50 watts
MAA—maximum authorized IFR altitude
MAC—mean aerodynamic chord
MAG—magnetic
MAINT—maintain, maintenance
MAJ—major
MALS—medium intensity approach light system
MALS/SF—medium intensity approach light system with sequenced flashing lights
MALSR—medium intensity approach light system with runway alignment indicator lights
MAP—manifold pressure, missed approach point
MARSA—military authority assumes responsibility for separation of aircraft
MAX—maximum
MAX—maximum runway gross weight bearing capacity for all aircraft
MB—millbar(s)
MB—mooring buoys
MC—megacycles
MC—magnetic course
MCA—minimum crossing altitude
MDA—minimum descent altitude

MDF—manually operated radio direction finder
MDFY—modify
MDT—mountain daylight time, moderate
MEA—minimum en route (IFR) altitude
MEL—multi-engine land
MEML—memorial
MES—multi-engine sea
METO—maximum except takeoff
MF—medium frequency
MFV—forward visibility more than miles
MH—magnetic heading; also, non-directional radio beacon (homing) power less than 50 watts
mHz—megaHertz
MI—mile(s)
MID—middle
MIDN—midnight
MIN—minimum, minute
MIRL—medium intensity runway edge lights
MITO—minimum interval takeoff
ML—range (loop radiators); power less than 50 watts
MOD—modernization/modification
MOV—moving
MPG—miles per gallon
MPH—miles per hour
MRA—minimum reception altitude
MRKD—marked
MRKG—marking
MRL—Range (loop indicators), power 500 watts or more, but less than 150 watts
MRNG—morning
MRTM—maritime
MSL—mean sea level
MST—mountain standard time
MTI—minimum target indicator, radar
MTN—mountain
MUNI—municipal
MVFR—marginal VFR
MXD—mixed
N—the identification made for aircraft in the United States
NA—not authorized
NATL—national
NAVAID—navigational aid
NAVAIR—navigational air
NAVCOM—navigational-communication equipment
NCWX—no change in weather
NDB—non-directional radio beacon

NF—non-federal control tower
NAUTIMI—nautical miles
NGT—night
NM—nautical miles
NMAC—near mid air collision
NMI—nautical mile(s)
NMRS—numerous
NO—number/not operational
NOFIN—no further information
NOPT—no procedure turn required
NORST—no restrictions
NOS—National Ocean Survey
NOSUM—NOTAM summary
NOTAM—notice to airmen
NPRM—notice of proposed rule making
NR—number
NS—nimbostratus
NTE—not to exceed
NT MI—nautical mile
NTSB—National Transportation Safety Board
NWS—National Weather Service
NXT—next
OAT—outside air temperature
OBI—omnibearing indicator
OBS—omnibearing selector
OBSR—obscure
OBSTN—obstruction
OCFNT—occluded front
OCL—obstruction clearance limit
OCLN—occlusion
OCNL—occasional
OCR—occur
OCT—octane
OFSHR—off shore
OM—outer marker (ILS)
ONC—Operational Navigational Chart
ONSHR—on shore
OPER—operate
OPERG—operating
OPN—operation
OTLK—outlook
OTP—on top
OTR—other
OTS—out of service
OUTBND—outbound
OVC—overcast
OVR—over

OVRN—overrun
P—polar (air mass); also precipitation ceiling
PA—pressure altitude
PAR—Precision Approach Radar
PATN—pattern
PATWAS—Pilots Automatic Telephone Weather Answering Service
PBL—probable
PCA—positive control area
PCL—pilot controlled lighting
PCPN—precipitation
PD—period
PDT—Pacific Daylight Time
PERMLY—permanently
PIC—pilot in command
PIREPS—pilot weather reports
P-LINE—power line
PMSN—permission
POSN—position
PPI—plan position indicator, radar
PPO—prior permission only
PPR—prior permission required
PRCTN—precaution
PRES—pressure
PRESFR—pressure falling rapidly
PRESRR—pressure rising rapidly
PROG—prognostic, prognosis, progress
PSBL—possible
PSF—pounds per square foot
PSG—passing, passage
PSI—pounds of pressure per square inch
PSN—position
PSR—packed snow on runway
PST—Pacific Standard Time
PT—point
PTCHY—patchy
PTLY—partly
PTN—portion
PVL—prevail
PWI—pilot warning instrument, also proximity warning indicator
PWR—power
PWRNO—power failure
PWROK—power restored
Q—denotes passing of squall
QDM—bearing to facility
QDR—bearing from facility

QFE—altitude above ground based on station pressure
QNE—altimeter setting 29.92 inches HG
QNH—altitude above sea level based on station pressure
QUAD—quadrant
R—range (adcock, vertical radiators) power 150 watts or more
R—rain; also, runway
RACFI—radio and communications facilities inoperative
RACON—radar beacon, a form of radar in which the aircraft signal triggers the radio beacon on the ground
R/A—radius of action
RAD—radial
RADAR—radio detection and ranging
RAFL—rainfall
RAIL—runway alignment indicator light system
RAPCON—radar approach control
RAREP—radar weather report
RATCC—radar air traffic control center (VSN)
R/B—relative bearing
RBN—radio beacon, non-directional
RBS—radar bomb scoring
R/C—rate of climb
RCC—Rescue Coordination Center
RCH—reach
RCLS—runway centerline system
RCO—Remote Communications Outlet
RCR—runway condition reading
RCV—receive
RCVG—receiving
RCVR—receiver
R & D—research and development
R/D—rate of descent
RDG—ridge
RDO—radio
RECONST—reconstruction
REG—operates on request
REIL—runway and identification lights
RELBI—reliable
RELCTD—relocated
RESTR—restrict
RF—en route charts, formerly known as radio facility charts
RF—radio frequency

RG—retractable gear
RGD—ragged
RGN—region
RGT—right
RH—relative humidity
RL—range (loop indicators)
RLA—restricted loading area
R/M—relative movement
RMI—radio magnetic indicator
RMN—remain
RNAV—area navigation
RNG—range
RNWY—runway
RPD—rapid
RPRT—report
RPT—repeat
ROC—rate of climb
RON—remain (or rest) overnight
RPM—revolutions per minute
RR—low or medium frequency radio range station
RR TOP—Restricted Operators Permit
RSG—rising
RSOPH—resumed operation
RSTR—restrict
RTCA—radio technical commission for aeronautics
RTE—route
RTRD—retard
RTRN—return
RUF—rough
RVO—runway visibility by observer
RVR—runway/visual range
RVV—runway visibility value
R/W—runway
RWA—relative wind angle
RWC—regional weather center
S—simultaneous range, home signal, and/or voice
S—snow; also, storage
S—storage (in AIM)
S—straight-in landing minimums
S—Superior—the symbol for a warm, dry air mass that has its origin aloft
SA—standard altitude
SA—service A, as shown in the heading of an hourly weather sequence report
SABH—non-directional radio beacon having limited navigational use; provides automatic weather broadcasts

SAGE—Semi-automatic Ground Environment
SALS—short approach light system
SAR—(also SARCC)—Search and Rescue
SAS—stability—augmentation system
S/B—National Aeronautics and Space Administration
SC—strato cumulus
SCATANA—Security Control of Air Traffic and Navigational Aids
SCS—single-channel-simplex
SCTD—scattered
SCTR—sector
SDP—standard datum plane
SEC—second, section
SEL—single-engine load
SELS—severe local storm
SELS—severe local storms forecast center
SES—single-engine sea
SFA—single frequency approach
SFAR—Special Federal Aviation Regulation
SFC—surface
SFERICS—atmospherics
SFL—sequenced flashing
SFO—simulated flameout
SHFT—shift
SHLW—shallow
SHTDN—shutdown
SHWR—shower
SID—Standard Instrument Departure
SIF—Selective Identification Feature (of the basic Mark X radar Beacon system)
SIGMET—significant meteorological information
SIR—snow and ice on runway
SKED—schedule
SL—sea level
SLD—solid
SLGHT—slight
SLMM—simultaneous middle marker compass locator and tower voice transmission
SLO—slow
SLOM—Simultaneous Outer Marker Compass and tower voice transmission
SLP—slope
SLR—slush on runway
SLS—self-launching sailplane
SLS—side lobe suppression
SLT—sleet
SM—statute mile

SMK—smoke
SMOH—(hours) since major overhaul
SMTH—smooth
SMWHT—somewhat
SNFLK—snowflake
SNW—snow
SNWFL—snowfall
SOB—souls on board
SPI—special position identification
SPL—special
SPRD—spread
SOP—standard operating procedure
SPC—single pilot certification
SQAL—squall
SQLN—squall line
SR—sunrise
SS—sunset
SSALS—simplified short approach light system
SSALSR—simplified short approach light system with runway alignment indicator lights
SSR—secondary surveillance radar
SST—supersonic transport
ST—stratus
STAR—standard terminal arrival route
STBL—stable
STC—supplemental type certificate
STDY—steady
STG—strong
STM—storm
ST MI—statute mile
STN—station
STOL—short takeoff and landing
SUPSD—supersede
SVC—service
SVFR—special visual flight rules
SVR—severe
SVRL—several
SYS—system
T—takeoff minimums
T—total time, fuel hours available; also, thunderstorms
T—transmits only
T—true (after a bearing); also, tropical (air mass)
TACAN—Tactical Air Navigation
TAS—true airspeed
TBO—time between (major) overhauls
TC—true course
TC—type certificate

TCA—terminal control area
TCU—towering cumulus
TDA—today
TDZ/CL—touchdown zone/ center line lights
TDZL—touchdown zone light system
TEMP—temperature
TERPS—terminal instrument procedure
TET—tetrahedron
TFC—traffic
TFC INFO—Traffic Information Service
TH—true heading
THDR—thunder
THK—thick
THN—thin
THRFTR—thereafter
THSD—thousand
THRU—through
THRUT—throughout
TIAS—true indicated airspeed
TIL—until
TKOF—takeoff
TLWD—tailwind
TMPRY—temporary
TMPRLY—temporarily
TMW—tomorrow
TN—true north
TNDCY—tendency
TNGT—tonight
TOVC—top of overcast
TPS—traffic pattern altitude
TPG—topping
TR—track
TRACON—terminal radar approach control facility
TRANS—transcribed
TRAS—terminal radar advisory service
TRML—terminal
TRNG—training
TROF—trough
TROP—tropopause
TRRN—terrain
TRSA—Terminal Radar Service Area
TSHWR—thundershower
TSGLS—thundersqualls
TSMT—transmit
TSMTG—transmitting
TSMTR—transmitter
TSO—technical standard order

TSMT—thunderstorm
TT—total (hours of) time (on engine)
TURB—turbulence
TURBT—turbulent
TV—television
TVOR—very high frequency terminal omni-range station
TWO—toward
TWEB—transcribed weather broadcast
TWR—tower
TWRG—towering
TWY—taxiway
U—unlimited; unrestricted; also intensity unknown
UDDF—up and down draft
UFA—until further advised
UFN—until further notice
UHF—ultra high frequency (300–3,000 MHz)
UNAVBL—unavailable
UNCTLD—uncontrolled
UNICOM—Aeronautical Advisory Service
UNKN—unknown
UNL—unlimited
UNLGTD—unlighted
UNMON—unmonitored
UNMKD—unmarked
UPR—upper
UPSLP—upslope
UNRELBL—unreliable
UNRSTD—unrestricted
UNSATFY—unsatisfactory
UNSBL—unseasonable
UNSTBL—unstable
UNSTDY—unsteady
UPR—upper
USA—United States Army
USAF—United States Air Force
USN—United States Navy
USWB—United States Weather Bureau
UWNDS—upper
V—Victor airway; also, variable
VA—design maneuvering speed
VAR—magnetic variation
VAR—visual-aural range
VASI—visual approach slope indicator
VCNTY—vicinity
VFR—visual flight rules
VFR ADV—VFR advisory service
VFRSA—VFR restrictions still apply
VFY—verify
VH—maximum speed in level flight with rated rpm and power
VHF—very high frequency
VIS—visibility
VLE—maximum landing gear extended speed
VLF—very low frequency
VLNT—violent
VLO—maximum landing gear operating speed
VLOF—lift-off speed
VLY—valley
VOR—very high frequency omni-directional range radio equipment
VOR DME—collocated VOR navigational facility and UHF standard navigational facility and UHF standard distance measuring equipment
VORTAC—very high frequency omnidirectional range radio equipment
VOT—a VOR receiver testing facility
VR—rotation speed
VRBL—variable
VSBY—visibility
V Speeds—see index
V/STOL—vertical/short takeoff and landing
VTOL—vertical takeoff and landing
VV—runway visibility
WA—airmet
WAC—airmet continued
WAC—World Aeronautical Chart
WCA—wind correction angle
WDLY—widely
WEA—weather
WH—hurricane advisories
WI—within
WIBIS—will be issued
WILCO—will comply
WIP—work in progress
WK—week; weak
WKN—weaken
WL—will
WND—wind
WO—without
WP—way point
WR—wet runway
WRM—warm
WRNG—warning

WS—Sigmet
WSHFT—wind shift
WSO—Weather Service Office
WT—weight
WV—wave

WW—severe weather watch bulletin
WX—weather
YDA—yesterday
Z—ZULU—(Greenwich Mean Time)

INDEX

above ground level, 16.2
accelerated stall, 23.12
acceleration error, 18.5
accident prevention, 51.1 et seq.
accident reports, 52.1 et seq.
acrobatic flight, 20.11
ADF, 37.1 et seq.
ADIZ, 19.12
aeronautical charts
    airport symbols, 25.1, 47.10
    airport traffic areas, 31.1
    airspace information, 19.14
    index of, 47.7
    local, 47.5
    planning, 47.5
    radio aids, 29.10
    sectional charts, 47.7
    symbols, 47.8
    world, 47.5
agonic line, 18.2
ailerons, 5.2
AIM, see Airman's Information Manual
aircraft call sign, 30.17
air defense identification zone, 19.12
Air Defense Low Altitude Training Routes, 19.11
Airman's Information Manual, Sec. 58
airmets, 21.2, 39.12
airport advisory area, 25.10
airport advisory service, 25.10, 29.3
airport lighting, 26.1 et seq.
airports, 25.1 et seq., 47.18
airport traffic area, 25.11, 31.1
airship, right-of-way, 20.6
airspeed
    calibrated, 17.2
    caution range, 17.5
    flap operating range, Fig. 17.2
    ground, 17.3
    indicated, 17.2
    indicator, 17.6
    indicator markings, 17.5
    maneuvering, 17.4
    maximum, Fig. 17.2

    normal range, 17.5
    true, 17.2
    V speeds, 17.4
alcohol, 51.6
Alert Area, 19.9
alphabet, phonetic, 30.3
alternator, 7.12
alternator malfunction, 42.5
altimeter, 13.11, 15.11, 16.4, 16.5, 16.6
altimeter, encoding, 38.2
altitude, 16.2, 16.3, 16.7
altitudes of flight, 16.8
amber light, flashing, 25.6
ambiguity meter, 36.7
ammeter, 7.13
angle of attack, 23.
annual inspection, 57.6
approach control, 31.1, 31.5, 31.6
area forecast, 39.9
arrival stall, 23.11
artificial horizon, 6.3, 44.4
ATIS, 35.1
attitude indicator, 6.3, 44.4
automatic altitude reporting, 38.2
automatic direction finder, 37.1 et seq.
automatic terminal information service, 35.1
auxiliary lights, 26.3
aviation weather report, 39.8
avoiding mid-air collisions, 51.12
axis
    lateral, 5.3
    longitudinal, 5.2
    vertical, 5.4

balloon, right-of-way, 20.6
bank, 15.5
barometric pressure, 14.28, 16.5
batteries, 7.12
best angle of climb airspeed, 14.14, 17.5
best rate of climb airspeed, 14.15, 17.5
biennial flight review, 57.7
birds, 21.5
blip, 38.1

brake horse power, 17.9
broken clouds, 39.5
buzzing, Sec. 58

calibrated airspeed, 17.2
call sign, ground station, 30.18
call up, 30.13
carbon monoxide, 21.8
carburetor, 7.8
carburetor heat, 13.18, 21.1
carburetor icing, 21.1
careless flying, 20.3
carrying passengers, 57.3, Sec. 58
caught on top, 39.18
CDI, 36.7
ceiling, 39.5, 39.10
ceiling, service, 16.10
center of gravity, 8.2
center of gravity moment envelope, 8.6
certified flight instructor, see flight instructor
Cessna 152/150
   airspeed, 17.5
   altimeter, 16.4
   capacity, 4.3
   ceiling, 4.9
   Continental engine, 4.1
   controls, 5.1 et seq.
   cruise performance, 17.9
   electrical system, 7.11 et seq.
   empty weight, 8.2
   engine, 4.1
   engine ignition, 4.6
   engine speed, 7.1 et seq.
   fuel capacity, 7.3
   fuel consumption, 7.1 et seq.
   glide distances, 43.3
   glide speed, 43.3
   gross weight, 4.2
   landing distance, 27.29
   load, 8.2
   Lycoming engine, 4.1
   maneuvers permitted, 20.11
   maximum weight, 4.2
   normal rate of climb, 17.8
   oil consumption, 4.8
   oil pressure, 17.
   Pilot's Operating Manual, see Pilot's Operating Manual
   power plant, 7.1
   range, 4.7
   service ceiling, 4.9
   stall speeds, 23.1
   takeoff performance, 29.1
   weight, 4.2
chart, sectional, see aeronautical charts
checkpoints, 47.13
circle, segmented, 25.6
clearances, 25. 31.2
climbing stall recovery, 44.9
climb, normal, 15.9
closed runway, 25.5
closing flight plan, 48.9
clouds, 16.2, 16.13, 39.4, 39.5
cloud separation
   controlled airspace, 9.6
   uncontrolled airspace, 9.5
clouds, letting down through, 39.25
codes, 38.3
collision avoidance, 51.11 51.12
commercial flights, 57.3
compass, 18.1
compass heading, 47.21
compass rose, 18.1
computer
   azimuth, 47.19
   grommet, 47.19
   ground speed, 47.19
   true airspeed, 17.7
   wind correction angle, 47.19
contamination of fuel, 7.3
continental control area, 9.3
control of lighting systems, 26.6
control zone, 9.3, 9.6
controlled airspace, 9.3, 9.6
control tower, 14.5
control wheel, 5.3
convection currents, 39.3
coordinated turn, 6.2, 15.6
course deviation indicator, 36.7
course selector, 36.7
cowling, checking under, 10.6
cross-country flight
   certifying for, 47.3
   charts, 47.5
   checkpoints, 47.13
   computing time en route, 47.24
   emergencies,
   flight test, 56.14, 56.15
   flying, 47.1 et seq., 49.1 et seq.
   fuel requirements, 47.25
   making the, 49.1 et seq.
   planning, 47.11
   requirements, 47.4
   terrain, 47.15

crosswind component, 14.30
crosswind landing, 27.26
crosswind, maximum, 14.30
crosswind takeoff, 27.25
cruise performance, 17.9
cruising speed, 17.9
cumulonimbus cloud, 39.4
cumulus clouds, 39.4

dead reckoning navigation, 49.6
defensive flying, 51.4
density altitude, 16.3
departure control, 31.1, 31.4
departure stall, 23.10
designated code, 38.1
deviation, 18.3
deviation card, 18.3
DF steer and approach, 41.1 et seq.
directional gyro, 15.10, 18.6
direction finding station, 41.1 et seq.
direction indicator, landing, 25.6
disaster area avoidance, 16.9
disorientation, 21.2
displaced runway, 25.5
distance measuring equipment, 36.11
ditching, 43.9
DME, 36.11
dome light, 7.16
door open in flight, 42.9
downdraft, 39.3
dragging the area, 43.7
dropping objects, 20.7
drugs, 51.6, 51.8

eights across a road, 50.4
eights along a road, 50.3
eights around pylons, 50.7
electrical fire, 42.6
electrical system, 7.11
electrical system malfunction, 42.5
elevator, effect, 5.3
elevator trim tab, 5.5
elevator trim tab inoperative, 42.10
ELT, 20.10
emergencies
    engine failure, 14.16, 14.17
    forced landing, 43.1 et seq.
    frequency, 43.5
    over water, 43.9
    report to Administrator, 20.3
emergency locator transmitter, 20.10

emergency operations
    complete power failure, 42.2
    fuel starvation, 42.3
    magneto check, 42.1
    partial loss of power, 42.1
empty weight, 8.2
encoding altimeter, 16.10, 38.2, 38.5
engine failure, 42.2
engine fire in flight, 42.4
en route charts, 47.6
en route flight advisory service, 39.16

fatigue, 51.5
FBO, 2.4
Federal Aviation Agency, 1.1
Federal Aviation Regulations, 1.1,
fire, electrical, 42.6
fire, engine, 42.4
fixed base operator 2.4
flaps, 24.1 et seq.
flap operating speed, 17.4, 24.7
flashing amber light, 25.6
flight altitudes, 16.8, 16.9
flight instructor, 2.2
flight into unfavorable weather, 39.21, 39.22
flight log, 47.13
flight, normal, 15.1 et seq.
flight plan, 48.1 et seq.
flight review, 57.7
flight rules, sample test, 46.2
Flight Service Station, 29.3, 30.20, 39.15
flight test
    airplane used, 54.3, 54.4, 54.5
    documents required, 55.6
    examiner, 54.2
    flying the test ride, 56.1 et seq.
    general requirements, 1.7
    oral quiz, 55.7
    preparation for, 54.1 et seq.
    requirements for, 54.1
    retesting, 54.8
    sample, 46.2
    taking, 55.1 et seq.
flight time, 20.2
flight watch, 39.16
flying defensively, 51.4
flying schools
    FAA approved, 2.3
    non-approved, 2.4
forced landing, 43.1 et seq.
forecasts, weather, 39.9, 39.10
forecast winds aloft, 39.14

foreign exchange telephone service, 39.15
formation flight, 20.5
four Cs, 40.2
FSS, see Flight Service Stations
fuel capacity, 7.3
fuel contamination, 7.3
fuel grades, 7.3
fuel mixture, see mixture control
fuel selector, 11.8
fuel shutoff valve, 11.8
fuel starvation, 42.3, 51.10
fuel system, 7.2

G, 23.6
generator malfunction, 42.5
gethomeitis, 39.21
glide distances, 43.3
glider, right-of-way, 20.6
glide speed, 43.3
GMT, see Greenwich mean time
grades of fuel, 7.3
gravity, 23.6
green arc, 17.5
Greenwich Mean Time, 30.4, 48.4
grommet, 47.19
gross weight, 8.2, 14.28
ground control, 31.1, 31.2
ground effect, 14.28
ground loop, 27.10
ground roll, 14.28
ground school, 2.1
ground speed, 17,3, 47.19, 47.23
ground station call sign, 30.18
Group I TCA, 32.2
Group II TCA, 32.3
gusty wind, 21.3
gyro compass, 18.7
gyro horizon, 6.3
gyroscopic flight instruments, 6.1

heading, indicator, see directional gyro
headwind component, 14.28
health, 51.7
hemispherical rule, 16.8
high intensity runway lights, 26.5
high performance aircraft, 57.2
home study, 2.1
homing, 37.6
hood time, 44.1 et seq.
horizon, artificial, see artificial horizon
horsepower, 17.9
humidity, 14.28

hundred hour inspection, 57.6
hyperventilation, 21.7
hypoxia, 21.6

ice, 21.9
ice, carburetor, 21.1
ident, 38.1
impact pressure, 17.6
improper loading, too far forward, 8.7
indicated airspeed,
indicated altitude, 16.3
indicator, wind direction, 25.6
inoperative elevator trim tab, 42.10
instructor, see flight instructor
instrument flight, 44.1 et seq., 57.3
instrument flying, simulated, 44.4
insurance, Sec. 58
Intensive Student Jet Training Area, 19.7
interior lights, 7.16
isogonic lines, 18.2

kilometers per hour, 17.1
Kollsman window, 14.28, 16.5

landing
  bounce recovery, 27.15
  crosswind, 27.26
  direction indicator, 25.6
  distance, 27.29
  forced, 43.1 et seq.
  normal, 27.1 et seq.
  procedures, 27.1 et seq.
  procedures after, 28.1 et seq.
  short field, 27.24
  slip to, 27.27
  soft field, 27.25
  stall, 27.10
  strip indicator, 25.6
  touch and go, 27.23
landing light, 7.15
landing strip indicator, 25.6
large aircraft, 57.2
lateral axis, 5.3
leaning procedures, 15.12
left-right indicator, 36.7
legal cloud separation, 39.19
letting down through clouds, 39.25
lighting of airports, 26.1 et seq.
lights, auxiliary, 26.3
light signals, 31.7
line of sight reception distance, 29.2
load factor, 23.6

load limit factor, 23.6
loading graph, 8.5
logbook, 53.1 et seq.
longitudinal axis, 5.2
lost certificate, 57.1
lost procedures, 40.1 et seq.
low altitude en route charts, 47.6
low intensity runway lights, 26.5
L-shaped indicator, 25.6

magnetic compass, 18.1 et seq.
magnetic course, 16.8, 47.21
magnetic bearing, 37.7
magnetic dip, 18.6
magnetic North Pole, 18.2
magnetic variation, 18.2
magneto, 4.5, 13.17, 42.1
malfunction of electrical system, 42.5
maneuvering speed, 17.4
maneuvers, required
   eights across a road, 50.4
   eights along a road, 50.3
   eights around pylons, 50.7
   rectangular course, 50.5
   S-turns along a road, 50.2
   turns about a point, 50.6
map light, 7.16
marking of runways, 25.5
master switch, 7.12
maximum flap extended speed, 17.4
maximum structural cruising speed, 17.4
maximum window open speed, 17.4
maximum weight, 4.2
mayday, 40.5, 43.4
mean sea level, 16.2
medical certificate,
   combined with Student Pilot Certificate, 3.2
   physicians, 1.3
   requirement, 1.3, 57.1
medical deficiencies, 57.1
medium bank, 15.7
medium intensity runway lights, 26.5
mid-air collision avoidance, 51.11, 51.12
miles per hour, 17.1
military airports, 25.1
Military Operations Area, 19.8
minimum altitudes, 16.7
mixture control, 7.5, 11.10, 15.12
MOA, 19.8
modes, 38.2
moment, 8.6
Morse Code, 30.2

mountain flying, 57.9
MSL, 16.2
multicom, 29.9
multi-engine aircraft, 57.2

National Transportation Safety Board, 52.4
near collision reports, 52.1 et seq.
negative sensing, 36.10
never exceed airspeed, 17.4
night flying, 45.1 et seq.
night flying prohibited, 57.8
night flying, recency requirement, 57.5
normal climb, 15.7
normal flight, 15.1 et seq.
normal rate of climb, 15.6
normal turns, 44.8
northerly turn error, 18.6
notam, 47.17

obscuration, 39.5
obstacle clearance, 16.11, 47.15
obstruction lighting, 26.4
octane rating, 7.3
oil, 4.7, 7.10, 10.6
oil pressure gage, 7.6
oil sump, 7.10
oil temperature gage, 7.7
Olive Branch Routes, 19.11
omni, 36.1 et seq.
omnibearing selector, 36.7
one hundred eighty degree turn, 44.5
open door in flight, 42.6
operating near other aircraft, 20.5
opportunities in flying, Sec. 58
opposite sensing, 36.10
oscillation error, 18.4
other aircraft, operating near, 20.5
overcast, 39.5
overvoltage light, 42.5
overvoltage sensor, 7.14
oxygen, 16.10

pan, 40.5
panic avoidance, 40.8
parallel runways, 25.4
parking brake, 11.5, 11.6
partial loss of power, 42.1
pattern altitude, 27.1
PATWAS, 39.15
PCL, 26.6
P factor, 14.11
phonetic alphabet, 30.3

physicians, 1.3
pilotage, 49.5
pilot controlled lighting, 26.6
pilot in command, 20.1
pilot operations, 55.2
pilots automatic telephone answering service, 39.15
pilot's logbook, 53.1 et seq.
pilot's operating manual, 4.1
pilot weather reports, 39.17
pitch axis, 5.3
pitot heat, 4.6
pitot-static system, 4.6, 16.4
pireps, 39.17
position lights, 7.15
position reports, 48.6
positive control area, 16.10
power-off stalls, 23.11
power-on spiral recovery, 44.10
power-on stalls, 23.10
precession, 15.10
precipitation, 39.7
preflight check, 10.1 et seq.
pressure altitude, 14.28, 16.3
prevailing visibility, 39.6
prevention of accidents, 51.1 et seq.
primer, 7.9, 11.12
private pilot certificate
   age requirements, 1.4
   commercial flights, 7
   destroyed, 57.1
   eligibility requirements, 1.4
   English language requirements, 1.4
   experience requirements, 1.6
   expiration of, 57.1
   flight check ride, 1.7
   general requirements, 1.2 et seq.
   limitations, 57.1 et seq.
   lost, 57.1
   preparation for, 2.1 et seq.
   suspension, 57.1
   qualifications for, 1.2
   replacement, 57.1
   revocation, 57.1
   written test, 1.5
private pilot, limitations
   commercial flights, 57.3
   high performance aircraft, 57.2
   large aircraft, 57.2
   multi-engine aircraft, 57.2
private pilot written examination, 1.5
professionalism, Sec. 58
prohibited area, 19.4

propeller, 17.9
proper sensing, 36.10

radar services, 33.1 et seq., 34.1 et seq.
radar traffic information, 31.1, 33.6, 33.7, 33.11
radial, 36.2
radio
   frequencies, 29.4, 29.7, 29.9
   reception distances, 29.2
   technique, 30.1 et seq.
   Unicom, 29.7
radio procedures
   contacting FSS, 29.3
   departure, 31.3
   landing, 25.10
   technique, 30.1 et seq.
   tower control, 25.10
   vocabulary, 30.12
radio telephone permit, 1.3
rate of climb, 15.9
rate of climb indicator, 15.9
recent flight experience requirements
   to carry passengers, 57.5
   to fly at night, 57.5
reckless flying, 20.4
recovery from unusual attitudes, 44.9, 44.10
rectangular course, 50.5
red line, 17.5
relative bearing, 37.8
reporting accidents and near collisions, 52.1 et seq.
required maneuvers, see maneuvers, required
restricted area, 19.5
restricted radiotelephone operator permit, 1.3
reverse sensing, 36.10
rheostat light controls, 7.16
right of way rules, 20.6
roll axis, 5.2
rotating beacon, airplane, 7.15
rough running engine, 42.1
rudder, 5.4
runup, 12.10, 13.1 et seq.
runway, closed, 25.5
runway, displaced, 25.5
runway, lighting, 26.5
runway markings, 25.5
runway numbering, 25.4
runways, 25.3
runway threshold, 25.5

safety rules, 51.13
scuba diving, 51.9
Search and Rescue, 43.5, 48.10

seat belt, 20.8
sectional chart, see aeronautical charts
segmented circle, 25.6
sense indicator, 36.7
service ceiling, 16.10
sequence reports, 39.13
severe weather advisory, 39.11, 39.12
shallow bank, 15.5
shallow climbing turns, 44.7
shallow descending turns, 44.6
sharing expenses, 57.3
short field landing, 27.24
short field takeoff, 14.26
sigmets, 21.20, 39.11
simulated instrument flying, 44.4
skid, 15.6
slip, 15.6, 26.26, 27.28
slip to landing, 27.27
slow flight, 23.1 et seq.
smoke, 42.6
smoking, 21.9
soft field landing, 27.25
soft field takeoff, 14.27
solo flight
    certification for, 46.4
    logbook endorsement, 46.8
    preparing for, 46.1 et seq.
    requirements, 46.1
    sample test, 46.2
spark plug fouling, 42.1
spatial disorientation, 21.2
special equipment suffixes, 48.5
special VFR clearance, 25.12
speed, see airspeed
squawk, 38.1
Stage I Radar Service, 34.2
Stage II Radar Service, 34.3
Stage III Radar Service, 34.3
stall
    accelerated, 23.12
    approach, 23.11
    arrival, 23.11
    attitude in, 23.5
    cause, 23.4, 23.5
    departure, 23.10
    flaps, effect of, 23.5
    frost, effect on, 23.5
    ice, effect on, 23.5
    indicated airspeed, 23.5
    landing, 23.11
    load factor, 23.6
    recovery, 23.10 et seq.
    snow, effect on, 23.5
    speeds, 23.5
    weight as cause, 23.5
standard-rate turn, 44.7
starting procedures, 11.1 et seq.
static pressure, 17.6
steep bank, 15.7
straight and level flight, 15.5
strobe lights, 7.15
student pilot
    business flights, 3.4
    carrying passengers, 3.4
    commercial flights, 3.4
    crew member, 3.4
    prohibited activities, 3.4
Student Pilot Certificate
    application for, 3.2
    combined Medical Certificate, 3.2
    expiration of, 3.3
    how to obtain, 3.2
    need for, 1.6
    requirements for, 1.6, 3.2
S-turns along a road, 50.2
suction gage, 6.1, 13.19
suffixes, special equipment, 48.5
sump, oil, 7.10
surface aviation weather reports, 39.12
switch, master, 7.12

takeoff
    clearance to, 14.5
    crosswind, 14.30
    distance required, 14.3, 14.28, 14.29
    emergencies,
    intersection, 14.3
    normal, 14.1 et seq.
    procedures, 14.1 et seq.
    short field, 14.26
    soft field, 14.27
    traffic pattern, 14.23
takeoff distance chart, 14.29
taxiing
    brakes, 12.3
    crosswind, 12.5
    downwind, 12.4
    procedures, 12.1 et seq.
    quartering wind, 12.5
    speed, 12.3
taxi light, 6.15, 26.5
taxiways, 25.5
TCA, see terminal control area
technique, radio, 30.1 et seq.

temperature, effect on takeoff, 14.28
terminal control area, 9.3, 31.2, 32.1 et seq.
terminal forecast, 39.10
terminal radar programs, 34.1 et seq.
terminal radar service area, 34.4
terrain, 47.15
tetrahedron, 25.6
thermal, 39.2
third class medical certificate, see medical certificate
threshold of runway, 25.5
throttle, 7.4, 11.16
tiedown procedures, 28.7
time zones, 48.4
to-from indicator, 36.7
torque, 14.11
touch and go landings, 27.23
tower control, see control tower
tower controlled airports, 31.1 et seq.
traffic control light signals, 31.7
traffic pattern, altitude, 27.1
traffic pattern indicator, 25.6
transcribed weather briefing, 39.15
transponder, 33.5, 38.1 et seq.
transponder phraseology, 38.4
trim tab, 5.5, 15.3, 42.10
TRSA, 34.4
true airspeed, 17.2, 17.7
true airspeed indicator, 17.7
true altitude, 16.3
true bearing, 37.7
true course, 47.21
true heading, 47.21
true North Pole, 18.1
turbulence, 21.4
turbulence, wake, 22.1 et seq.
turn and bank indicator, 6.2
turn needle, 6.2
turns
   about a point, 50.6
   coordinated, 6.2, 15.6
   eights across a road, 50.4
   eights along a road, 50.3
   eights around pylons, 50.7
   normal, 44.8
   shallow climbing, 44.7
   shallow descending, 44.6
   standard rate, 44.7
   S-turns along a road, 50.2
   two minute, 44.7

uncontrolled airspace, 9.3
Unicom, 29.4

United States time zones, 48.4
unusual attitudes, 44.9, 44.10
updraft, 39.3
useful load, 9.2

vacuum pump, 6.1
vacuum system, 6.1
variation, 18;2
VASI, 26.7
vertical axis, 5.4
vertical speed indicator, 15.9, 17.8
vertigo, 21.2
very high frequencies, 29.2
VFR, see visual flight rules
VFR Low Altitude Training Routes, 19.10
VHF, 29.2
Victor Airways, 47.12
visibility, 39.6
visual flight rules, 9.1
visual approach slope indicator, 26.7
vocabulary, radio, 30.12
VOR, 36.1 et seq.
VORTAC, 36.11
vortex movement, 22.2
vortices, 22.2
VSI, 15,9, 17.9
V speeds, 17.4

WAC, 47.5
wake turbulence, 22.1 et seq.
walk around, 10.1
warning area, 19.6
weather
   checking, 9.1
   generally, 39.1 et seq.
   required knowledge, 1.5
weather bureau, 39.15
weather information, test upon, 55.9
weather reports, 39.8
weather signs, 39.23
weather stations, 39.8
weight
   empty weight, 8.2
   gross, 8.2
   maximum allowable, 8.2
   useful load, 8.2
weight and balance, 8.1
weight and balance data, 8.5
weight and balance, flight test, 55.8
white arc, 17.5
wind
   aloft forecast, 16.10, 39.14

correction angle, 47.19
direction, determining, 9.7
direction indicator, 25.6
generally, 39.2
gusts, 9.7
sock, 25.6
tee, 25.6
velocity, 9.7
winds aloft forecast, 16.10, 39.14

yaw axis, 5.4
yellow arc, 17.5